ROBERT TRESSELL - A LIFE IN HELL

The Biography of the Author and His Ragged Trousered Philanthropists

IAN HERNON

Red Axe Books

ISBN: 978-0993218323

© Ian Hernon

Red Axe Books: find us at www.dogstailbook.co.uk

DEDICATION

For Reuben, Freya and Theo, our grandchildren

Dedicated to the memory of the late Fred Ball

Robert Tressell, probably in 1908.

ACKNOWLEDGEMENTS

This book is the result of a 45-year-old labour of love since I started work as a teenage reporter on the *Hastings and St Leonards Observer*, immortalised by Robert Tressell as *The Mugsborough Obscurer*. I was involved in the campaign to save one of Tressell's last remaining artistic works and then first met the late F.C. (Fred) Ball, Tressell's first biographer, to whom I owe the biggest debt. But over subsequent decades away from Hastings there were many more who shared information based on a shared passion for a man who never knew the posthumous impact he would have on the labour and trade union movement. They cross party and class divides and are too numerous to mention.

I would like to single out the following, however: the late J.V. Cornelius, my first editor and a deep-seated Tory who nevertheless spotted that Tressell's life was a "cracking good story"; the late Eric Heffer MP; the late Lord (Norman) Hogg of Cumbernauld; the late John Smith MP; the late Robert Rhodes James MP; Steve Rotheram MP; Lord (John) Reid; my publisher David Wheeler; Jim Mowatt of Unite Education; and Mark Metcalf, freelance journalist and political activist.

And, as always, my family.

CONTENTS

PREFACE

By Len McCluskey, General Secretary of Unite

It was my dad who introduced me to *The Ragged Trousered Philanthropists* in my early teens, telling me that he had read it during the War. I later learned that this book had been passed around in the trenches and is commonly regarded as one of the reasons why the returning soldiers voted *en masse* for the Labour Party and a brave new world.

The central character in the book is a skilled painter and decorator - just like my dad - but whose skills, again like my dad, were never properly used or valued.

I read the book again in my early twenties and it had a dramatic effect on my political thinking and my class consciousness. "The money trick" is still one of the greatest and simplest exposes of the obscenity of capitalism.

It is to me, one of the great books everyone should read if they want to know about the world of work, understand the grinding relationships between master and servant and appreciate the nature of the western society in which we live.

And by a curious coincidence, 10 years later, after reading 'The Ragged Trousered Philanthropists', a group of ordinary union branch officers (not academics) discovered that author Robert Tressell was buried in Liverpool, in an unmarked grave - in a paupers' grave with ten others!

A great comrade of mine, John Nettleton, then our convenor at Courthaulds, organised the campaign for recognition and acknowledgement of Robert Tressell and in June 1977 we turned up in our thousands outside Walton Prison wall to commemorate Tressell with a truly marvellous headstone - a small replica of which adorns the UNITE North West headquarters, Jack Jones House in Liverpool.

But to my mind, the best celebration of Robert Tressell is to enthuse individuals, new generations, to read and be inspired by *The Ragged Trousered Philanthropists.*

Len McCluskey

General Secretary, Unite

INTRODUCTION

"the best book ever."

IN EARLY February 2011 around 100 "mourners" attended a recreation of the funeral 100 years earlier of an Irish jobbing house painter and decorator. He had been buried with a dozen other unfortunates in a mass pauper's grave a few yards from the walls of Walton Gaol and close to the former Liverpool Workhouse.

He was unrecognised in his lifetime but at the centenary event the city council's Labour Leader Joe Anderson spoke passionately of his legacy. The Irishman's name was Robert Noonan but his pen name was Robert Tressell. After the simple ceremony Walton Library hosted readings from his one book, published posthumously, *The Ragged Trousered Philanthropists*.

It concerned a painter and decorator in Hastings in the early 1900s struggling to support himself and his child, and constantly frustrated by the unwillingness of his workmates - the "Philanthropists" - to organise against corruption and exploitation, better their own lives and those of their families, and break the cycle of poverty and poor wages to benefit their children. The characters work, play, and battle poverty of body and spirit over a year on building sites in and around a coastal resort town in Edwardian England. There are no clever plot devices, little sex and violence, and only minimal narrative structure. What there is in abundance is rage and humour and a realism which many modern writers can rarely aspire to. Robert sub-titled his book: "Being the story of twelve months in Hell, told by one of the damned, and written down by Robert Tressell." His pen name was based on the wooden table used for wallpapering in his trade.

Its author never knew of its publication and his daughter received just £25 for a book than has sold well over a million copies worldwide. The fictionalised but true-to-life novel of ordinary working men struggling to provide for their families had arguably more influence on the rise of Labour and the trade union movement than Marx or Engels. It has been credited with helping Labour win its 1945 general election landslide - battered copies of the abridged form were stuffed in the knapsacks of many returning soldiers - and can therefore be said to have played a part in the creation of the National Health Service and the welfare state. Trade union veteran Jack Jones, as Labour unity fractured in the 1970s, warned: "Ignorance and division will stand in the way of a rapid advance to the socialism of Bob Noonan's dreams."

The novel was an inspiration across the UK and the Commonwealth. The late Eric Heffer, formerly MP for Walton and a carpenter by trade, was given a copy when he was an apprentice. "It had a profound influence," he said decades later. "For the first time it showed what the world of work was really like and how the workers were exploited. It influenced generations of socialists and trade unionists." (1) Author Alan Sillitoe said that the subject of the book was class war and that many people familiar with it "talk about the characters as if they knew them, recount incidents from it as if they had happened to themselves only the other day."(2) Novelist Margaret Drabble described it as the "classic text of the Labour movement" which exposes the "widespread corruption and hypocrisy" inherent in rampant capitalism. Author Raphael Samuel described it as "Socialism's one serious contribution to English literature."

Academic Jonathan Hyslop wrote: "No book shaped the 20th century British labour movement as Robert Tressell's *The Ragged Troosered Philanthropists* (RTP). In the 70 years from its first, posthumous, publication amidst the syndicalist fervour of 1914, to the defeat of industrial unionism in the miners' strike of 1987, it was the Left's semi-underground classic, its copies passed from one activist to another, and hence from one political generation to another. Tressell's tale of the lives of a group of house painters in the southern English town of 'Mugsborough' brilliantly combined socialist propaganda with vitriolic satire, slapstick humour and stories of deep pathos, to achieve an enduring popular appeal." Liverpool seaman's union activist John Nettleton said: "It's a common saying in Liverpool socialist circles that for every person brought into the movement by Marx, there's 10 brought into the movement by Robert Tressell." (3)

Mervyn Jones wrote in 1955: "Go into any meeting room of the working class movement in Britain and you will probably find at least one man present who could say: 'That book brought me into the movement. That book made me a convinced socialist. That book altered the whole course and direction of my life.'" (4)

Author Jack Mitchell wrote in 1969: "No other work of fiction, possibly no other book of any kind, has taken up such secure quarters in the imagination of succeeding generations of militant British workers. It is our one real working class classic." *(5)*

Scouse actor and former union militant Ricky Tomlinson was more succinct: "It's the best book ever."

Much has been written of Tressell's influence, the relevance of his book to successive generations of working class activists, and its effect on the various Leftist factions which have continually splintered from the mainstream of Labour politics. But the life of the man himself has been surrounded by myth, false information and gaping holes in his personal narrative. The late Fred Ball, who pieced together the original manuscript and who wrote two early biographies, did sterling and pioneering work, but was hampered by the paucity of firm facts then available to him. That said, however, this book and others could not have been written without Fred's life-long efforts. Most of the recollections of Tressell's workmates and contemporaries were gathered by him, and I have plundered that archive shamelessly. In my own defence, he interviewed them from the 1930s onwards and when I arrived on the scene in 1970 most of them were long dead and those surviving would not have spoken in such detail to a callow 17-year-old trainee reporter.

The following is my attempt to tell the straightforward story of a remarkable man. There remain many gaps, but Robert insisted that every incident in his novel happened in front of his own eyes. That allows much missing detail to be supplied by the man himself in extracts, reproduced in italics, from his remarkable book.

CHILDHOOD

"always a bit of mystery about him."

THE man posthumously known as Robert Tressell and by his workmates as Robert Noonan was born Robert Croker. His origins are shrouded in mysteries partly of his own making. Possibly due to his adventures in South Africa at the height of Empire, where he was involved in what the authorities would have considered sedition, he told friends and families wildly conflicting stories. He was born in Dublin. Or Liverpool. Or off London's Tottenham Court Road. Rumours abounded that he was the bastard son of an aristocrat. Or a soldier. Or a policeman.

His daughter Kathleen believed that her paternal grandfather was Sir Samuel Croker, an army officer seriously wounded by Fenian rebels and who carried a silver plate in his skull for the rest of his life. But no records of a "Sir Samuel" date from that city at that time. Robert's birth certificate from Dublin's south city district shows that Robert was born on April 18 1870. He was baptised a little over a week later in St Kevin's church. The priest noted that the father, a "pensioner" approaching 80 called Samuel Croker, was not a Catholic, unlike his mother Mary Croker, formerly Noonan, of Wexford Street. But the priest tactfully did not dispute the marital status of the infant's parents.

Samuel Croker was born in 1791 and joined the Royal Irish Constabulary in his 20s. By 1825 he was effectively the police chief of Dungarvan, County Waterford, and later of Carrickbeg, County Tipperary. He retired on an annual pension of £400 in 1840 but continued maintaining law and order as resident magistrate in Ennis, County Clare, for another three years. *(1)* Such posts were immensely lucrative. A share of fines was pocketed by legal right, while even more advantage could be made through business contacts who tipped well for favours and the occasional blind eye. Samuel certainly enjoyed a degree of affluence. In 1862 he secured the mortgage on ramshackle Inverine Castle, but continued living comfortably in Dublin. He was able to read the Greek testament and was said to have studied law. (2)

During his career and its aftermath he was married to Jane Usher Croker who bore him numerous children, of whom three sons and two daughters survived. But at some point he took Mary as his mistress and she was to bear two sons, Robert included, and three daughters, all of whom claimed Samuel as their father.

In1873 Samuel conveyed a commercial property he owned in Great Britain Street to Mary who then received £27.13s.10d (£27.69 – about £3,000 in today's money) a year in rent. The following year he granted her a £100 annuity from his pension. Mary stayed in Wexford Street while the real Mrs Croker lived in the more upmarket Winslow Terrace. So far this was a classic tale of Victorian hypocrisy and class division tempered by some degree of responsibility and devotion. Samuel was a stalwart of the Establishment holding sway over Ireland and would today be considered an exploiter as well as a randy old goat. But he took his responsibilities seriously and risked social ostracism, although admittedly as a retiree he perhaps could not have cared less about that. Mary was his "liaison lady."

It is not clear whether Samuel lived full-time with either of his "wives" or simply flitted between two homes. But Robert's niece reported that the small Robert was very fond of his father who only beat him once for staying out too long.

Robert was a "very sensitive and impressionable child." He was raised a Catholic and, thanks to both maternal devotion and paternal cash, was well-fed, properly clothed and decently educated. His sisters were schooled in a Dublin convent, although there is no record of where Robert was tutored. By most accounts the family had a comfortable existence, albeit on the fringes of respectability. Times may occasionally have been tight, but this was no upbringing of grinding poverty. One relative said many years later: "I have told you quite truthfully that Robert was not born into the working class. He would have had a much happier life, no doubt, had he been."

But sometime before Christmas 1875 Samuel died, reportedly of a condition that left him "raving." Robert, approaching six, "grieved very deeply despite his tender age, and never forgot his father." Mary lost her annuity and married, with what some regarded as indecent haste, a John O'Reilly. He does not appear to have liked his step-children, although he took responsibility for the younger ones as a price of the marriage. Robert in particular was deeply unhappy. He once ran away from home dressed in a sailor suit and was brought home by a policeman who had found him sleeping in a park while hugging a loaf of bread and a butcher's knife. Significantly, the children who feature in RTP have loving, if desperately poor, parents. Robert's childhood was less idealised.

His older siblings moved out one by one - his sister Mary married at 16 - leaving Robert isolated. His niece, Alice Meiklejon, recalled family stories of that time: "His mother married again, sooner than was then thought proper, and apparently the family was split up, and certainly this marriage had a profound effect on Robert, who never, I believe, agreed with it nor took to his stepfather, and the stepfather never took kindly to the children. Also, Robert's education seems to have been seriously interrupted, for he complained in later life of his stinted schooling, that is compared with that received by his brothers and sisters when his father was alive." (3)

There is no evidence of any severe ill-treatment from his step-father beyond what was the norm in such 19th century households, but Robert later suggested that O'Reilly was either a thuggish rent-collector or an absentee landlord whose Irish tenants starved. He probably invented such stories, creating a caricature of despotism from which he needed to escape. Robert never told his daughter Kathleen that he had had a step-father, and family stories confused the two men. But someone told her that her grandmother Mary was "frivolous, vain and proud of her tiny feet" and had married off her eldest daughter "at a very early age because a girl of that age dated the mother."

Kathleen believed that the family had estates elsewhere in Ireland and that "the father left the collecting of rents to agents and lived in comfort himself" with no concern for his tenants. Robert left home because he "could not live on the rentals of absentee tenants." (4) That is dubious. Robert's well-respected father and more disreputable step-father appear to have been merged. And the absentee landlord may have been invented by her father to justify his leaving the family home.

Kathleen insisted that Robert had enrolled as a student at Trinity College, Dublin, but did not start his studies. (5) Trinity have no record or that, but Robert was certainly adept in several languages, which suggests, like other inconsistencies in Robert's version of his family history, that he disguised his own background, embellishing some aspects of his early life, exaggerating others, and deleting even more. He was possibly ashamed of his illegitimacy and, later among the workmen he related to so strongly, of his relatively comfortable, even privileged, youth.

Another reason for the smokescreen, which will be discussed later, was that he regarded himself a fugitive from British oppression in both Ireland and South Africa. Whether that was real or imagined remains cloudy. Tressell's biographer, Fred Ball, who tracked down and interviewed his surviving relatives from the 1930s to 1980s, wrote: "There was always a bit of mystery about him as if he had secrets in his past that he didn't want to talk about, and what he *did* tell people, or what they *said* he told them, didn't always tally.

"He complained to others about his poor schooling; he once joked that his ill-health was due to the age of his parents, and he told friends that he had not been apprenticed to a trade – a most unlikely omission if he had been born into a working-class family of any standing." (6)

Robert honed his skills as a painter and sign-writer, although it is not known where and who taught him the basics. Alice was convinced he never had formal training, much less an apprenticeship, but developed his talent on the basis of childhood lessons. By the age of 16 he was earning his own living away from home and, although he never saw his mother again, switched his surname from Croker to Noonan in 1886. Alice reported: "It was always taken for granted throughout his life that Robert would go off somewhere and then reappear at long intervals giving no explanation. None of his family (ever) knew where he was or how he earned his living in earlier years. He was a true rolling stone." She said: "Robert was extremely self-willed and in my opinion left home in youth unable to bear living at home." (7)

What is clear is that Robert deliberately cut himself adrift not because of any single argument or cataclysmic row, but due to disappointment at his mother's "betrayal" and dislike of his step-father. His elder brothers and sisters had all completed their educations and had either entered professions or marriage. Ball wrote: "He was launched into the world a callow, half-educated youth suddenly finding between himself and the future little but his own brains and energy. What he undoubtedly did have were the severe handicaps which his upbringing would impose on him in these changed circumstances. He was now a working man without having been nurtured as one."

These were tumultuous times in Ireland, whatever one's class, trade or religion. In 1882, when Robert was 12, Fenian assassins murdered Lord Frederick Cavendish on his first day as newly-appointed Lord Lieutenant, and his permanent under-secretary, Thomas Henry Burke. The hunt for the Phoenix Park murderers led to riots and further repression. Throughout Robert's early life the Irish land war raged with uprisings against absentee landlords and their unscrupulous agents, all put down with bloody ferocity. Robert's reading material would have certainly included newspapers and pamphlets which blazed against injustice and exposed infamy. He later quoted Theobald Wolfe Tone: "If the men of property will not, then we must depend upon that numerous and respected class, the men of no property."

On both sides of the Irish Sea the bitter campaign for home rule gathered momentum and the 1885 elections saw 86 Nationalists sent to Westminster. Such issues must have influenced Robert's politics and added to his own sense of confusion - he was a Catholic whose family had relied on cash provided by the Protestant judicial hierarchy. And in 1887 the Fenian case was set back a generation when *The Times* printed a forged letter purporting to show that nationalist leader Charles Stewart Parnell had embraced terrorism and was tacitly involved in the so-called Jubilee Plot to murder Queen Victoria.

All this was against the bitter background of the Great Famine a generation before which had seen Ireland's population reduced by a third through starvation and emigration. Robert, in one of RTP's few references to his homeland, wrote, in Owen's response to an ignorant workmate: *"Four million of people have been exterminated by famine or got rid of by emigration, but they haven't got rid of poverty. P'raps you think that half the people in this country ought to be exterminated as well." (RTP 26)*

Robert's mind, always impressionable and volatile, would have been in turmoil. There was nothing to keep him in Ireland and he left it forever.

Noonan's niece Alice told Fred Ball that her uncle "probably" went first to England. "Whether he left without leave or whether with parents' assent as he was under age, I don't know," she said. "Some of his sisters and probably his brothers had already left Ireland for England and I don't know whether Robert found a home with any of them, but he never saw his mother again and by tacit consent her name was never mentioned among members of the family afterwards." (8

Robert embarked for Liverpool and in 1890 he was a sign writer living in lodgings in Queen's Road, Everton. In nearby Courtney Road, Great Crosby, his niece was a servant in the home of a prosperous shipping agent, Charles Fay Junior. According to documents recently uncovered, Robert was in May charged with 'housebreaking and larceny' at the house, and stealing 'an electro-plated coffee service, tea-pots, cream jugs and other articles to the value of £50' (worth around £4,800 today) on May 27. His alleged confederate, Frances Wilson of Perth Street, Everton, was charged with trying to pawn property she knew to be stolen. On 10 June he appeared at Liverpool County Intermediate Sessions court at Islington, Liverpool after previously having pleaded guilty. He tried to take all of the blame, but he and 25-year-old Wilson, who had no occupation, were sentenced to six months in Walton Gaol. There are several problems with this account. Robert was described as 19, when he had turned 20. His name was common in the area then and now – Liverpool court records are peppered with namesakes from 1890 to 2015. Robert's honesty were remarked on by every person he worked with. His diatribes against the ruling classes were dominated by their dishonesty and hypocrisy. The idea that he engaged in common burglary goes against the nature of the man {although the idea that he tried to take full blame to save a woman from gaol does not). And there is no hint in any of his writings or remembered conversations of a traumatic spell in what was a harsh environment. However, I accept that as a young man burning with resentment at his family circumstances, he may have slipped. It would also explain his capacity to constantly reinvent his own background. Despite the documentary evidence, for me the jury is still out. Whatever the truth, it is clear that Robert regarded Liverpool as a staging post. He wanted a frontier land of sunshine and opportunity. He chose South Africa.

SOUTH AFRICA

"a good little fellow"

ROBERT worked his passage to Cape Colony. It was a boom time, thanks to the discovery in 1867 of diamonds at Kimberley on the border with the neighbouring Orange Free State, and of gold on the Rand in 1886. He arrived in Cape Town, a bustling port-city and major station for the Royal Navy.

Sudden prosperity had increased political tensions. Britain was engaged with the other major Western powers in carving up Africa. It was a race with Portugal, Germany, Belgium and France. The two neighbouring Boer states of the South African Republic, called the Transvaal by the British, and the Orange Free State were caught in the middle. Initially the main motivation had been to control the trade routes to India, but the discovery of diamonds and gold upped the ante. In 1877 the British had annexed the Transvaal and British and other foreign "Uitlanders" flooded in. That resulted in the short but sharp First Boer War of December 1880 to March 1881. The British suffered a near-massacre at Majuba Hill and the government of William Gladstone agreed to give the Transvaal Boers self-governance with nominal allegiance to the British Crown.

Cape Town was mushrooming when Robert arrived, no later than 1890. Its population had risen from 28,400 in 1845 to 67,000 and there was no sign of any let-up - by 1904 it reached 171,000. Most newcomers were young single men from Britain and the colonies who found Cape Town remarkably, and unusually, lacking in racial segregation. White Europeans mixed with Malays and the descendants of Khosa tribesmen and those of both African and Asian slaves. The franchise was based on property qualifications rather than race, so the electorate included a significant minority of "coloureds." But that was changing. The colonial upper crust was moving towards formalised racial divisions. And British artisans were introducing craft and trades unions. White members began to demand protection against blacks and coloureds under-cutting their wages.

Robert first appears in surviving records on October 15 1891 when he married 18-year-old Elizabeth Hartel, a local girl, with one parent's consent in the Protestant Holy Trinity Church. For some reason he gave his age as 23 rather than 21, his trade as "decorator" and his address at 78 Strand Street. The couple lived in the middle-class suburb of Rosebank, Mowbray. (1) Kathleen was born on September 17 1892. The couple were happy for a few years until Robert suspected she was having an affair with a man called Saunders. She denied it, and he had no proof, but Robert remained suspicious and, partly due to those doubts and partly because "business was bad," he left for Johannesburg to find more work and a new home for his family.

Kathleen was baptised on April 7 1895 in the Protestant St Peter's, Mowbray, but later that year she was left with nuns in a convent while Elizabeth travelled to join her husband in Johannesburg. By December she was back "on holiday" in Cape Town where she had an affair with a local man of German descent, 30-year-old Thomas Lindenbaum, a senior cart driver. When Robert returned to Cape Town in April 1896 she was noticeably pregnant. Elizabeth insisted on her innocence until her second child was born in August. Robert again had his suspicions but he again ignored his doubts and "did nothing." Hearing that she was sick, Robert returned again to Cape Town and found her "delirious." In such a delirium, she named Lindenbaum as the father. (2)

On November 11 Robert filed for divorce on the grounds of his wife's adultery. The case was heard on February 27 1897 in the Supreme Court before the Chief Justice Sir John Henry De Villiers. Lindenbaum testified that he had intercourse with her and "used to pay her when I was with her." Robert won his divorce and got custody of Kathleen, while Elizabeth was declared to have forfeited all benefits arising from the marriage "in community of property." She and her child possibly returned to her family, although that is not certain. Typically, when she was older, Robert told his daughter that her mother was a French Catholic called Madeleine who died of typhoid. Kathleen was puzzled about her middle name - Elizabeth. (3)

Robert may have won the case and custody of his daughter, but he harboured some regrets and guilt about the break-up of his marriage. He felt that he must have neglected Elizabeth and so driven her into the arms of another man. That is clear from a tragic sub-plot to his later novel. In RTP the wife and mother of one young child, Ruth Easton, is seduced and has a second child by the religious bigot Alf Slyme. The book's central character,

Frank Owen, berates her husband instead of sympathising with him as a wronged man. Owen challenges William Easton to accept some share of responsibility, saying *"...you treated (her) with indifference and exposed her to temptation. What has happened is the natural result of your neglect and want of care for her. The responsibility for what has happened is mainly yours, but apparently you wish to pose now as being very generous and to "forgive her" - you're "willing" to take her back; but it seems to me that it would be more fitting that you should ask her to forgive you.' (RTP 559)* It is not hard to read into that Robert's own sense of guilt. Or to see the evil Slyme as a disguised portrait of Lindenbaum.

Historian Jonathan Hyslop was convinced. He wrote: "The similarities between Noonan's court-room account of his marriage, and his fictional account of Ruth and William, suggests that in both instances he was telling the same story." (4) He went on: "The Ruth narrative may be understood as Robert's intense attempt to grapple with the experience of his marriage. But he used that engagement to try to think through the relation between personal and social morality. This is a neglected dimension of the (book's) social and political vision." (5)

Leaving Kathleen to be schooled in the convent, Robert returned to Johannesburg. It was a rough and ready place. Its population had doubled to almost 100,000 in three years, and most of them were single men, the majority British, a vociferous minority Irish. In just a decade it had grown from a shanty town to one of the world's richest, the district providing instant wealth for the mining bosses and even more riches for the speculators. The teeming population included Boer oligarchs, the super-rich "Randlords" who ran the mining consortia, British, Australian and American miners, African labourers, Afrikaaner cab drivers, Zulu washermen, Asian coolies, East European prostitutes. Oliver Schreiner described it as a "great, fiendish, hell of a city ....which for glitter and gold and wickedness - carriages and palaces and brothels and gambling halls, beats creation." Robert initially considered it no place to take a five-year-old girl until he was established with a home.

He found work in the town's biggest decorating business, Herbert Evans & Co., founded 1889, which operated from a yard in Kerk Street. Evans, a Shrewsbury painter, had worked for several years in Natal but saw in Johannesburg much greater opportunities. The city was expanding rapidly and the number of new buildings erected almost doubled from 1,236 in

1894 to 2,358 the following years. Evans became the leading painter and decorating firm, thanks in part to the ruthlessness of its boss. In February 1896 that became clear when a train carrying 150 tons of dynamite blew up at Braamfontein goods yard, killing many and shattering windows across the city. Evans immediately telegraphed every glass manufacturers in southern Africa and bought every pane. He then had a monopoly of window replacements across Johannesburg and his staff worked around the clock to keep up with demand. Evans must have provided at least part of the character of Rushton, the ruthless boss in RTP, and Noonan used the Kerk Street address in his novel.

The Transvaal politics that Robert encountered was a three-way struggle between the Boer ruling classes who keenly protected the independence of the Transvaal; the miner owners and the middle classes who were equally keen to incorporate the country into the British Empire; and the exploited immigrant labour force. The imperial lobby of the South African League pumped out propaganda suggesting that British subjects were living under a despotic Boer yoke. The Kruger administration responded by highlighting the exploitations and excesses of the mining barons, and by introducing reforms in workplace practices. They were needed. Black and Asian workers may have been at the bottom of the pile, living in sordid and squalid compounds, but the white miners suffered high mortality rates from lung disease deep underground and from the effects of the cyanide extraction process used. They were paid better than the natives but that was undercut by high transport costs and inflation leading to high living costs. That led in turn to tensions between the various workforces and a sceptical attitude to the imperial case against the Boers amongst white incomers.

Hyslop wrote: "If Robert Noonan had deliberately set out to select a city where he could examine the worst excesses of capitalism, he surely could not have found one so appropriate for that purpose anywhere on this planet. Johannesburg was already a byword for greed, commercial swindles, and wanton disregard for human life."

For three years Noonan worked under and alongside foreman Stewart Ogilvy who found him "a very good signwriter, indeed, the best I have ever known." Ogilvy reckoned he had "the makings of a brilliant artist." Robert must have been made a junior foreman himself when the company created a separated signwriting department because he was earning £7 or more a week when the wage for an ordinary tradesman was £5 for a five-and-a-half day week. Ogilvy described him: "Noonan was short and well built. We used to call him 'little Noonan.' He walked with a sharp energetic step and a slight roll or sway. His speech was good and his accent very slightly Irish. He did not mix much with his fellow employees, but on the whole he was a good little fellow."

Ogilvy recalled that Robert was "an interesting and entertaining companion" with a "brilliant and versatile mind." Robert appears to have been in demand as a talker in a town which "offered little, outside hard drinking, in the way of amusement." Ogilvy added: "He was an extremely pleasant fellow, and the best company, and we became very friendly." Robert, he said, "lived in a little world of his own and was very fond of writing, especially articles dealing with everyday life." (6)

One such piece, "All meals a shilling," appeared in a local magazine. Robert "had an eye for queer characters, and would follow them about, endlessly listening to their conversations, and taking voluminous notes of how they looked and what they said. When, many years afterwards, a copy of his book came into my hands, I had no difficulty whatever in identifying some of the characters portrayed as being derived from the oddities Noonan had subjected to such close examination and study during the years he lived on the rand."

At the time Robert told his foreman that he had planned to write a book about his impressions of the people of Johannesburg, but that had to be shelved because of "troubled times." He did not say whether that was a reference to his domestic life or the impending crisis in South Africa.

Robert was also attracted to get-rich-quick gold mining schemes and land speculation, but found himself an innocent swimming amongst sharks. The opening up of the gold-fields had sparked an astonishing bubble in land prices, regardless of whether there was gold on the property. After the Boers had driven out the natives, they sold land amongst each other for as little as a farthing an acre. After the gold strikes it rose to £1 an acre, while when Robert was in town one lot in Johannesburg sold for £40,000. In June 1898 Robert leased Lot No 16, Block No 2 of farmland in the Witwatersrand goldfield, in Heidelberg district. The 99-year lease was registered with the

Robert Noonan and Kathleen, studio portrait

Registrar of Mining Right, but it gave him no mineral rights, only costly responsibilities. He had to pay £3 a year in advance and was required, under the lease's terms, to fence the property and to accept that no building valued at less than £200 should be erected on it - a measure that made it impossible to erect a shack with which to pursue mining. Moreover, he had to agree never to sell, sub-lease or hire out the land to "any Malay, Chinese, Coolie, Indian, or other coloured person." (7) Robert paid up to the end of 1899, but never built on the land, and he lost possession of it. Robert described such deals as "swindles."

By the time of his abortive foray into land speculation, Robert had sent for Kathleen and installed her in the Convent of the Holy Family in Regent Street, Johannesburg, which was run by the Holy Sisters of Bordeaux. The Convent was Roman Catholic, while Kathleen's baptism had been Protestant. Robert had "no use" for organised religion, but sent her there either because it provided the most "suitable" education for a young girl, or because of a promise to his own mother. He took his child on an outing every Sunday. Kathleen remembered the school as "far from being cheap" and was clearly a place for the relatively affluent. Day girls would be brought to school in carriages, while Kathleen was given, presumably from her father, a necklace with a diamond, a ruby and a pearl. She has a nurse, Mary Eulalie, while Robert himself employed a servant called Sixpence of whom Robert was "quite fond." All of which points to Robert building up a relatively prosperous, comfortable life for himself and his daughter

But despite the niceties and veneer of a late Victorian colonial community, Johannesburg was at heart still a rough frontier town.

In the early hours one morning, having been at a party, Robert saw a man apparently insensible through drink or accident lying in the road. He went to offer aid and to move him to the side of the road to prevent him being run over by horses and carriages. But as he bent down to help the man and his cronies set upon him in a classic muggers' set-up. He was battered and robbed. Kathleen recalled: "I don't know how he got to hospital, but he was found to have a broken nose and was operated upon. While under the anaesthetic, although unable to move, he heard the doctors saying 'The books describe this as an easy operation but we're not finding it so.' When it was all over Robert said, 'You didn't find it as simple as you expected, eh?', and a doctor replied, "Perfectly simple," and Robert surprised them by repeating their conversation. It seems our family doesn't take well to anaesthetics. My Aunt Mary Jane was treated with morphine as a pain-killer for neuritis and the doctor told her she had taken enough to kill anyone else." (8)

Kathleen never knew whether Robert had christened his servant Sixpence or whether it was his birth name because *they had all kind of, to us, funny names." She recalled that Sixpence once stole a green and gold sash and Robert "used to imagine him strutting in front of his wives, wearing nothing but his loin-cloth." (9) Robert never begrudged the minor theft, and Kathleen insisted that the "colour question" never arose although she remembered that a man was "attacked by Kaffirs at a farm near the convent." But colour did feature in Robert's first recorded foray into trade union activism.

Robert had not belonged to a union in Cape Town, but by the end of 1897 he helped form the Transvaal Federated Building Trades Council with himself as secretary. It was his first act as a trade union organiser and active socialist. Its first public act, however, was to protest "against the employment of black skilled labour." Faced with the threat of action, architects behind Johannesburg's building boom insisted that only white skilled workmen would be employed in future. It was a victory for white supremacy but Robert and his fellows should not be judged by today's standards. Throughout industrialisation bosses had sought to undercut wages by employing the ill-organised and the despised, whether blacks ...or Irish. White supremacy sits uncomfortably with socialism but it can be seen as a necessary evil for those struggling to maintain and improve pay and conditions. The infant trade unions later in Britain bitterly opposed many Suffragette ideals and ambitions, including the right to work alongside men, because they correctly feared that women were prepared to work for less.

Robert's next moves were overtly political. He went to the launch of the International Independent Labour Party (IILP), formed by British trade unionists and German Socialists, in his capacity as trades council secretary. The inaugural meeting or around 60 members elected Robert to the steering committee. The IILP had a real impact on Transvaal politics and came close to persuading the Boer Parliament to enact legislation introducing an eight-hour working day. (10)

The IILP regarded the Boers as victims of British imperialism and Robert was only elected to the committee after vigorously denying allegations that he had mocked President Kruger. Common cause with the Boers was also merging with Irish Nationalism, and Robert was elected to the Transvaal executive committee of the Centennial of 1798 Association. That commemorated the revolt, brutally crushed 100 years earlier, of the United Irishmen. Ogilvy said: "Although he was British, Noonan was very much opposed to the war." The pieces which formed the "Ragged-Trousered" author - Socialist, trade unionist, Republican - were coming together.

To modern, liberal sensibilities following the apartheid era, it can be difficult to understand Robert's advocacy of the Boers. They were God-fearing racists, but the British were imperialistic freebooters. Dissent amongst the Uitlanders, mainly British, of their lack of rights in the Transvaal under Boer self-governance was exploited by the expansionist Cecil Rhodes who had made his fortune out of mining. He became prime minister of Cape Colony in 1890 and dreamed of British African rule "from the Cape to Cairo." He was largely behind the disastrous and ignominious Jameson Raid by 500 adventurers aiming to oust the Boer leadership and replace them with men who supported Rhodes' ideal of a federated South Africa.

Tensions rose throughout the 1890s and were coming to a head when Robert was engaged in Johannesburg. Robert, a free spirit, an Irishman and a romantic, was drawn to the Boer side due to a hatred of British imperialism, not of the British themselves. Legally, of course, he was a Briton but it was easy in those time for Irish and Boers, both essentially farming nations with strong religious ties, to find common cause.

Ball wrote: "Robert must have watched the growing tension between Boers and English with alarm and with his Irish anti-British sentiments it wasn't far to becoming a pro-Boer. Indeed, it appeared to many liberal-minded people in England that Britain, as she had done all through the nineteenth century, was waging another colonial war against a small nation. The cover story used by the British in the quarrel with the Boers concerned the limitations on civil rights and restrictions on the franchise imposed on the Uitlanders. But in reality both British and Boers were determined upon gaining control of South Africa for themselves. Apart from the historical rivalry between the two people, the very logic of the economic conflict, in this virtually 'undeveloped' sub-continent, between two ways of life, industrial and pastoral, made war inevitable." (11) Robert's Irish sentimentality and burning anti-imperialism, was drawing him into the conflict.

A fellow-member of the 1798 centennial committee was the wealthy Pretorian baker Sol Gillingham who linked the Irish Republican Brotherhood - a forerunner of the Irish Republican Army (IRA) - to the Boers. Another, John MacBride, was later shot by the British after the 1916 Easter Rising. An ordinary member, Arthur Griffith, was to become President of Sinn Fein. Robert was in volatile, and dangerous, company. Ogilvy was certain that Robert was "active in the formation of the Irish Brigade", a clandestine organisation which began recruiting for men to fight on behalf of the Boers in the event of a second war. Ogilvy recalled Robert railing against the war during its approach, blaming British aggression and imperialism.

Robert had rooms on Pritchard Street and he "and a lot of other wild Irishmen used to meet and concert their plans" in a small cleaners and dyers' shop in the same street. (12) For six weeks from early August 1899 the group met every Sunday - the miners' day off - and debated how best to help the Boers. MacBride consistently advocated armed resistance.

On September 3 a proposal was made to take up arms with the Boers. Three days later the Boer leadership authorised the creation of the First Irish Transvaal Brigade. Its commander was John Joseph Mitchell, whose premises the group used for their secret meetings, with MacBride as second-in-command. On October 2 the pair travelled across the border to Pretoria to receive their commissions while in Johannesburg recruits enlisted in Pritchard Street, the new Brigade's temporary HQ. Most were Irish or Irish-American miners. On the 5th they marched to the railway station and entrained to the Natal border. War broke out less than a week later.

Robert was certainly involved to some degree in the Irish Brigade. During that early period, whenever Kathleen asked him where he was going he would reply: "To see a man about a dog." (13) The big question is: did he enlist, and if so, did he fight against the British? Robert was himself tight-lipped on the subject throughout his life. If he had fought, that would be explained by fear of state repercussions in response to a treasonous act. If not, he may not have wanted to be seen merely as a talker, not a fighter.

The balance of probability is that he did not enlist but was active in its creation. That would explain his reticence throughout his life and his reluctance later to sign his name to anything. Henry Evans' business had shut down in August, so he was out of work with a child to support, and service in the Brigade was unpaid. He was also suffering ill-health, so maybe he was turned down as unfit for active service. He partially blamed his weak chest on the advanced age of his parents, as we have seen. But Kathleen also remembered her father repeatedly blaming his condition on "drinking whiskey to keep warm when riding across the veldt at nights, and getting chilled."

The question of enlistment cannot be answered with total certainty either way because no full muster rolls for the Irish Transvaal Brigade survive. But there was no mention of a Robert Noonan in detective branch papers written during intensive undercover scrutiny. But it is a fair bet that Robert's involvement did not go unnoticed by the authorities and Ogilvy recalled that his friend "disappeared into the blue very shortly before the Boer War broke out." (14)

There has been intense speculation that if Robert did enlist, then he was captured and imprisoned before the last Brigade train left Johannesburg, and was behind bars for the rest of the war before being deported. Such speculation is unfounded. The story Robert told his niece Alice and later workmates was that he had joined the sometimes panicky civilian exodus in the last days before the outbreak of war. He left on October 9 1899 on the last train heading south to Cape Town. He said that the journey had been "terrible" with between 70 and 100 people packed into open "Kaffir-trucks" normally used for blacks, or cattle, or coal, not white people. For three days and nights he was "exposed to the spring rain, and covered in mud and coal dust." The Irish Nationalist Michael Davitt recorded the panic as somewhere between 30,000 and 40,000 Uitlanders fled Transvaal: "Trains for Natal and Delagoa Bay were crowded every day with refugees. They rushed off in mindless panic before the war broke out. No immediate risk menaced their persons or liberties - they rushed into cattle trucks in their hurry to be off. They fought for places."

But that story, too, was at odds with Kathleen's recollections. She remembered that her father had considered remarrying but the object of his affection could not stomach the responsibility of raising someone else's child.

In 1897 he had written to his widowed sister, Adelaide Rolleston, who had emigrated to Santiago, Chile, where her late husband had worked in the British consulate. When her husband died she supported herself and their son Arthur in Valparaiso by teaching English in a convent school. He asked her to join him in South Africa to keep house for him and "be a mother to" Kathleen. In return he would "be a father to" her son, and support the whole family. He sent her the fare to South Africa but Adelaide spent it on visiting family in England instead of taking direct passage. Robert then sent her the fare from England to Cape Town.

During the months of delay war grew closer and Kathleen believed that Adelaide's behaviour was another reason for putting Robert's pro-Boer sympathies to one side. Her selfishness may well have saved his life. Adelaide and Arthur arrived in September 1899 and Robert left Johannesburg the next month to meet them and "to arrange for a house for us all in Rondesbosch, near Cape Town." Adelaide was used to personal maids and house servants and there was never any question that she would deign to join Robert and Kathleen in the still rough mining town. Kathleen insisted that her father's leaving of Johannesburg "had nothing to do with the Irish Brigade" and that he left "on his own and not under duress."

The clincher is that Robert left Kathleen behind in Johannesburg. Everything known about Robert points to a loving and responsible father who would never have abandoned his child in a general panic. Either Robert later made up the cattle truck story or, which is possible, he returned to Johannesburg on business just before the outbreak of war.

Kathleen stayed on at the convent for several more weeks after the war began and, due to her father's tirades that the real reason for the war was diamonds and gold mines, she was herself outspoken against it. At morning assembly "everyone would be praying for the British to win, and I would be praying for the Boers. When an English officer gave all the children Union Jack buttons, she threw hers to the ground and stamped on it. When a rousing chorus of God Save the Queen began, she sat down. (13) Clearly she could not stay.

The nuns asked a Frenchwoman, Mme Vailant, to take her to her father in Cape Town. They travelled comfortably by train to Durban, and completed the journey by boat. When they reached her new home Kathleen mistook her "vain" Aunt Adelaide for a maid. Kathleen recalled: "My aunt turned up in a white tailored suit which, no doubt, looked like a maid's uniform to me. I was used to people with a more fussy kind of clothes. I would only remember that I'd expected my daddy to come for me and absolutely refused to go with a woman I'd never seen. My whole trip from Johannesburg had probably been one long anticipation of seeing my father again." (15) Adelaide never forgave the imagined slight from the precocious seven-year-old.

Robert and Kathleen, Adelaide and Arthur, lived in the Cape Town suburb. They appear to have lived mainly off savings, but were comfortable enough to employ a "dark girl" as a maid. Robert probably took on personal contracts for painting and signwriting, as no record of employment with a major firm exists. But the war had produced a slump in the trade, and Robert would have devoured reports of the war's progress. And it is not hard to imagine his sense of shame when news came of the exploits of the Irish Transvaal Brigade.

On December 15 1899 they played a pivotal part in the humiliating defeat of the British at the battle of Colonso, covering Boer movements. The British fatalities included Lt. the Hon. Freddy Roberts, only son of Field Marshall Lord Roberts. At the siege of Ladysmith they serviced the Boer artillery piece Long Tom, which gave them a huge range advantage over the defenders. As miners they were renowned demolition experts and were credited with delaying the British advance of Pretoria by blowing up bridges. In the 12 months to September 1900 they fought in around 20 engagements and suffered 18 dead and around 70 wounded out of a strength that was never more than 500 at any one time. When they disbanded, partly due to Boer reversals and partly due to internal divisions, most crossed the border into Mozambique, a neutral Portuguese colony.

The war dragged on and in October 1900 Kitchener stationed troops in Cape Town and its environs. The following year the horrors of his concentration camps became well known internationally. Robert joined in the overwhelming revulsion. He decided to leave South Africa and start again in England.

In late September the two adults and two children spent several days at the Hotel La France in Cape Town - Kathleen was bitten by a pet monkey which she had petted in defiance of her father's instructions - before embarking on the Union Castle line's brand new *SS Galician*, a 6,897-ton vessel build at the Belfast shipyard Harland and Wolff.

Kathleen was told that the reason was to ensure she had a full and proper education. She recalled: "There probably were good schools both in Cape Town and Johannesburg but colonials living abroad nearly always brought their children home to be educated. I do not think that there was any question of his not being able to afford to send me to a good school in South Africa. The convent was far from being cheap. He did not know the great difference he would find in English conditions and by that time it was too late to return to South Africa." (16)

Robert certainly considered his daughter's education of utmost importance. He was always embarrassed at his lack of formal education beyond his mid-teens and throughout his life took every step possible to widen his knowledge. As his political opinions gelled, he also saw education as a way to break the cycle of poverty to which working-class families were condemned. In his novel he railed against "despicable" workmates who seemed content to continue that cycle.

Hyslop wrote: "It was not in Hastings, but in Johannesburg that Robert Noonan was drawn into labour organization and socialist politics. His scepticism towards the British social order had also been fostered in Johannesburg by involvement with some of the leading protagonists of Irish nationalism. "

English friends later gave other explanations for the family's return from South Africa. One said that Robert left because things were "upside down" during the war. Another agreed, saying: "During the war business became so dislocated that he came to this country." Another said that Adelaide insisted on going to England where her sisters had settled. (17) Whichever was true, and they probably all are to differing degrees, it still seems strange that Robert should go to the country he had railed against across two hemispheres. Fred Ball wrote: "I wonder about his feelings as he left South Africa. It had given him and taken away his wife; it had given him a daughter. And he had seen the Boer cause defeated by numbers 10 times their own ...at a cost of over 120,000 British soldiers dead, missing or invalided out, or twice the number of the entire Boer forces." (18)

During the first few days on board Robert appears to have been under some strain as he smacked Kathleen for the first and last time for cheeking a fellow passenger. As the voyage progressed at a rate of 12 knots he became his old self again, playing practical jokes on both family members and passengers. One jape saw him wetting one of Adelaide's fur stoles and putting it in his victim's bed where it looked like a large black snake. She was terrified and not amused. Robert apologised. (19) Robert organised his daughter's ninth birthday party in transit. He also produced several editions of a news and gossip newsletter. The flimsy, hand-written sheets he titled *The Evening Ananias*, after the Biblical character who "fell down and gave up the ghost after being found out a liar." Given Robert's sardonic humour and occasional self-mocking, it is easy to believe that the title reflected his own meek exodus after so many brave words.

The S.S. Galician

HASTINGS, OR MUGSBOROUGH

"a vast whited sepulchre"

Robert, Kathleen, Adelaide and her son Arthur arrived in England in late 1901 as the Boer War was coming to its drawn-out conclusion and as the country was still coming to terms with a new age following the death of Queen Victoria.

They stayed first in London and Robert joined a branch of the Painters' Union. There is no record of him finding work there. He roamed the cold, wet streets which did not suit him, having been told by a South African doctor that he had tuberculosis. He suffered from lung and chest troubles and Kathleen later recalled that he had "recurrent attacks of bronchitis and would cough and cough."

Friends and workmates he made in the months that followed described him as a "compact" five foot and three inches weighting about nine stone, thinning hair on top, a sandy moustache, on the frail side. William Ward said that his eyes "seemed to have a light behind them" which he put down to ill-health. Others noticed "the pink spots which appeared on his cheeks in moments of excitement." (1)

The building and decorating trade was in a periodic slump, and Robert's savings must soon have diminished. A 1922 article in the union publication *Painter's Journal* said that "he remained some time in London where, his physique being against him, he had a bitter struggle for an existence." But Kathleen thought they only stayed in the capital for a few weeks. Robert decided to seek help from family on this side of the Irish Sea. He had two sisters living in England, Ellie in Liverpool, and Mary Jane in a south coast health resort. The latter wrote to him urging him to come to "dear, sunny Hastings." Robert took up the offer and, with Adelaide and the two children, rattled down of the South Eastern and Chatham railway.

They stayed with Mary Jane at 38 Western Road, St Leonards. As an elderly lady Kathleen was asked for how long." I don't know," she replied, "but my aunt probably thought we had money and when she found out we hadn't our welcome wore out." During that stay the family was visited by Ellie, who travelled down from Liverpool. It was the last time the four siblings got together. Despite the thawing family welcome, Robert decided to stay in Hastings. The town was recommended to sufferers of pulmonary weakness. He found a house to rent at 1 Plynlimmon Road, on the West Hill overlooking Hastings town centre, the ancient cliff-top castle and the gasworks.

The gasworks have since gone, but the view of the railway and numerous pubs still remain. As do the town hall, various meeting places, some churches, the library, the out-of-town cemetery, work premises and many of the houses Robert worked on.

Hastings remains best-known for the battle fought a few miles inland in which William the Conqueror defeated Harold and sealed the Norman Conquest. Its importance in early medieval times was its status as a Cinque Port which contributed ships and sailors to the royal navy. In 1339 and 1377 it was sacked by the French, but the port continued to serve, sending the 70-ton *Anne Bonaventure* to help defeat the Spanish Armada. But repeated raids and turbulent seas wrecked the harbour and the town became an impoverished fishing port. In 1656 the harbour was completely swept away. The fishing fleet remained (it is still Europe's largest beach launched fleet) because of the fertile fishing grounds in nearby Rye Bay and Hastings became a hub for smuggling luxury goods, from brandy to silks, from continental Europe. The conclusion of the Napoleonic Wars saw that illicit trade dwindle.

But in the late 18th century Hastings appeared to have a new lease of life thanks to the craze for sea-bathing amongst the gentry and ruling classes. In 1771 the landlord of the Swan Inn realised the opportunities and advertised that his accommodation had been upgraded to serve visitors of taste and discrimination. That summer the better-off swarmed to Hastings and the boom continued as more facilities, including bathing machines, were provided. By 1815 the town was firmly established as a premier seaside resort, but the lack of accommodation of suitable quality, for both visitors and permanent settlers, became a severe problem.

The property speculator James Burton saw his opportunity in the adjoining hamlet of St Leonards. He designed a new town fit for gentlemen to live in. His first project was the seafront St Leonards Hotel, now the Royal Victoria, a wedding-cake confection. Behind and around it

Better-off strollers on St Leonards' sea-front, c. 1908

he built fine mansions fit for wealthy commuters. In Hastings itself the period saw such elegant constructions as Wellington Square, Pelham Crescent and St Mary-in-the-Castle cut into the cliff face. Such developments spread along the promenade to join up with St Leonards.

But the railway, which arrived in Hastings in 1846, was not fast or efficient enough - partly due to some dodgy cost-cutting in the construction of tunnels - and it took three hours from London rather than the one hour to the town's bigger rival at Brighton. That was crucial for the first generation of gentlemen rail commuters. In 1851 the *Hastings News* reported: "The houses that are now being built on the Carlisle Parade and elsewhere are intended for families whose dinner hour is generally fixed from six to seven o'clock." A direct line was built in 1852, but communications remained a problem. (2)

Nevertheless, the town's population quadrupled to just over 50,000 and by 1881 was the second largest resort after Brighton. A decade later it topped 57,000 following the development of Bohemia, St Mary's and Silverhill. The tourism industry dwarfed fishing, which was hit by competition from East Coast industrialised ports. The chief handicap was the lack of a proper harbour and an 1897 attempt to build a new one was uncompleted when, due to financial irregularities, the money ran out. (3)

In 1888, following reform of local government, Hastings became a county borough and its council became responsible for all local services independent of the surrounding county. It was an advance for both democracy and for get-rich-quick entrepreneurs who swiftly dominated the authority. Corruption mushroomed.

Hastings may have once been a magnet for genteel families seeking fresh sea air, but when Robert and his family arrived it was a hell-hole for those seeking work. He could not have arrived at a worse time. Hastings may have become a "superior" resort but faced stiff competition not just from Brighton but from the newer resorts of Bexhill, Eastbourne and Bournemouth. The town's standing as a resort was waning, partly due to the local council's refusal to invest in modern facilities during a recession. The posher visitors were outraged that the town's hospital was opposite the pier, forcing promenaders to look at the sick and crippled.

A correspondent to the *Hastings Observer* wrote: "Our local band and promenade fairly 'take the cake.' It is nothing short of a scandal. It is so indescribable, so utterly ridiculous an attempt at resort organisation that words fail to express one's contempt. Imagine an open, windswept place, washed over by seas as high as houses, at times draughty, or sun-baked, at others dusty or puddly, with a band of really good artistes doing their level best to give pleasure to those seeking rest, repose and refinement. On one side there are puddles of water, dogs are barking in all directions, trams are passing every minute with a noise like thunder, nursery maids are wriggling all over the place in hysteric convulsion of brainless giggling, bits of girls from local slums flaunt about with motor veils on their hatless hair, charwomen talk at the top of their cracked voices, while the conductor struggles with the Prelude in Lohengrin." (4) Others complained that "common" weekenders who filled the pubs of the Old Town, always a boisterous fishing village, deterred visitors of a "better class." One local newspaper editorialised: "The day tripper in multitude deteriorates Hastings and St Leonards as a watering place; and that so long as the railway company drafts thousands of Londoners into our borough at a ridiculously cheap rate so long Hastings will continue to suffer." (5)

Jack Mitchell wrote: "While the newly-rich paraded the promenades of such fashionable resorts as Hastings, the standard of life of the people dropped dramatically." (6)

Robert portrayed the scene as unemployment rose: *Most of them just walked about aimlessly or stood talking in groups in the streets, principally in the neighbourhood of the Wage Slave Market near the fountain on the Grand Parade. They congregated here in such numbers that one or two residents wrote to the local papers complaining of the `nuisance', and pointing out that it was calculated to drive the `better-class' visitors out of the town. After this two or three extra policemen were put on duty near the fountain with instructions to `move on' any groups of unemployed that formed. They could not stop them from coming there, but they prevented them standing about.* (RTP 335)

Working men, in their spattered overalls, were also considered a blot on the landscape: *Quite a common spectacle - for gods and men - was a procession consisting of a handcart loaded up with such materials being pushed or dragged through the public streets by about half a dozen of these Imperialists in broken boots and with battered, stained, discoloured bowler hats, or caps splashed with paint and whitewash; their stand-up collars dirty, limp and crumpled, and their rotten second-hand misfit clothing saturated with sweat and plastered with mortar.*

Even the assistants in the grocers' and drapers' shops laughed and ridiculed and pointed the finger of scorn at them as they passed.

The superior classes - those who do nothing - regarded them as a sort of lower animals. A letter appeared in the Obscurer one week from one of these well-dressed loafers, complaining of the annoyance caused to the better-class visitors by workmen walking on the pavement as they passed along the Grand Parade in the evening on their way home from work, and suggesting that they should walk in the roadway. When they heard of the letter a lot of the workmen adopted the suggestion and walked in the road so as to avoid contaminating the idlers. (RTP 392-393)

Crucially, Hastings had no basic industries to fall back on. The only industrial structures were the gasworks retort-houses belching foul smoke over the town centre. Alf Cobb wrote in 1907: "Hastings is a non-industrial town, which dependents entirely upon its visitor for its prosperity. Forsaken by our wealthy classes, we must rely on the tripper, or holiday class."(7) Ball wrote that it had an economy "best described as taking in one another's washing." The pier and promenade was where the gentry paraded, and the Old Town still had a fishing fleet, but ordinary working families relied on the local Corporation, the railway, the public utilities, domestic service, shop work and, at the bottom of the pile, the building trades.

The last was at a low ebb. Over 50 years the borough's population had increased substantially, but much of the building work had been completed during that time. There was a high proportion of the retired and elderly and the fine Burton houses in St Leonards were fast being split into small homes for spinsters. House prices fell by up to 40 per cent in the century's first decade. The elaborate homes which had sprung up on the West Hill, Mount Pleasant and Clive Vale were finished. There was no room to expand in a borough geographically clinging to the sides of parallel valleys and, given the straitened times, the population was slipping. Between 1901 and 1911 it fell 4,000.

The end of the Boer War brought its own decline in building and the competition became stiffer. Few full-time building firms were left when Robert arrived and those still engaged in construction diversified into redecoration, shop fronts and funeral directorships. They became the inspiration for RTP's "Bodgers" and "Rushtons," skimping on materials, cheating customers and cutting pay and conditions to maintain profits. Their best customers were sweatshop traders who cared only for cheapness, not quality.

Certain crafts within the trade remained relatively secure with firms keeping a permanent core of bricklayers, joiners and carpenters, but other hands were paid by the hour and could be laid off at any time with no more notice than that.

Mike Matthews wrote: "Because Hastings had no industrial base it lacked any tradition of organised trade unionism and collective support. The development of mutual aid and working class solidarity was greatly restricted and working men were at the mercy of unscrupulous employers. Wage-slavery and oppressive working conditions flourished. There were accusations that the Corporation sweated its labour force, ignoring the fair wage clause written into every employees' contract." (8)

The wages in the painting, decorating and building trades varied from 5d to 8d an hour, which meant that in even good times income varied between 18 shillings and one pound five shillings a week. Every workman was in debt – rent arrears, rates, personal loans and 'tick' from shops which got them through periods, even for the most secure, when they were seasonally laid off. Robert, a great advocate of balance sheets to make a point, broke down the Hastings working man's income and outgoings. The figures fluctuated due to inflation and living costs, but they applied throughout the decade he was writing about: *How much rent do we owe now?' asked Easton.*

`Four weeks, and I promised the collector the last time he called that we'd pay two weeks next Monday. He was quite nasty about it.'
`Well, I suppose you'll have to pay it, that's all,' said Easton.
`How much money will you have tomorrow?' asked Ruth.
He began to reckon up his time: he started on Monday and today was Friday: five days, from seven to five, less half an hour for breakfast and an hour for dinner, eight and a half hours a day - forty-two hours and a half. At sevenpence an hour that came to one pound four and ninepence halfpenny.
`You know I only started on Monday,' he said, `so there's no back day to come. Tomorrow goes into next week.'
`Yes, I know,' replied Ruth.
`If we pay the two week's rent that'll leave us twelve shillings to live on.'
(RTP 52-53)

The couple reckoned up. They owed the baker 4s for bread delivered during the breadwinner's period of unemployment and another 12 shillings in groceries. Rent arrears, at 6s a week came to 24s. Another 4/8d was owed to the milkman, 2/7d to the butcher, around £6 was owed for the hire purchase of furniture and final demands for the rates totalled £1 4s 1d. The couple tried to work out what they could, or would have to, pay: two weeks' rent 12s, baker and butcher arrears 2s each, furniture repayments 12s, milkman 1/1d, grocer 1s. That might put off the bailiffs, but they needed to feed and warm themselves and their baby: a hundredweight of coal 1/6d, a piece of meat and a week's worth of bread and vegetable 3s, other foodstuffs including tea and butter 3s. They had nowhere near enough for the basic necessities, never mind clothing and little luxuries.

In the week before Christmas, a time when paid hours were cut, Owen had earned 19/3d for a 33-hour week. He and his wife totted up – 7s for rent, 1/3d for bread, 1½s for milk, 1/8 for coal, five pence three-farthing's for their son's socks, 4d for paraffin oil, 1s on potatoes and other vegetables. Luckily most of their week's food supply, including meat, was provided by various Christmas Clubs into which they had been paying throughout the year. They were left with four shillings and sevenpence halfpenny for the festive season and their priority was to buy toys for their little son. They bought a clockwork train engine for 1s, a box of dolls from Japan for 6d, and assorted items, including a paint box, for 1/6d. That left them with just over a shilling to enjoy seasonal cheer themselves. (RTP 297) It was still a happy family Christmas.

Unemployment was, of course, a constant dread throughout the decade, subject to troughs and peaks. The brunt was invariably borne by the building trades. The Hastings Distress Committee one year broke down the town's registered jobless as follows: navies and general labourers 283, carpenters 13, painters 73, masons 3, bricklayers 13, plasterers, carters and carman 12, gardeners 5, plumbers mates 2 and one apiece amongst gas fitters, butchers, night-watchmen, scaffolders, upholsterers, decorators, blacksmiths, store dressers, tinsmiths, printers, machine minders, needlewomen, mineral water manufacturers, furniture packers and porters. (9) The 434 total was well short of the true tally, as it only included the registered unemployed who had filled in the necessary forms and not the large numbers of casual and seasonal workers whose names rarely appeared on electoral rolls.

The vacancies column of the *Observer* in one edition the previous year graphically showed the meagre opportunities for both sexes: there were 13 vacancies for men and 16 for boys, but 103 for females. All the latter were in the domestic trade – dressmakers, ironers, millinery apprentices, maids, servants, housekeepers and helpers. (10)

The poorest parts of Hastings were Halton, Ore and the Old Town. Matthews refers to a Wesleyean pastor, one of the few churchmen from the period to emerge with any credit, speaking out in 1902 on behalf of congregation members living on four shillings a week, from which 2s 6d went on rent and the pitiful remainder had to cover food, clothing, lighting and heat. He said that such poverty was endemic across the borough, but sometimes disguised by "a frantic effort to keep up appearances." The pastor added: "Let it be remembered that in Old Hastings the only appearance which is kept up is that which corresponds to the grim reality of poverty and hunger – at this moment I am visiting those who are sick, the doctors urge nourishment: they might as well urge the moon." (11)

Ore, a rural village swallowed up by the expanding borough, was so poverty-stricken that in 1905 a doctor said the levels of deprivation was worse anything he had seen while practicing in the slums of London's East End. During the winter the Penny Dinner Fund gave free food on schooldays to 200 ragged, emaciated children (12)

For the unemployed and their families there was no safety net save Poor Law Relief and ultimately the workhouse. Both were administered by the local worthies who, as Robert pointed out, were responsible for creating the conditions of poverty. They doled out meagre payments to those they deemed suitable, while "chronic" cases were sent to the workhouse. There men and women and children were housed separately. Hastings workhouse was built in Cackle Street, now Frederick Road, in 1836 as part of a national network created after the poor law amendment act two years earlier which was aimed at weeding out the "workshy." On average during the 1905-06 it contained 396 permanent or semi-permanent inmates and 217 'vagrants' who had to work for overnight shelter. Robert described the effect on the elderly and recently-redundant Jack Linden and his wife:

One week about the middle of February, when they were in very sore straits indeed, old Jack applied to the secretary of the Organized Benevolence Society for assistance. It was about eleven o'clock in the morning when he turned the corner of the street where the office of the society was situated and saw a crowd of about thirty men waiting for the doors to be opened in order to apply for soup tickets. Some of these men were of the tramp or the drunken loafer class; some were old, broken-down workmen like himself, and others were labourers wearing corduroy or moleskin trousers with straps round their legs under their knees.

Linden waited at a distance until all these were gone before he went in. The secretary received him sympathetically and gave him a big form to fill up, but as Linden's eyes were so bad and his hand so unsteady the secretary very obligingly wrote in the answers himself, and informed him that he would inquire into the case and lay his application before the committee at the next meeting, which was to be held on the following Thursday - it was then Monday.

Linden explained to him that they were actually starving. He had been out of work for sixteen weeks, and during all that time they had lived for the most part on the earnings of his daughter-in-law, but she had not done anything for nearly a fortnight now, because the firm she worked for had not had any work for her to do. There was no food in the house and the children were crying for something to eat. All last week they had been going to school hungry, for they had had nothing but dry bread and tea every day: but this week - as far as he could see - they would not get even that. After some further talk the secretary gave him two soup tickets and an order for a loaf of bread, and repeated his promise to inquire into the case and bring it before the committee.

As Jack was returning home he passed the Soup Kitchen, where he saw the same lot of men who had been to the office of the Organized Benevolence Society for the soup tickets. They were waiting in a long line to be admitted. The premises being so small, the proprietor served them in batches of ten at a time.

On Wednesday the secretary called at the house, and on Friday Jack received a letter from him to the effect that the case had been duly considered by the committee, who had come to the conclusion that as it was a 'chronic' case they were unable to deal with it, and advised him to apply to the Board of Guardians. This was what Linden had hitherto shrunk from doing, but the situation was desperate. They owed five weeks' rent, and to crown their misfortune his eyesight had become so bad that even if there had been any prospect of obtaining work it was very doubtful if he could have managed to do it. So Linden, feeling utterly crushed and degraded, swallowed all that remained of his pride and went like a beaten dog to see the relieving officer, who took him before the Board, who did not think it a suitable case for out-relief, and after some preliminaries it was arranged that Linden and his wife were to go into the workhouse, and Mary was to be allowed three shillings a week to help her to support herself and the two children. As for Linden's sons, the Guardians intimated their Intention of compelling them to contribute towards the cost of their parents' maintenance. (RTP 320-321)

The local Charity Organisation Society's report for 1902 said: "The year that has just ended has been one of the most trying for the poor of this borough. Although the weather at the beginning of 1902 was not unusually severe, owing to a lack of employment, the distress was exceptionally acute.

"Many of the men, before applying to this Office, had pawned nearly all their tools, and but for the fact that they were nearly half-starved would not have applied. For a borough like ours, where the working classes depend so much on the fluctuation of the building trade, we cannot hope to be exempt from periods of exceptional and widespread distress." (13)

Such periods saw the establishment of soup kitchens. One report in November 1903, when there were 789 official cases of unemployment in the approach to a harsh winter, said: "Applications to the Board of Guardians have been more numerous, and the Waterworks Road soup kitchen, which Mr L.H. Elford and Miss P. Garrett founded, has had to open its doors on November 9, a fortnight earlier than usual, and the number of men women and children provided with meals is three or four times greater than at this period last year." (14) That report was repeated, almost word for word, in RTP. Later he described one soup kitchen - there were several in the town – as *really an inferior eating-house in a mean street. The man who ran this was a relative of the secretary of the OBS. He cadged all the ingredients for the soup from different tradespeople: bones and scraps of meat from butchers: pea meal and split peas from provision dealers: vegetables from greengrocers: stale bread from bakers, and so on. Well-intentioned, charitable old women with more money than sense sent him donations in cash, and he sold the soup for a penny a basin - or a penny a quart to those who brought jugs. (RTP 337-338)*

Justice reported: "This is a health resort for plutocrats but not for the unemployed workers and their hungry children." (15)

Those in work could still be reduced to squalor. Local railway workers, for example, earned 16 shillings a week but rents could eat up 12 shillings of that. Station porters were unpaid and relied on tips. Even the top local artisans had to pay at least a third of their wages for a decent home for their families.

Houses in and around the Bourne in the Old Town were judged unfit for habitation but still families were crammed into them, often a family to each room, because they had nowhere to go. The journalist Henry H. Hunt wrote: "Many houses in Hastings are horrible hovels: old, insanitary and disgusting; quite unfit for chicken houses, let alone men, women and children. I have seen in some homes bugs hanging from the four walls of the rooms in clusters as large as the top of a teacup...

"...and yet some of these same homes are regarded as picturesque, beautiful, something to elevate one's mind and thoughts to look upon. Visitors would rather look down on the huddled mass of bricks and tiles,

45

bugs and worm-eaten woodwork, narrow passages and thoroughfares with their cramped-in hovels breeding filth and disease and aiding all kinds of degeneration which should disgust any kind of civilised being... No bathroom, leaky roofs, but little or no back yards and from six to a dozen or even more persons forced to live in them. I have known some of their little children having to sleep on the shelves of the kitchen cupboard." (16)

Queen's Road, Hastings, showing tower of St. Andrew's

Slums were not confined to the cities and many of the stories told by RTP characters read like thinly exaggerated reportage: *Philpot remembered working in a house over at Windley; the people who lived in it were very dirty and had very little furniture; no bedsteads, the beds consisting of dilapidated mattresses and rags on the floor. He declared that these ragged mattresses used to wander about the rooms by themselves. The house was so full of fleas that if one placed a sheet of newspaper on the floor one could hear and see them jumping on it. In fact, directly one went into that house one was covered from head to foot with fleas! During the few days he worked at that place, he lost several pounds in weight, and of evenings as he walked homewards the children and people in the streets, observing his ravaged countenance, thought he was suffering from some disease and used to get out of his way when they saw him coming. (RTP 139)*

In another, more straightforward piece of reportage, Robert wrote: *To reach the house one had to go down a dark and narrow passage between two shops, the house being in a kind of well, surrounded by the high walls of the back parts of larger buildings - chiefly business premises and offices. The air did not circulate very freely in this place, and the rays of the sun never reached it. In the summer the atmosphere was close and foul with the various odours which came from the back-yards of the adjoining buildings, and in the winter it was dark and damp and gloomy, a culture-ground for bacteria and microbes. (RTP 294)*

The plight of the destitute inevitably led to desperate prostitution, as Robert alluded to: *Harlow remembered the case of a family whose house got into such a condition that the landlord had given them notice and the father had committed suicide because the painters had come to turn 'em out of house and home. There were a man, his wife and daughter - a girl about seventeen - living in the house, and all three of 'em used to drink like hell. As for the woman, she COULD shift it and no mistake! Several times a day she used to send the girl with a jug to the pub at the corner. When the old man was out, one could have anything one liked to ask for from either of 'em for half a pint of beer, but for his part, said Harlow, he could never fancy it. They were both too ugly.*
The finale of this tale was received with a burst of incredulous laughter by those who heard it.
`Do you 'ear what Harlow says, Bob?' Easton shouted to Crass.
`No. What was it?'
`'E ses 'e once 'ad a chance to 'ave something but 'e wouldn't take it on because it was too ugly!'
`If it 'ad bin me, I should 'ave shut me bl--y eyes,' cried Sawkins. `I wouldn't pass it for a trifle like that.' (RTP 140)

Suicides amongst the desperate were common. In September 1907 a Hastings man, James Loveday, was washed up on the beach at nearby Bexhill. Unable to find work, he had walked into the sea after local police refused to let him play his penny-whistle for coins. The local press regularly reported other tragedies. The sea offered one way out, but others were plentiful: a cutthroat razor, the tall buildings clinging to the hillsides, the cliffs above the beaches, the railway lines and the reservoirs at the top end of Alexandria Park.

Suicide, murder-suicide and the contemplation of suicide feature repeatedly in RTP, as do newspaper cuttings alluding to tragedy. Owen,

Robert's alter ego, considers killing himself and, in one dark passage, his child: *As he looked down upon the little, frail figure trotting along by his side, Owen thought for the thousandth time that it would be far better for the child to die now: he would never be fit to be a soldier in the ferocious Christian Battle of Life.*

Then he remembered Nora. Although she was always brave, and never complained, he knew that her life was one of almost incessant physical suffering; and as for himself he was tired and sick of it all. He had been working like a slave all his life and there was nothing to show for it - there never would be anything to show for it. He thought of the man who had killed his wife and children. The jury had returned the usual verdict, `Temporary Insanity'. It never seemed to occur to these people that the truth was that to continue to suffer hopelessly like this was evidence of permanent insanity. (RTP 229)

This, then, was the town which Robert arrived at and which he later christened "Mugsborough." In his appendix to RTP he summed up much of what had gone before. He changed the names and locations, switched the compass points from east to west, and placed his town 200 miles from London, possibly fearing libel at a time when he believed the book would make his fortune. But no-one, then and now, doubted that Hasting was the location. He described it as a sheltered valley with to the west a beautiful suburb with the homes of "the wealthy residents and prosperous tradespeople, and numerous boarding-houses for the accommodation of well-to-do visitors." The other side was where working people lived.

Robert wrote: *"Years ago, when the facilities for foreign travel were fewer and more costly, Mugsborough was a favourite resort of the upper classes, but of late years most of these patriots have adopted the practice of going on the Continent to spend the money they obtain from the working people of England. However, Mugsborough still retained some semblance of prosperity. Summer or winter the place was usually fairly full of what were called good-class visitors, either holiday-makers or invalids. The Grand Parade was generally crowded with well-dressed people and carriages. The shops appeared to be well-patronized and at the time of our story an air of prosperity pervaded the town. But this fair outward appearance was deceitful. The town was really a vast whited sepulchre; for notwithstanding the natural advantages of the place, the majority of the inhabitants existed in a state of perpetual poverty which in many cases bordered on destitution." (RTP 588)*

MISERY

"the lid of a coffin"

The 31-year-old Robert was a genuine craftsman but the little work available was for "jobbers" who could hammer a nail or slap whitewash on bricks. There appeared to be little call for his specialist skills.

Robert was often asked why he didn't set up in business for himself as a self-employed sign-writer and decorator, but he replied that he was under-funded and would have stood no chance in a town where working men often literally fought for short-term jobs, and the established firms crushed competition. His daughter Kathleen in later life insisted that there was "no puzzle in his not attempting to 'better' himself, since he was there to find out the TRUE facts of working conditions and to find out how they could be improved."

But late in 1901 or early in the following year Robert did find employment. And both Tressell's fictionalised truth and his central character of Frank Owen, to all intents a self-portrait, were born.

Bruce and Company, electrical sanitary engineers and builders, were based at 2 York Buildings, slap in the town centre close to the now-demolished Clock Tower. Colleagues recognised much of Mr Bruce in Robert's description of the fictional boss Rushton: "*about thirty-five years of age, with light grey eyes, fair hair and moustache, and his complexion was a whitey drab. He was tall - about five feet ten inches - and rather clumsily built; not corpulent, but fat - in good condition. He appeared to be very well fed and well cared for generally. His clothes were well made, of good quality and fitted him perfectly. He was dressed in a grey Norfolk suit, dark brown boots and knitted woollen stockings reaching to the knee. He was a man who took himself very seriously. There was an air of pomposity and arrogant importance about him which - considering who and what he was - would have been entertaining to any observer gifted with a sense of humour.*" (RTP 120)

Bruce and Co had a reputation for under-cutting rivals by cutting wages and scrimping on materials, just like Rushton and Co in RTP which beat off the competition – Pushem and Sloggem, Bluffum and Doemdown, Dodger and Scampit, Snatcham and Graball, Smeeriton who were themselves masters of the art of exploiting both employees and customers.

At first Robert worked in the shop selling paper-hangings, glass and wood grain and told a colleague that he "had not been used to trade work." Apprentice Bill Gower remembered seeing the new hand working on the shop window and exchanged a few pleasantries which, although Gower could never remember exactly, struck him as "unusual coming from a working man." (1) The next time the spoke at any length was when the boy arrived on a job at a professor's home in St Leonards and found Robert graining the front door. "He was wearing a house-painter's apron and a stetson hat," said Gower. Robert never wore a cloth cap to work.

By then Robert was on the firm's top rate for workmen – seven pence halfpenny an hour - as his reputation for skilled work meant that the company could take on detailed interior decoration contracts which previously had been done by London-based craftsmen. Robert showed his boss samples of what he could do, and for once the boss responded intelligently.

Robert was diffident about his talents. He had assumed in South Africa that standards would be high in England, and was surprised that he was considered better-than-average. Paint in pots had only just been introduced, and Robert was adept at mixing and matching colours as well as gilt and varnish. It was skilled work, even before the first lick of paint was applied. Paints and varnishes were prepared in the builder's yard before embarking on a job. Horses and carts delivered kegs of linseed oil, turpentine and white lead from the railway sidings. The raw materials were mixed and ground down by brush-hands, and then skilled painters like Robert would mix to colours to the customer's specifications. Robert described the paint-shop:

At one end was a fireplace without a grate but with an iron bar fixed across the blackened chimney for the purpose of suspending pails or pots over the fire, which was usually made of wood on the hearthstone. All round the walls of the shop - which had once been whitewashed, but were now covered with smears of paint of every colour where the men had `rubbed out' their brushes - were rows of shelves with kegs of paint upon them. In front of the window was a long bench covered with an untidy litter of dirty *paint-pots, including several earthenware mixing vessels or mortars, the sides of these being thickly coated with dried paint. Scattered about the stone floor were a number of dirty pails, either empty or containing stale whitewash; and standing on a sort of low platform or shelf at one end of the shop were four large round tanks fitted with taps and labelled `Boiled Oil', `Turps', `Linseed Oil', `Turps Substitute'. The lower parts of the walls were discoloured with moisture. The atmosphere was cold and damp and foul with the sickening odours of the poisonous materials. (RTP 238-239)*

Robert was well aware, however, that massed-produced materials would remove many of the old skills of which he was a master.

The pettiness of the tyranny Robert found at Bruce and Co constantly rankled. Smoking at work could be a sacking offence, even going to the privy outside meal breaks was frowned upon. Work sites were run on the basis of fear. The extremes were to be found in two RTP characters clearly based on Bruce and Co employees. The first was Bert White, the apprentice, for whom Bill Gower was a model. Robert wrote of the youngster:

Bert White was a frail-looking, weedy, pale-faced boy, fifteen years of age and about four feet nine inches in height. His trousers were part of a suit that he had once worn for best, but that was so long ago that they had become too small for him, fitting rather lightly and scarcely reaching the top of his patched and broken hob-nailed boots. The knees and the bottoms of the legs of his trousers had been patched with square pieces of cloth, several shades darker than the original fabric, and these patches were now all in rags. His coat was several sizes too large for him and hung about him like a dirty ragged sack. He was a pitiable spectacle of neglect and wretchedness as he sat there on an upturned pail, eating his bread and cheese with fingers that, like his clothing, were grimed with paint and dirt. (RTP 16)

Later Robert added to that description:

He had light brown hair and hazel grey eyes, and his clothes were of many colours, being thickly encrusted with paint, the result of the unskilful manner in which he did his work, for he had only been at the trade about a year. Some of the men had nicknamed him `the walking paint-shop', a title which Bert accepted good-humouredly.

This boy was an orphan. His father had been a railway porter who had worked very laboriously for twelve or fourteen hours every day for many years, with the usual result, namely, that he and his family lived in a condition of perpetual poverty. Bert, who was their only child and not very robust, had early shown a talent for drawing, so when his father died a little over a year ago, his mother readily assented when the boy said that he wished to become a decorator. It was a nice light trade, and she thought that a really good painter, such as she was sure he would become, was at least always able to earn a good living. Resolving to give the boy the best possible chance, she decided if possible to place him at Rushton's, that being one of the leading firms in the town. At first Mr Rushton demanded ten pounds as a premium, the boy to be bound for five years, no wages the first year, two shillings a week the second, and a rise of one shilling every year for the remainder of the term. Afterwards, as a special favour - a matter of charity, in fact, as she was a very poor woman - he agreed to accept five pounds. (RTP 95)

Robert continued:

"He soon became a favourite with Owen, for whom he conceived a great respect and affection. Bert in his artful way would scheme to be sent to assist Owen, and the latter whenever possible used to ask that the boy might be allowed to work with him."

And so it was with Robert and Gower. The lad recognised that the older man was not run-of-the-mill, had been properly educated and was unafraid of expressing strong opinions. Gower wrote later: "I was myself something of a critic of existing conditions, and I did not hesitate to express my youthful opinions to the men on the job there. I used to like to start arguing with Noonan to hear his answers, and we became great friends. I always endeavoured to get myself sent on jobs with him and so did the other lads. He always treated us kindly and was an interesting man to work with." (2)

The second employee to become a RTP template, albeit as a composite, was the chief foreman at Bruce and Co, later to be dubbed Nimrod, Hunter and, most famously, "Misery." His first top foreman was not a considerate man and, as many employees attested to in the decades that followed, treated his men "worse than blacks might have expected" in Robert's former stamping ground. Some recalled that the real-life Misery once sacked a man for presuming to approach him on the street about a work project. Others said that the RTP description was accurate: *"If one were to make a full-face drawing of his cadaverous visage it would be found that the outline resembled the lid of a coffin." (RTP 33)*

The foreman was an embittered man, a bully and a victim, as was made clear in RTP:

This man had been with Rushton - no one had ever seen the `Co.' - for fifteen years, in fact almost from the time when the latter commenced business. Rushton had at that period realized the necessity of having a deputy who could be used to do all the drudgery and running about so that he himself might be free to attend to the more pleasant or profitable matters. Hunter was then a journeyman, but was on the point of starting on his own account, when Rushton offered him a constant job as foreman, two pounds a week, and two and a half per cent of the profits of all work done. On the face of it this appeared a generous offer. Hunter closed with it, gave up the idea of starting for himself, and threw himself heart and mind into the business. When an estimate was to be prepared it was Hunter who measured up the work and laboriously figured out the probably cost. When their tenders were accepted it was he who superintended the work and schemed how to scamp it, where possible, using mud where mortar was specified, mortar where there ought to have been cement, sheet zinc where they were supposed to put sheet lead, boiled oil instead of varnish, and three coats of paint where five were paid for. In fact, scamping the work was with this man a kind of mania. It grieved him to see anything done properly. Even when it was more economical to do a thing well, he insisted from force of habit on having it scamped. Then he was almost happy, because he felt that he was doing someone down. If there were an architect superintending the work, Misery would square him or bluff him. If it were not possible to do either, at least he had a try; and in the intervals of watching, driving and bullying the hands, his vulture eye was ever on the look out for fresh jobs. His long red nose was thrust into every estate agent's office in the town in the endeavour to smell out what properties had recently changed hands or been let, in order that he might interview the new owners and secure the order for whatever alterations or repairs might be required. He it was who entered into unholy compacts with numerous charwomen and nurses of the sick, who in return for a small commission would let him know when some poor sufferer was passing away and would recommend Rushton & Co. to the bereaved and distracted relatives. By *these means often - after first carefully inquiring into the financial position of the stricken family - Misery would contrive to wriggle his unsavoury carcass into the house of sorrow, seeking, even in the chamber of death, to further the interests of Rushton & Co. and to earn his miserable two and a half per cent.*   *It was to make possible the attainment of this object that Misery slaved and drove and schemed and cheated. It was for this that the workers' wages were cut down to the lowest possible point and their offspring went ill clad, ill shod and ill fed, and were driven forth to labour while they were yet children, because their fathers were unable to earn enough to support their homes*

Fifteen years!
Hunter realized now that Rushton had had considerably the best of the bargain. In the first place, it will be seen that the latter had bought over one who might have proved a dangerous competitor, and now, after fifteen years, the business that had been so laboriously built up, mainly by Hunter's energy, industry and unscrupulous cunning, belonged to Rushton & Co. Hunter was but an employee, liable to dismissal like any other workman, the only difference being that he was entitled to a week's notice instead of an hour's notice, and was but little better off financially than when he started for the firm. Fifteen years!
Hunter knew now that he had been used, but he also knew that it was too late to turn back. He had not saved enough to make a successful start on his own account even if he had felt mentally and physically capable of beginning all over again, and if Rushton were to discharge him right now he was too old to get a job as a journeyman. Further, in his zeal for Rushton & Co. and his anxiety to earn his commission, he had often done things that had roused the animosity of rival firms to such an extent that it was highly improbable that any of them would employ him, and even if they would, Misery's heart failed him at the thought of having to meet on an equal footing those workmen whom he had tyrannized over and oppressed. It was for these reasons that Hunter was as terrified of Rushton as the hands were of himself. (RTP 33-34)

Misery, or Nimrod, or Mr Hunter, or his other incarnations, came to represent to Robert both the physical and spiritual misery of a working-man's life and toil. That is summed up in many passages of TRP, highlighting both the hardness and pettiness of life on the job:

"The basement of the house was slightly below the level of the ground and there was a sort of trench or area about three feet deep in front of the basement windows. The banks of this trench were covered with rose trees and evergreens, and the bottom was a mass of slimy, evil-smelling, rain-sodden earth, foul with the excrement of nocturnal animals. To second-coat these basement window, Philpot and Harlow had to get down into and stand in all this filth, which soaked through the worn and broken soles of their boots. As they worked, the thorns of the rose trees caught and tore their clothing and lacerated the flesh of their half-frozen hands.

"As they stood there working most of the time they were almost perfectly motionless, the only part of their bodies that were exercised being their right arms. The work they were doing required to be done very carefully and deliberately, otherwise the glass sould be 'messed up' or the white paint of the frames would 'run into' the dark green of the sashes, both colours being wet at the same time, each man having two pots of paint and two sets of brushes. The wind was not blowing in sudden gusts, but swept by in a strong, persistent current that penetrated their clothing and left them trembling and numb with cold. It blew from the right; and it was all the worse on that account, because the right arm, being in use, left that side of the body fully exposed. They were able to keep their left hands in their trouser pockets and the left arm close to their sides most of the time. This made a lot of difference. Another reason why it was worse when the wind strikes upon one from the right side is that the buttons of a man's coat are always on the right side, and consequently the wind gets underneath. Philpot realised this all the more because some of the buttons on his coat and waistcoat were missing....
""'If I thought Nimrod wasn't comin', I'd put my overcoat on and work in it,' remarked Philpot, 'but you never know when to expect the b----r, and if'e saw me in it, it would mean the bloody push.' (RTP 254-255

In another graphic passage, Robert described the fear the workman had of a bully who could sack them on a whim or, as accurately depicted in the book, to make way for a cut-rate hand:

As he looked at them the men did their work in a nervous, clumsy, hasty sort of way. They made all sorts of mistakes and messes. Payne, the foreman carpenter, was putting some new boards on a part of the drawing-room floor: he was in such a state of panic that, while driving a nail, he accidentally struck the thumb of his left hand a severe blow with his hammer. Bundy was also working in the drawing- room putting some white-glazed tiles in the fireplace. Whilst cutting one of these in half in order to fit it into its place, he inflicted a deep gash on one of his fingers. He was afraid to leave off to bind it up while Hunter was there, and consequently as he worked the white tiles became all smeared and spattered with blood. Easton, who was working with Harlow on a plank, washing off the old distemper from the hall ceiling, was so upset that he was scarcely able to stand on the plank, and presently the brush fell from his trembling hand with a crash upon the floor.

Everyone was afraid. They knew that it was impossible to get a job for any other firm. They knew that this man had the power to deprive them of the means of earning a living; that he possessed the power to deprive their children of bread. (RTP 41-42)

And yet another passage describes the constant surveillance under which the men worked:

During the next four weeks the usual reign of terror continued at `The Cave'. The men slaved like so many convicts under the vigilant surveillance of Crass, Misery and Rushton. No one felt free from observation for a single moment. It happened frequently that a man who was working alone - as he thought - on turning round would find Hunter or Rushton standing behind him: or one would look up from his work to catch sight of a face watching him through a door or a window or over the banisters. If they happened to be working in a room on the ground floor, or at a window on any floor, they knew that both Rushton and Hunter were in the habit of hiding among the trees that surrounded the house, and spying upon them thus There was a plumber working outside repairing the guttering that ran round the bottom edge of the roof. This poor wretch's life was a perfect misery: he fancied he saw Hunter or Rushton in every bush. He had two ladders to work from, and since these ladders had been in use Misery had thought of a new way of spying on the men. Finding that he never succeeded in catching anyone doing anything wrong when he entered the house by one of the doors, Misery adopted the plan of crawling up one of the ladders, getting in through one of the upper windows and creeping softly downstairs and in and out of the rooms. Even then he never caught anyone, but that did not matter, for he accomplished his principal purpose - every man seemed afraid to cease working for even an instant. The result of all this was, of course, that the work progressed rapidly towards *completion. The hands grumbled and cursed, but all the same every man tore into it for all he was worth. Although he did next to nothing himself, Crass watched and urged on the others. He was `in charge of the job': he knew that unless he succeeded in making this work pay he would not be put in charge of another job. On the other hand, if he did make it pay he would be given the preference over others and be kept on as long as the firm had any work. The firm would give him the preference only as long as it paid them to do so.*

As for the hands, each man knew that there was no chance of obtaining work anywhere else at present; there were dozens of men out of employment already. Besides, even if there had been a chance of getting another job somewhere else, they knew that the conditions were more or less the same on every firm. Some were even worse than this one. Each man knew that unless he did as much as ever he could, Crass would report him for being slow. They knew also that when the job began to draw to a close the number of men employed upon it would be reduced, and when that time came the hands who did the most work would be kept on and the slower ones discharged. It was therefore in the hope of being one of the favoured few that while inwardly cursing the rest for `tearing into it', everyone as a matter of self-preservation went and `tore into it' themselves. (202-203)

Given Nimrod/Misery's petty but absolute tyranny, it was certain that they would clash. Ball wrote: "Robert was a man who wore his heart on his sleeve, where it ought to be, and by all accounts, and as Gower noticed upon their first meeting, he had a completely open and natural manner with people, but kindly and considerate of people. And openness of character is the last thing required in our society, and poor Tressell, I believe, made a discovery in England that he hadn't made before. Not because he was naive, but he had been a self-employed man in South Africa, was highly skilled, was well-read and of considerable education and, I believe, had had no direct experience of English class society and working conditions and could not know that, as in the armed services, for a man to even look intelligent is considered an affront."

Bruce and Co's Misery targeted Robert as soon as he realised that the new employee was both a skilled worker and, increasingly, a radical. This Misery was a chapel-goer and regarded any criticism of the established order as akin to blasphemy. He was also jealous of Robert's talents and the fact that they had been recognised by the boss of both of them. Those talents meant that Robert was kept on during slack periods when others were laid off. During such periods Misery would give him every dirty job he could invent. One former hand told Ball he remembered Robert whitewashing a filthy cellar while another, less talented, painter worked on the upstairs rooms. Another recalled Robert painting garden railings while Misery/Nimrod lectured him on the dependency of the man of independent mind.

In RTP Robert chronicled the growing antagonism in a conversation with the under-foreman Cross and the terrified worker Easton:

You know,' Cross went on, confidentially. `Between me an' you an' the gatepost, as the sayin' is, I don't think Mr bloody Owen will be 'ere much longer. Nimrod 'ates the sight of 'im.' Easton had it in his mind to say that Nimrod seemed to hate the sight of all of them: but he made no remark, and Cross continued: ''E's 'eard all about the way Owen goes on about politics and religion, an' one thing an' another, an' about the firm scampin' the work. You know that sort of talk don't do, does it?'
`Of course not.'
''Unter would 'ave got rid of 'im long ago, but it wasn't 'im as took 'im on in the first place. It was Rushton 'imself as give 'im a start. It seems Owen took a lot of samples of 'is work an' showed 'em to the Bloke.'
`Is them the things wot's 'angin' up in the shop-winder?'
`Yes!' said Cross, contemptuously. `But 'e's no good on plain work. Of course 'e does a bit of grainin' an' writin' - after a fashion - when there's any to do, and that ain't often, but on plain work, why, Sawkins is as good as 'im for most of it, any day!' (RTP 99)

A key factor in RTP and in real life was the foreman's fear that a better man might take his job:

`Of course we all know what's the matter with 'im as far as YOU'RE concerned,' Easton went on. `He don't like 'avin' anyone on the firm wot knows more about the work than 'e does 'imself - thinks 'e might git worked out of 'is job.'

Owen laughed bitterly.
`He needn't be afraid of ME on THAT account. I wouldn't have his job if it were offered to me.'
`But 'e don't think so,' replied Easton, `and that's why 'e's got 'is knife into you,' `I believe that what he said about Hunter is true enough,' said Owen.

'Every time he comes here he tries to goad me into doing or saying something that would give him an excuse to tell me to clear out. I might have done it before now if I had not guessed what he was after, and been on my guard.' (RTP 104)

Robert was a gentle man, almost placid in his regard for others, but his relationship with the real Misery veered towards outright violence. Former workmates told Ball of one incident when Robert was working with a gang on the Post Office in King's Road, St Leonards. Robert arrived a little late and was reprimanded publicly and in an uncompromising manner. Robert, who had walked two miles for the six am start, was seething with rage by the time he arrived on site. There were two 40-foot ladders at each end of the PO and the gang were working on the roof. From that vantage point they saw Misery approaching. Robert shocked his colleagues by grabbing a length of lead piping, cursed, and said: "If that bastard comes up this ladder and starts again I'll knock his brains out with this." One mate said that there was a look of such passion in his eyes that they all feared that murder would be done. Luckily Misery went up the farther ladder and Robert, his anger subsiding, said: "Thank God for that." His mates asked whether he would actually have brained him and Robert replied: "Yes I would have done, but thank God he went up that side.

In RTP a visit by the fictionalised Misery to Owen's work-site is clearly based on the real-life King's Road PO incident. Owen is working alone, blowtorch in hand, when *"he began to feel conscious of some other presence in the room; he looked around. The door was open about six inches and in the opening appeared a long, pale face with a huge chin, surmounted by a bowler hat and ornamented with a large red nose, a drooping moustache and two small glittering eyes set very closely together. For some seconds this apparition regard Owen intently, then it was silently withdrawn, and he was alone again... (Owen) trembled with suppressed fury, and longed to be able to go out there on the landing and hurl the lamp into Hunter's face... he would like to take him by the throat with one hand and smash his face in with the other... he would seize him by the collar with his left hand, dig his knuckles into his throat, force him up against the wall and then, with his right fist, smash! smash! smash!" (RTP 42)* What held him back, in both fiction and reality, was what would happen to his family if he was hanged for murder.

Given the tensions between craftsman and foreman, it is astonishing that Robert's tenure with the company lasted a year or so. It was bound to end badly and after such a period – the company's work records are incomplete and do not include his termination date - the inevitable happened. Robert was either sacked or walked off the job. His workmates could only recall that he "left under a cloud."

Robert, out of work, returned to London on his own without Kathleen or his sister or his nephew, but could not find anything which could provide for them all. In RTP Owen did the same and *"found London, if anything, worse than his native town. Wherever he went he was confronted with the legend: 'No hands wanted.' He walked the streets day after day; pawned or sold all his clothes save those he stood in ...sometimes starving and only occasionally obtaining a few days' work. At the end of that time he was forced to give in. The privations he had endured, the strain on his mind and the foul atmosphere of the city combined to defeat him (RTP 65-66)*

There remains some confusion about whether what he described pertained to his first experience of London when he disembarked from South Africa, or his second visit between Hastings jobs. All the, admittedly meagre, evidence points to the latter. Robert was genuinely shocked by his experience at Bruce and Co., and wouldn't have been if he had first experienced conditions in the capital to any great degree.

Fred Ball has no doubt that the gestation of RTP was at Bruce's, having interviewed at length surviving workmates. It "cured him of any illusions about work in England, and the status of the workman, whether craftsman, artist or labourer. And it wasn't his temperament alone which made him detest the set-up and the lack of a real human relationship between employers and men. All the old men (and their wives) I interviewed had evil memories of the three main firms he worked for: the mildest of them spoke in terms of disapproval of the bosses and many of the foremen and the wrongness of it, and some of them damned them out of hand in bitter language, and all spoke of the low wages and harsh conditions imposed on them... It is from the shock of his experiences with Bruce and Co. that I date the real origin of the passionate sense of outrage which was to inspire and light up *The Ragged Trousered Philanthropists;* and, perhaps, the beginning of the deep sense of loss which he was to feel over the rest of his short life." (3)

Robert was hardly naive when he arrived in Hastings - he had sought his fortunes on the other side of the globe, had learnt a trade and become a master of it, and had survived the hurly-burly of frontier life while starting a family. He had always been a free spirit and a free thinker, having grown up in an atmosphere of Republican passions and sensibilities. But he was deeply shocked by his experiences in the south of England, at the crushing of the working man's spirit and their conservative attitudes to their own subjection.

For Robert, it wasn't going to get any better.

FAMILY LIFE

"Children should always be told the truth"

Shortly after leaving Bruce's, Robert moved to the top flat of Grosvenor Mansions at 115 Milward Road, not far from his previous accommodation, with Kathleen, Adelaide, who acted as housekeeper, and her son Arthur. Flat 5 consisted of three gabled attics, cheaper than those on the lower floors.

The arrangement allowed for a small bedroom each for Robert and Kathleen, another for mother and son, and a communal living room. Four flights of stairs had to be climbed on top of the long, steep flight of stone steps which rose up the West Hill from Queen's Road. From the distinctive gabled windows they had views over the railway bridge near the southern end of Alexandria Park, the gasworks and the roofs of the homes and commercial buildings of the Queen's Road thoroughfare.

In RTP Robert puts Frank Own and his family in a similar property, the top flat of a house that had once been a large private dwelling but now converted into four floors of fats. The location is probably an amalgam of those he stayed at in both St Leonards and Hastings but the Milward Road site has the strongest claim: *At one time this had been a most aristocratic locality, but most of the former residents had migrated to the newer suburb... Notwithstanding this fact, (it) was still a most respectable neighbourhood, the inhabitants being of a very superior character: shop-walkers, shop assistants, barber's clerks, boarding house keepers, a coal merchant, and even two retired jerry-builders."(RTP 76)* The 1903 street directory shows that there were indeed insurance salesmen, builders and carpenters listed. (1)

Robert's humour is evident in this passage, but the tone grows darker and more sarcastic as he describes the social order even in such relatively humble surroundings:

The most exclusive set consisted of the families of the coal merchant, the two jerry-builders and Mr Trafaim (a shop-walker in 'Sweater's Emporium'), whose superiority was demonstrated by the fact that, to say nothing of his

French extraction, he wore - in addition to the top hat - a frock coat and a pair of lavender trousers every day. The coal merchant and the jerry-builders also wore top hats, lavender trousers and frock coats, but only on Sundays and other special occasions. The estate agent's clerk and the insurance clerk, though excluded from the higher circle, belonged to another select coterie from which they excluded in their turn all persons of inferior rank, such as shop assistants or barbers. "The only individual who was received with equal cordiality by all ranks was the tallyman's traveller. But whatever differences existed amongst them regarding each other's social standing they were unanimous on one point at least: they were indignant at Owen's presumption in coming to live in such a refined locality.

"This low fellow, this common workman, with his paint-bespattered clothing, his broken boots, and his generally shabby appearance, was a disgrace to the street; and as for his wife she was not much better, because although whenever she came out she was always neatly dressed, yet most neighbours knew perfectly well that she had been wearing the same straw hat all the time she had been there." (RTP 77)

It is easy to see Robert's seething indignation, tinged perhaps with some shame, as he wrote that. For Owen's wife, read Robert's sister Adelaide. But the passage speaks with pride of the children in the family, daughter and nephew, who were merged into one in RTP:

"In fact, the only tolerable one of the family was the boy, and they were forced to admit that he was always well-dressed; so well indeed as to occasion some surprise, until they found out that all the boy's clothes were home-made. Then their surprise was changed into a somewhat grudging admiration of the skill displayed, mingled with contempt for the poverty which made its exercise necessary." (RTP 77)

In Robert's actual flat there were no carpets but Robert painted intricate designs on the bare boards which showed between rugs and pieces of linoleum. The curved ceilings, Kathleen recalled, were "painted in the style of Louis XIV period with cherubs and scrolls, and things." Her room had wallpaper covered in poppy motifs on which she pencilled faces "because I saw faces everywhere." (2)

The apprentice Gower visited often and said that the flat, like all others he saw, was poorly furnished with some furniture being merely boxes. But in Robert's room books were piled on most flat surfaces. Robert fashioned a writing table from a large box, using a tower of heavy books as a stool. The only proper table in the flat, by a window, was used by the family for eating and by Kathleen for homework. Kathleen remembered that it had a green-shaded lamp in its centre. Gower also said that the only luxury item was an Irish harp on which Robert would strum old Irish songs, although Kathleen insisted it was an Italian harp, with carved rams' heads around the top of a fluted column, with only five strings. "I was supposed to learn the harp at one time, but one day my aunt was in a temper and slashed the five strings and that was the end of the harp," she said, suggesting that Adelaide found the cramped family circumstances often difficult to bear. Kathleen recalled locking herself in a lavatory to avoid a spanking after she had taught Arthur how to pour water onto the heads of people toiling up the stone steps outside.

The coal box was, Kathleen recalled, half the size of a large packing-case and covered with 'Lincrusta' paper as though it was an Oriental piece. In it she and Arthur kept imaginary creatures, including Leprechauns and changelings. "Entering into our make-believe must have been a relief from the tragedy of everyday life," she said. (3) But she also had other "visitors" - birds which used to get into her bedroom through the roof. And her father was a constant delight to her, singing with a deep voice, telling stories and playing jokes.

"He had a wonderful sense of humour," she told Ball. "He rarely called us by name - always by some funny or insulting one, 'Funny Face' or some outlandish name he'd invented. When out walking with us he would make up names from signs and notices to amuse us... and he used to come home and for little Arthur's benefit hang his hat on an imaginary nail on the wall and walk away and of course it would fall to the floor. I can remember Arthur and I doing drawings and sticking them on the wall, and underneath we had written, 'Drawn by hand', and Dad coming in and saying about them, good thing we had put 'by hand' or people may have thought we had done them with our feet."

"Then there was a Christmas time when Santa Claus used to come and see us and I remember he was always 'annoyed' because, although my father knew he was coming, he always used to go out. I believed faithfully in Santa

Claus. There was one time when Santa Claus had a glass of magic wine and he gave it to us each to drink and none of us could drink it. It was a magic glass of wine all right for when he took it he emptied it straight away. It was probably a wine-glass with a hollow stem, corked. We of course couldn't drink it - Santa removed the cork surreptitiously and no doubt caught the liquid in a handkerchief.

"For Christmas presents Dad often used to give me prints of famous pictures. I remember I had a whole lot of Gainsborough's. And then I had a print of the engraving showing Dr Johnson coming to the rescue of Oliver Goldsmith from his landlady who wouldn't let him leave his room until he paid the rent. Dr Johnson sent a guinea for immediate relief until he could call but when he called later that day Oliver had already changed the guinea to buy a bottle of wine." (4)

Robert's child-friendly sense of humour shines from the pages of RTP, particularly his description of a Christmas party: *Philpot - who had got a funny-looking mask out of one of the bon-bons - started a fine game pretending to be a dreadful wild animal which he called a Pandroculus, and crawling about on all fours, rolled his goggle eyes and growled out he must have a little boy or girl to eat for his supper.*

He looked so terrible that although they knew it was only a joke they were almost afraid of him, and ran away laughing and screaming to shelter themselves behind Nora or Owen; but all the same, whenever Philpot left off playing, they entreated him to `be it again', and so he had to keep on being a Pandroculus, until exhaustion compelled him to return to his natural form. (RTP 300)

As Robert's physical condition deteriorated he found it increasingly hard to climb the long flight of stone steps to Milward Road, then another four flights to the flat. This is reflected in RTP:

'Dad!' cried Frankie, rushing to the door and flinging it open. He ran along the passage and opened the staircase door before Owen reached the top of the last flight of stairs. `Why ever do you come up at such a rate,' reproachfully exclaimed Owen's wife as he came into the room exhausted from the climb upstairs and sank panting into the nearest chair.

`I al-ways-for-get,' he replied, when he had in some degree recovered. As he lay back in the chair, his face haggard and of a ghastly whiteness, and with

the water dripping from his saturated clothing, Owen presented a terrible appearance.

Frankie noticed with childish terror the extreme alarm with which his mother looked at his father. `You're always doing it,' he said with a whimper. `How many more times will Mother have to tell you about it before you take nay notice?' (RTP 84)

When they arrived in Hastings Kathleen first went to the private Aylsham House School run by a Mrs Glenister in Milward Crescent. Some savings, family help and frugal living meant that for some time Kathleen was sent to a private boarding school, St Ethelburga's, in Deal. She remembered that when she arrived "a little boy spit at me and called me a pro-Boer." (5) But she was generally happy there. The money ran out when she was approaching 12 and she then, despite being baptised a Protestant, went to the Convent of the Sacred Heart RC school over the other side of the West Hill in Old London Road. Robert encouraged in her a love of reading, had a high opinion of her ability and told a friend that he hoped she would become a teacher.

Kathleen, who had lead a somewhat gypsy life, was as strong-willed as her father and that must have added to the strains of single parenthood. She recalled one incident: "I remember doing an awful thing once. I was usually a good girl with him, obedient because I loved him very much, but I don't know what I had done this time but I was really mad. I can't remember whether I had left a note but I made up my mind that I wasn't coming home when I left to go to school, and of course by the time I came out of school I didn't know where to go and I hung around here and there and probably went into the park. Anyway, it was getting dark and I don't know how late it was and I decided I had better go home and I met him just on his way to the police station. I can imagine the hell I went through. I used to have a terrible temper." (6)

Robert treated Arthur as his own son and the little boy reciprocated, watching out for him as he returned from work and throwing his arms around his neck. Kathleen recalled of her cousin: "Arthur had long curls and was a very pretty and attractive little boy. I remember we used to go out together and he always believed in fairies and goblins and when he wouldn't do what I wanted him to do I used to knock on the railing posts to get the goblins listening and tell them all about him and then he would do what I wanted to do." (7)

There were always games in the house, even if they could only involve a small piece of chalk and a lot of imagination. Robert's fictionalised son expects to be entertained whenever his exhausted father returned from work. Disappointed that they can't play 'a game of trains' the boy is happy to prepare for the following evening:

`All right, then,' said the boy, contentedly; `and I'll get the railway station built and I'll have the lines chalked on the floor, and the signals put up before you come home, so that there'll be no time wasted. And I'll put one chair at one end of the room and another chair at the other end, and tie some string across for telegraph wires. That'll be a very good idea, won't it, Dad?' and Owen agreed. (RTP 86-87)

Gower told of Robert's easy way with both children. One Sunday morning, when visitors were chatting in the flat, Arthur got a bit boisterous. Robert said to him: "Now Arthur, you just go to the door, will you, and close it on the outside." Ball's verdict, based largely on conversations with Gower, was that Robert "was always full of fun and gaiety with children, believing that they must be made happy when they were young, for the future would bring suffering enough without them having it inflicted on them in childhood."

Gower also recalled that Robert often used to stand over both children when they were sleeping and spoke many times with bitterness and sadness about the drudgery and hunger that lay ahead for so many of them, together with the loss of happiness and fine perceptions.

Robert's fears for the next generation comes over clearly in one of RTP's darkest and most uncharacteristically bitter passage, put into the thoughts of Owen:

And the future, as far as he could see, was as hopeless as the past; darker, for there would surely come a time, if he lived long enough, when he would be unable to work anymore. He thought of his child. Was he to be a slave and a drudge all his life also? it would be better for the boy to die now. As Owen thought of his child's future there sprung up within him a feeling of hatred and fury against the majority of his fellow workmen. THEY WERE THE ENEMY. Those who not only quietly submitted like so many cattle to the existing state of things, but defended it, and opposed and ridiculed any suggestion to alter it.

THEY WERE THE REAL OPPRESSORS - the men who spoke of themselves as 'The likes of us,' who, having lived in poverty and degradation all their lives considered that what had been good enough for them was good enough for the children they had been the cause of bringing into existence.

He hated and despised them because the calmly saw their children condemned to hard labour and poverty for life, and deliberately refused to make any effort to secure for them better conditions than those they had themselves.   It was because they were indifferent to the fate of THEIR children that he would be unable to secure a natural and human life for HIS. It was their apathy or active opposition that made it impossible to establish a better system of society under which those who did their fair share of the world's work would be honoured and rewarded. Instead of helping to do this, they abased themselves, and grovelled before their oppressors, and compelled and taught their children to do the same. THEY were the people who were really responsible for the continuance of the present system.
Owen laughed bitterly to himself. What a very comical system it was. Those who worked were looked upon with contempt, and subjected to every possible indignity. Nearly everything they produced was taken away from them and enjoyed by the people who did nothing. And then the workers bowed down and grovelled before those who had robbed them of the fruits of their labour and were childishly grateful to them for leaving anything at all
No wonder the rich despised them and looked upon them as dirt. They WERE despicable. They WERE dirt. They admitted it and gloried in it. (RTP 45-46)

Once, when walking with Gower, they passed some ragged youngsters and Robert said with passion: "God is a devil who lets little children suffer." (8)

Such thoughts led Robert into clashes with his sister Adelaide. She "sternly rebuked" him when he attacked organised religion in front of the children. Robert replied: "Children should always be told the truth." He despised, as RTP shows, those who insisted that religious instruction was right for children, regardless of whether it was true or not. "My father had a great love of truth and truthfulness," said Kathleen, "'A lie is a cowardly thing,' he would say. 'Never lie to get yourself out of trouble." (9) Relations between the brother and sister were strained. The cramped conditions must have been one factor, her disappointment at not being able to lead a genteel, comfortable life was undoubtedly another. Kathleen remembered that while every other adult called him Bob, she would never deviate from

Robert.

Adelaide also believed that Robert's increasing radicalism would infect her own child. From her standpoint, she may have had a point. In RTP Owen's fictional wife gently teaches the little boy Frankie about the evils of capitalism:

But how do the people who never do any work manage to get lots of money then?' added Frankie.
`Oh, there's lots of different ways. For instance, you remember when Dad was in London, and we had no food in the house, I had to sell the easy chair.'

Frankie nodded. `Yes,' he said, `I remember you wrote a note and I took it to the shop, and afterwards old Didlum came up here and bought it, and then his cart came and a man took it away.'
`And do you remember how much he gave us for it?' `Five shillings,' replied Frankie, promptly. He was well acquainted with the details of the transaction, having often heard his father and mother discuss it. `And when we saw it in his shop window a little while afterwards, what price was marked on it?'
'Fifteen shillings.'
`Well, that's one way of getting money without working.' Frankie played with his toys in silence for some minutes. At last he said: `What other ways?' `Some people who have some money already get more in this way: they find some people who have no money and say to them, "Come and work for us." Then the people who have the money pay the workers just enough wages to keep them alive whilst they are at work. Then, when the things that the working people have been making are finished, the workers are sent away, and as they still have no money, they are soon starving. In the meantime the people who had the money take all the things that the workers have made and sell them for a great deal more money than they gave to the workers for making them. That's another way of getting lots of money without doing any useful work.' `But is there no way to get rich without doing such things as that?' `It's not possible for anyone to become rich without cheating other people.' (RTP 79-80)

There were many visitors to the flat. Kathleen said her father "used to bring people home to tea and was just as likely to bring somebody like a crossing-sweeper and the bishop at the same time." A priest, Father O'Callaghan, was a regular visitor and they would sit up half the night talking. Women would also stop by, to give Adelaide some company and, no doubt, to provide role models for Kathleen. They included the "Misses Haggard" who may have been the daughters of Sir Rider Haggard who lived in St Leonards at the time; a miniature painter called Marie le Verrier; and a "Miss Lowe" who would draw Arthur and who is likely to have been Constance M. Lowe, the writer of books of children's verse with titles such as *Little Folks Fun* and *The Round and Round ABC*.

But the most frequent visitor, in the early days at least, was the apprentice Gower who appears to have idolised Robert. The lad was eager to learn what he had never learnt at school and Robert was both friend and teacher. Over a coffee pot which Robert replenished, they talked and talked. They never chatted about racing or women, the staple of conversations amongst other workmates. Instead Gower was enthralled by long, animated discussions of politics, economics, books, history, travel, flying and, increasingly, socialism. Gower later told Ball that he always felt that "some submerged genius lay in Robert." (10)

Robert was a voracious reader and would scour the second-hand book shops in the Old Town to buy volumes for pennies and lend them to Gower and other workmates who expressed interest. Gower gave Fred Ball a list of those authors he remembered Robert quoting - Charles Dickens, Jonathan Swift, William Shakespeare, Henry Fielding, Shelley, Byron, Oliver Wendell Holmes and others, plus his favourites, William Morris and John Ruskin. Robert lent the lad Edward Arnold's *Light of Asia* and Haeckel's *Evolution of Man*. But Gower reckoned the author who most influenced Robert was Dean Swift.

Robert's growing library of second-hand books included the classics — Plutarch's '*Lives*' and, the '*Poetics*' of Aristotle, Pliny and Plato — and the histories of Gibbon, as well as the most popular novels of the era — Sir Arthur Conan Doyle's Sherlock Holmes stories, Eugene Sue's '*Mysteries of Paris*,' and Bram Stoker's '*Dracula*.'

Gower and many others remembered fondly how Robert would use anything to hand to illustrate his arguments or back up a point - scoring maps in the beach sand with his walking cane, or in the shop-floor dust with a piece of wood. In public he carried pieces of chalk in his pocket for the same purpose. "So if you met him out for a walk on Sunday or met him anywhere, you might find yourself looking at the pavement while this little man drew diagrams in the dust for you illustrating the proportions of drones to worker-bees, or bishops to itinerant mendicants, and very likely to the great curiosity of passers-by, for the English as a rule aren't given to making themselves conspicuous." Gower talked of one time when Robert was chalking some point on the windows of the York Hotel and a policeman ordered him to erase it smartly otherwise he would run him "round the corner" to the police station.

Despite poverty and despair, disappointment and disillusionment, Rober'ts friends remembered him many decades later as a cheerful, dapper, happy man, brimming full of ideas. They recall him dressed smartly, sporting a buttonhole, walking jauntily along the seafront. Or peering into a florist shop, because he loved flowers. Or drinking in moderation in a local pub, often illustrating a point with the tip of his finger tracing spilled beer. He walked with a bit of a swagger, confident that he was as good as any other, and that jauntiness made people smile. Sixty-odd years later former painter Len Green wrote: "As I write this letter I can see Bob and hear his cheery laugh, he always seemed to be a very happy man. My Dad and him got on very well together. Our family always called him 'Dolphus'; he had a very hearty laugh, but he would put his hand on his chest and I asked him once what was the matter and he said he was 'One Lung' in Chinese, and I knew he was a tuberculosis victim." (11)

Given his illness, the manner of his living and the society he railed against, Robert's innate optimism was not infinite.

PAINTING AND BURYING

"Pad in, rain or snow"

After a year or so at his previous employers' and after a series of temporary jobs paying "a bob or two here and there", Robert in late 1902 or early 1903 began working for Burton and Co., building contractors, decorators and funeral directors of 88 Stonefield Road, Hastings, opposite the long flight of stone steps which took Robert to his Millward Road flat

Henry Burton who owned the firm was, like so many of his time, a pillar of the church, particularly when it suited business. He made a habit of getting dressed in the dark so that he could get to his workshops and check that no man was late and to issue his orders, before returning home to bed. He banned smoking at work and, unlike most firms, refused his men an annual "beano" or outing. Former employees told Fred Ball that they were convinced he used to watch his men at work from a telescope specially bought for the purpose. He found Robert a "difficult man" but the fact that he was hired and remained for the company for around four years is testament that Robert's skills were such it was worth putting up with a little bolshieness.

That bolshieness, generally leavened with humour, was often on display. On one job Robert and a gang found themselves working on a Hollington Hill mansion owned by a Mr Upton, a boot-manufacturer and a high Tory. He was hugely disliked and had an eye like a "stinking eel." He would watch them work, criticising everything they did before being driven along the promenade. The job was a long one and Robert and his gang, during his afternoon absences, reckoned they burnt three tons of Upton's coal and one of coke to "save him the bother" while they kept warm. On another occasion Robert got his revenge on a foreman-carpenter who claimed he could paint as well as the gang by creating a realistic effigy and placed in the drive to the house they were working on.

But such moments of light relief could not compensate for the gruelling work. Robert was once asked how much he earned and answered with a relatively high amount, adding: "That's not what I get - you asked me what

I earned." The men worked long hours but their payments only

Hastings coffin-makers, c. 1908

began when they arrived at a job. They were obliged to tramp anywhere within a rough 10-mile radius, to Crowhurst, Ninfield, Netherfield and other villages, which meant they would often have to leave at three or four am. Ball, who worked in similar conditions two decades after Robert, wrote that the men would "pad in, rain or snow, thunder of lightening, often arriving saturated, to work in empty houses or on building sites without fires for warmth or cooking... In summer you might be on a job for 13 or 14 hours, when you were at liberty to walk home, and if your wife was still up and hadn't locked you out, she would serve a meal for you."

Later Ball wrote: "One can picture the old building-workers, tramping through the dark overhung Sussex lanes, dressed in their drainpipe trousers, caps and bowlers, and a rare collection of second-hand clothes, the rain dripping off their walrus moustaches. One can sympathise with their imprecations on work and the weather and the size of the country, and the slowness of time." For those jobs certain to last a week or more, Robert and the men would pack food in a wicker basket and sleep of the property's floor amongst the dust, paint fumes and plaster. Dinner was bread, tea and onions, with any extras going into a communal pot. In rain, hail and slow it would have been a nightmare for a man, like Robert, with a weak chest. (1)

At Burton's, as was the case with the other two main firms Robert worked for, most of the work was in North St Leonards, particularly around the Green and Hollington Park Road, the borough's wealthiest areas. Peak wrote: "These were the homes of the rich. The well-off could also be found living in the surrounding parts of St Leonards, around the southern end of Alexandria Park and up through the Blacklands area to the St Helens part of The Ridge. The workers who were looking after all these delightful homes lived in their own impoverished districts: Hollington, Silverhill, Bohemia, Halton, the Old Town and, worse of all, Ore," (2)

From September 1903 to June 1904 most of Burton's painters, decorators, plumbers and labourers worked on the mansion Val Mascal, one of the biggest houses on the Hollington Park Estate, created in the 1870s for the borough's wealthiest elite. Each house was large, detached, well-designed and surrounded by impressive gardens, but by Robert's day were looking a bit tired and shabby. Such houses, during a period of economic boom and bust, often changed hands and needed upgrading. For Burton's they were a potential goldmine.

Val Mascal, built in 1891, is widely regarded as a template for The Cave, where much of RTP is set and where Owen painted the Moorish drawing room. But the house was owned by John H. Upson, who lived there until he died in 1910 and whose family continued living there until 1936. Upson lived by private investment, and there is no record of him being involved in local business or council politics, so it is unlikely that he was the template for Sweater, the prominent citizen, councillor, mayor and business mogul who bought the Cave. There was a prominent local boot manufacturer called Upton whose business premises adjoined Burton's, and Robert may have confused the two when working on the site.

The relatively anonymous Upson also owned West Dene, another large property in Hollington Park. In 1906 the council gave him permission to build an entrance lodge cottage and in May the following year contracted Burton's to do the work, including alterations to the main house. Robert and his workmate Len Green are known to have worked there.

The Cave looks certain to have been an amalgam of both Upson properties plus Filsham Lodge at the top of Filsham Road. It had been built around

1890 for a physician Adam Bealey who sold it in 1905 to Henry Philpot, who ran a draper's business which existed from the 1830s to the 1980s. The evidence that it was, at least in part, The Cave is 1906 planning permission to replace a cesspit with a sewer connecting to the main sewer in Hollington Park Road, as featured in RTP. (3)

At the completion of the work on the Cave, and most hands were laid off, Robert summed up the company's ethic: *'There it stands!' said Harlow, tragically, extending his arm towards the house. 'There it stands! A job that if they'd only have let us do it properly, couldn't 'ave been done with the number of 'ands we've 'ad, in less than four months; and there it is, finished, messed up, slobbered over and scamped, in nine weeks!'* (RTP 283)

Other sites which Robert is known to have worked on included St Andrew's Church, of which more later, and the Imperial public house adjoining the Burton's shop in Stonefield Road. He probably also worked on Kite's Nest, a large house in St Helen's Park Road, and Christ Church Ore.

At Bruce and Co Robert was given the RTP templates for Bert white the apprentice and Misery the foreman. At Burton's his cast list was extended, covering young and old, grotesques and delinquents, the exploiters and the exploited, the bosses' narks and the rebels. Most, in the book, were composites of people Robert worked with during his short career in Hastings. Others may have been complete pen-portraits of specific individuals. But they represented the whole structure of working life. They included:

Bob Crass, the painters' foreman: *Crass was the 'coddy' or foreman of the job. Considered as a workman he had no very unusual abilities; he was if anything inferior to the majority of his fellow workmen. But although he had but little real ability he pretended to know everything, and the vague references he was in the habit of making to 'tones', and 'shades', and 'harmony', had so impressed Hunter that the latter had a high opinion of him as a workman. It was by pushing himself forward in this way and by judicious toadying to Hunter that Crass managed to get himself put in charge of work.*

Although Crass did as little work as possible himself he took care that the others worked hard. Any man who failed to satisfy him in this respect he reported to Hunter as being 'no good', or 'too slow for a funeral'. The result was that this man was dispensed with at the end of the week. The men knew this, and most of them feared the wily Crass accordingly, though there were a few whose known abilities placed them to a certain extent above the reach of his malice. Frank Owen was one of these.

There were others who by the judicious administration of pipefuls of tobacco and pints of beer, managed to keep in Crass's good graces and often retained their employment when better workmen were `stood off'. (RTP 40-41)

Sawkins, the nark, was *not popular with any of the others. When, about twelve months previously, he first came to work for Rushton & Co., he was a simple labourer, but since then he had `picked up' a slight knowledge of the trade, and having armed himself with a putty-knife and put on a white jacket, regarded himself as a fully qualified painter. The others did not perhaps object to him trying to better his condition, but his wages - fivepence an hour - were twopence an hour less than the standard rate, and the result was that in slack times often a better workman was `stood off' when Sawkins was kept on. Moreover, he was generally regarded as a sneak who carried tales to the foreman and the `Bloke'. Every new hand who was taken on was usually warned by his new mates `not to let the b--r Sawkins see anything.' (RTP 17)*

Slyme, an abstemious religious zealot: *This young man had been through some strange process that he called `conversion'. He had had a `change of 'art' and looked down with pious pity upon those he called `worldly' people. He was not `worldly', he did not smoke or drink and never went to the theatre. He had an extraordinary notion that total abstinence was one of the fundamental principles of the Christian religion. It never occurred to what he called his mind, that this doctrine is an insult to the Founder of Christianity. (RTP 26)*

George Barrington, an educated man who, it was whispered, was the disgraced son of a gentleman and who had been hired by the boss as a favour to social superiors: *Whatever the explanation of the mystery may have been, the fact remained that Barrington, who knew nothing of the work except what he had learned since he had been taken on, was employed as a painter's labourer at the usual wages - fivepence per hour. He was about twenty-five years of age and a good deal taller than the majority of the others, being about five feet ten inches in height and slenderly though well and strongly built. He seemed very anxious to learn all that he could about the trade, and although rather reserved in his manner, he had contrived to make himself fairly popular with his workmates. He seldom spoke unless to answer when addressed, and it was difficult to draw him into conversation. At meal-times, as on the present occasion, he generally smoked, apparently lost in thought and unconscious of his surroundings.* (RTP 19)

Joe Philpot: *or as he was usually called, `Old Joe' - was in the habit of indulging freely in the cup that inebriates. He was not very old, being only a little over fifty, but he looked much older. He had lost his wife some five years ago and was now alone in the world, for his three children had died in their infancy* (RTP 27)

Jack Linden who *was about sixty-seven years old, but like Philpot, and as is usual with working men, he appeared older, because he had had to work very hard all his life, frequently without proper food and clothing. His life had been passed in the midst of a civilization which he had never been permitted to enjoy the benefits of. But of course he knew nothing about all this. He had never expected or wished to be allowed to enjoy such things; he had always been of opinion that they were never intended for the likes of him. He called himself a Conservative and was very patriotic.*

At the time when the Boer War commenced, Linden was an enthusiastic jingo: his enthusiasm had been somewhat damped when his youngest son, a reservist, had to go to the front, where he died of fever and exposure. When this soldier son went away, he left his wife and two children, aged respectively four and five years at that time, in his father's care. After he died they stayed on with the old people. The young woman earned a little occasionally by doing needlework, but was really dependent on her father-in-law. Notwithstanding his poverty, he was glad to have them in the house, because of late years his wife had been getting very feeble, and, since the shock occasioned by the news of the death of her son, needed someone constantly with her. (RTP 40)

William Easton was *a man of medium height, about twenty-three years old, with fair hair and moustache and blue eyes. He wore a stand-up collar with a coloured tie and his clothes, though shabby, were clean and neat. He was married: his wife was a young woman whose acquaintance he had made when he happened to be employed with others painting the outside of the house where she was a general servant. They had `walked out' for* *about fifteen months. Easton had been in no hurry to marry, for he knew that, taking good times with bad, his wages did no average a pound a week. At the end of that time, however, he found that he could not honourably delay longer, so they were married. That was twelve months ago.*

As a single man he had never troubled much if he happened to be out of work; he always had enough to live on and pocket money besides; but now that he was married it was different; the fear of being `out' haunted him all the time. (RTP 48)

Newman, a hard-up family man offered work by Misery if he agreed to work below rate: *Newman was taken by surprise and hesitated. He had never worked under price; indeed, he had sometimes gone hungry rather than do so; but now it seemed that others were doing it. And then he was so awfully hard up. If he refused this job he was not likely to get another in a hurry. He thought of his home and his family. Already they owed five weeks' rent, and last Monday the collector had hinted pretty plainly that the landlord would not wait much longer. Not only that, but if he did not get a job how were they to live? This morning he himself had had no breakfast to speak of, only a cup of tea and some dry bread. (RTP 36)*

Harlow, a sober and industrious family man who worked on his allotment before and after work, weather permitting: *He was not a teetotaller, but as he often remarked, `what the publicans got from him wouldn't make them very fat', for he often went for weeks together without tasting the stuff, except a glass or two with the Sunday dinner, which he did not regard as an unnecessary expense, because it was almost as cheap as tea or coffee.* (RTP 387)

And of course, there was Frank Owen. He, together with a little bit of Barrington, was the author's self-portrait, only thinly disguised. In RTP the passage which introduces Owen allowed Robert to vent his frustrations at his workmates:

He was generally regarded as a bit of a crank: for it was felt that there must be something wrong about a man who took no interest in racing or football and was always talking a lot of rot about religion and politics. If it had not been for the fact that he was generally admitted to be an exceptionally good workman, they would have had little hesitation about thinking that he was mad. This man was about thirty-two years of age, and of medium height, but so slightly built that he appeared taller. There was a suggestion of refinement in his clean-shaven face, but his complexion was ominously clear, and an unnatural colour flushed the think cheeks.

There was a certain amount of justification for the attitude of his fellow workmen, for Owen held the most unusual and unorthodox opinions on the subjects mentioned.

The affairs of the world are ordered in accordance with orthodox opinions. If anyone did not think in accordance with these he soon discovered this fact for himself. Owen saw that in the world a small class of people were possessed of a great abundance and superfluity of the things that are produced by work. He saw also that a very great number - in fact the majority of the people - lived on the verge of want; and that a smaller but still very large number lived lives of semi-starvation from the cradle to the grave; while a yet smaller but still very great number actually died of hunger, or, maddened by privation, killed themselves and their children in order to put a period to their misery. And strangest of all - in his opinion - he saw that people who enjoyed abundance of the things that are made by work, were the people who did Nothing: and that the others, who lived in want or died of hunger, were the people who worked. And seeing all this he thought that it was wrong, that the system that produced such results was rotten and should be altered. And he had sought out and eagerly read the writings of those who thought they knew how it might be done.

It was because he was in the habit of speaking of these subjects that his fellow workmen came to the conclusion that there was probably something wrong with his mind. (RTP 18)

Robert, on the other hand, was constantly frustrated at the ignorance of his workmates. He reserved his contempt for illiteracy, however, for the foremen and bosses. A good example is the list Crass gives Bert when told to pick up supplies:

I pare steppes 8 foot
1/2 gallon Plastor off perish
1 pale off witewosh
12 lbs wite led
1/2 gallon Linsede Hoil
Do. Do. turps

At Burton's Robert's pay was supplemented by writing coffin-plates. The extra money was welcome, but it was emotionally distressing because of the high mortality rate among infants and children. A friend of Robert's, decades later, still carried a contemporary newspaper cutting from the Weekly Despatch, headed: DEMENTED FATHER Kills His Children Because He Could Not See Them Starve. (4) A similar placard appears in RTP outside a newsagents' shop:

TERRIBLE DOMESTIC TRAGEDY
Wife and Two Children Killed
Suicide of the Murderer

It was one of the ordinary poverty crimes. The man had been without employment for many weeks and they had been living by pawning or selling their furniture and other possessions. But even this resource must have failed at last, and when one day the neighbours noticed that the blinds remained down and that there was a strange silence about the house, no one coming out or going in, suspicions that something was wrong were quickly aroused. When the police entered the house, they found, in one of the upper rooms, the dead bodies of the woman and the two children, with their throats severed, laid out side by side upon the bed, which was saturated with their blood. (RTP 88)

Funerals were an integral part of the business, as Robert showed in his description of the main office: *The windows were lit up with electric light, displaying an assortment of wallpapers, gas and electric light fittings, glass shades, globes, tins of enamel, paint and varnish. Several framed show-cards - `Estimates Free', `First class work only, at moderate charges', `Only First Class Workmen Employed' and several others of the same type. On one side wall of the window was a large shield-shaped board covered with black velvet on which a number of brass fittings for coffins were arranged. The shield was on an oak mount with the inscription: `Funerals conducted on modern principles'. (RTP 236)*

Robert explained that funerals were popular with the bosses because of the extra profits involved and with the men because of the bonuses involved. They were paid a shilling for lifting bodies into coffins - half as much again for high class affairs - and the foreman took a large cut. Robert's attitude can be guessed from the following extract:

"'I believe that nothing would please 'im so much as to see a epidemic break out," remarked Philpot. "small-pox, Hinfluenza, Cholery morbus, or anything like that.'

"'Yes: don't you remember 'ow good-tempered 'e was last summer when there was such a lot of Scarlet Fever about?' observed Harlow. "'Yes,' said Cross with a chuckle. 'I recollect we 'ad six children's funerals to do in one week. Ole Misery was as pleased as Punch because of course as a rule there ain't many boxin'-up jobs in the summer. It's in winter as hundertakers reaps their 'arvest.'" (RTP 127)

Such extras could mean the difference between eviction or rent paid, between food on the table or starving families. Robert knew that and made allowances. But such work must have grieved such a loving father.

On the other hand, Robert found humour when events showed that the rich and privileged were not immune from death, as in the following passage over the demise of a corpulent parson (see Religion chapter) who had taken a holiday courtesy of church funds:

'Who is this last party what's dead?' asked Harlow after a pause. `It's a parson what used to belong to the "Shining Light" Chapel. He'd been abroad for 'is 'ollerdays - to Monte Carlo. It seems 'e was ill before 'e went away, but the change did 'im a lot of good; in fact, 'e was quite recovered, and 'e was coming back again. But while 'e was standin' on the platform at Monte Carlo Station waitin' for the train, a porter runned into 'im with a barrer load o' luggage, and 'e blowed up.'
`Blowed up?'
`Yes,' repeated Philpot. `Blowed up! Busted! Exploded! All into pieces. But they swep' 'em all up and put it in a corfin and it's to be planted this afternoon.'

Harlow maintained an awestruck silence, and Philpot continued: `I had a drink the other night with a butcher bloke what used to serve this parson with meat, and we was talkin' about what a strange sort of death it was, but 'e said 'e wasn't at all surprised to 'ear of it; the only thing as 'e wondered at was that the man didn't blow up long ago, considerin' the amount of grub as 'e used to make away with. He ses the quantities of stuff as 'e's took there and seen other tradesmen take was something chronic. Tons of it!'

`What was the parson's name?' asked Harlow.
`Belcher. You must 'ave noticed 'im about the town. A very fat chap,'
replied Philpot. `I'm sorry you wasn't 'ere on Saturday to see the corfin plate. Frank called me in to see the wordin' when 'e'd finished it. It had on:

"Jonydab Belcher. Born January 1st, 1849. Ascended, December 8th, 19--"'
`Oh, I know the bloke now!' cried Harlow. `I remember my youngsters
bringin' 'ome a subscription list what they'd got up at the Sunday School to
send 'im away for a 'ollerday because 'e was ill, and I gave 'em a penny each
to put on their cards because I didn't want 'em to feel mean before the other
young 'uns.' (RTP 251)

Robert remained constantly frustrated that his talents were not being used.
J. Walsh wrote in 1922, after speaking to many of his workmates: "He was
a brilliant scenic painter and signwriter and also a grainer, and was in great
demand on decoration of local churches, where his work received much
admiration. He loved his Art for Art's sake. He shared with William Morris
and Walter Crane a desire to give to the world the best that was in him, so
that the beauty of his work should be an inspiration to all striving for that
which is most beautiful. Like Morris and Crane, he found himself in revolt
against the degrading conditions of labour imposed on the workers by
Capitalism. He had a hard struggle with failing health and poverty. His gifts
brought him little extra renumeration. Art was not wanted. Much of his
time was spent in the less skilled work of washing off, distempering, etc.
Nothing distressed him more than the scamping of his work. He, like the
rest of us, was not permitted to do his best. Everything is sacrificed to the
god of profit." (5)

Walsh may have over-egged his arguments as Robert did receive extra
payments, particularly for church murals and decoration which he often
painted in his own time, or as overtime. Commissions at Burtons included
painting the east wall of Christchurch, Ore, and stencilling at that church
plus St Thomas of Canterbury Catholic church and the Convent Chapel, St
Leonards. (6)

But such commissions which stretched his talents were rare and, like his
comrades, most of his job was drudgery disguised as professionalism. His
dislike of bodging, of cutting corners, of cheating both workers and
customers, is clear from RTP. One incident has Misery – there were Miserys
at every firm he worked - on the prowl in a house being redecorated   by
the firm and finds one of the men at work:

"The man was painting the skirting, and just then he came to a part that
was split in several places, so he took his knife and began to fill the cracks
with putty. He was so nervous under ...scrutiny that his hand trembled to

such an extent that it took him about twice as long as it should have done and (Misery) told him so with brutal directness. 'Never mind about puttying up such little cracks as them!' he shouted. 'Fill 'em up with the paint. We can't afford to pay you for messing about like that!'" (RTP 111-112)

Another incident showed the foreman Misery/Nimrod/Hunter again bawling out the same workman:

On going into Newman's room Misery was not satisfied with the progress made since the last visit. The fact was that Newman had been forgetting himself again this morning. He had been taking a little pains with the work, doing it something like properly, instead of scamping and rushing it in the usual way. The result was that he had not done enough. "'You know, Newman, this kind of thing won't do!' Nimrod howled. 'You must get over a bit more than this or you won't suit me! If you can't move yourself a bit quicker I shall 'ave to get someone else...'
"Newman muttered something about being nearly finished now, and Hunter ascended to the next landing - the attics, where the cheap man - Sawkins, the labourer - was at work. He had been slogging into it like a Trojan and had done quite a lot. He had painted not only the sashes of the window, but also a large part of the glass, and when doing the skirting he had included part of the floor, sometimes an inch, sometimes half an inch.
"The paint was a dark drab colour and the surface of the newly-painted doors bore a strong resemblance to corduroy cloth, and from the bottom corners of nearly every panel there was trickling down a large tear, as if the doors were weeping for the degenerate condition of the decorative arts. But these tears caused no throb of pity in the bosom of Misery: neither did the corduroy-like surface of the work grate upon his feelings. He perceived him not. He saw only that there was a Lot of Work done and his soul was filled with rapture as he reflected that the man who had accomplished all this was paid only five pence an hour." (RTP 111)

Robert was becoming increasingly radicalised and that caused friction both with his bosses and some workmates who were generally split between traditionalist lines - Tory and Liberal. His natural Irish openness, which had been magnified in colonial South Africa, made his views difficult to hide. Not that he ever tried. Ball wrote: "He wasn't unique in his habit of frankness but he was virtually a colonial to whom a free and easy manner was natural at the level of ordinary men. But his workmates knew their

England better than he did and only the undefeated, uncorrupted among them managed to keep their manhood intact. They recognized this incorruptibility in Robert and accepted the vulnerable colonial as an honest man." (7)

That fearless honesty got Robert into trouble on numerous occasions, and not just with his bosses. Hastings had a history of celebrating Guy Fawkes Night – its borough bonfire society was formed in 1860 – and RTP features the Mugsborough Skull and Crossbones Boys who collected pennies for Guys and set off firecrackers. The *Hastings Observer* reported in November 1905 that Robert was summonsed for obstructing a plainclothes police officer, PC Curtis, in the execution of his duty. The PC was confronted when he cautioned a lad, presumably Arthur, who was lighting a squib in Havelock Road. The report continued:

"Defendant interfered and called witness, who was in plain clothes, a coward. Defendant took his coat off, and put himself in a fighting attitude. He refused to give his name, but subsequently did at the station. Defendant, who referred to notes, cross-examined the witness, who said that Noonan was very excited, and it was owing to that that he declined to show his authority as a constable. He admitted that the boy complained that witness had hurt his shoulder. PC Hoadley said that the defendant was making a great disturbance, and there was a big crowd round. Mr Noonan, a decorator of 115 Milward Road, gave his version of the affair on oath. He had bought his children some Chinese crackers. One of them tried to light one, and he saw a man, apparently a civilian, come up to his boy, seize him violently by the shoulder, and began stamping on the squib. He interfered to protect the boy, and took off his overcoat with the intention of defending himself ...he did not give his name and address because Curtis did not treat him properly."

Despite such mitigation the summons was found by the magistrates to be "fully proved." Robert was fined 10 shillings and had to pay £1 9s costs or suffer seven days' hard labour. (8)

That brief newspaper report speaks volumes about Robert's character: his love of the children in his care, his refusal to bow down to authority, his marshalling of evidence, his determination never to give in to either wider injustice or petty despotism.

Nevertheless, the money he handed over to avoid prison must have been a hard blow. That Christmas he painted a mural in a ward of Buchanan hospital without charge, but on Christmas Day itself he was writing coffin plates for pay.

During this period Robert stormed out of Burtons and worked briefly for another St Leonards contractor, but told William Ward that he was "treated very badly by them" and was "off again because he could not put up with it."

Burtons had a contract to supply the municipal hospital with coffin plates for 6d each, and Robert returned to them. (9)

ART AND OTHER TALENTS

"hour speshul hartist"

Was Robert an artist, as so many of his workmates insisted many years later? He was certainly a talented artisan and craftsman with a determination to try every form available for the edification of those he loved and worked with. But scant evidence of genuinely artistic talents exist. There is a grainy, gloomy photograph of his extravagant murals, whitewashed over decades after he painted them, in St Andrew's Church, in Queen's Road, Hastings, which I watched being demolished. There is a single panel from those murals rescued, due to the efforts of Fred Ball and his supporters, in Hastings Museum. But other than the sad remnants of a few fading advertising signs in dark corners, and a few drawings of airships, there is nothing else that can be attributed to him.

It was at Burton's that he was given the nickname 'Raphael' and one foreman, presumably not Misery, said that he was an artist rather than a house-painter. (1) Gower, on at least one occasion, posed for him, but said that he was nervous about sketching the human frame. H.R. Poynton, writing in the *Daily Worker,* however, described him as "quick and bold" in sketching. (2) Robert's own home was decorated with murals worked out painstakingly and then stencilled to the walls. His sign-writing was florid, and suggested a man determined to do more than merely advertise. People long remembered a huge mural on a wall in Perth Road which included a small landscape of Hollington Church-in-the-Wood, where I married, and an inset with birds. He continuously studied technical books on the arts, interior decoration and mural design, plundering every form of printed works for inspiration.

Such talents were the reason why Burton's paid him for the commission to paint the murals for St Andrew's Church, a gift from the firm to the parish and church authorities. His task was to decorate the chancel with scrolls, religious imagery and floral bouquets. Robert embarked on it with gusto and, some remarked later, used it as an opportunity to show his ability to write any form of script and paint any form. Robert, in RTP, lampooned both the attitude of his workmates to anything that smacked of art, the contempt of the foremen to such undertakings, and his own lack of originality, in one of several scenes concerning the decoration of the Moorish drawing room in The Cave:

"'Well, wot do you think of it?'
'Think of what?' asked Easton.
'Why, hour speshul hartist,' replied Crass with a sneer. 'Do you think 'e's goin' to get through it?'
'Shouldn't like to say,' replied Easton guardedly.
'You know it's one thing to draw on a bit of paper and colour it with a penny box of paints, and quite another thing to do it on a wall or ceiling,' continued Crass. 'Ain't it?'
'Yes; that's true enough,' said Harlow.
'Do you believe they're his own designs?' Crass went on.
'Be rather 'ard to tell,' remarked Easton, embarrassed...
'If you was to ast me, quietly,' Crass added, 'I should be more inclined to say as 'e copied it all out of some book.'
'That's just about the size of it, mate,' agreed Harlow.
'It would be a bit of all right if 'e was to make a bloody mess of it, wouldn't it?' Crass continued with a malignant leer.
'Not arf!' (RTP 177)

Robert was paid an extra penny an hour for the work, taking his rate to eight pence, plus some overtime. But he worked long hours into the night, sometimes to three or four a.m., and much of that work was deemed his own time because he took such scrupulous care. He rifled through the Decorator's Journal for inspiration, particularly looking for Moorish designs, other books from the local Free Library with illustrations of the Pre-Raphaelites and exotica which could be adapted. He consulted The Practical Decorator and Ornamentalist and The Manual of Ornament which contained illustrations picked out in gold of the structual art of the Middle and Far East. Personal advantage or what he could get from them was not his main concern, Kathleen insisted, although the occasional extra commission would have helped with household bills. He was simply obsessed with doing the work to the best of his ability, while recognising that the same proud work ethic did not apply to those directly employing him.

Interior of the later-demolished St Andrew's Church, Queen's Road, Hastings, showing Robert Noonan's murals and decoration.

Robert, in the guise of Owen, spelt out his thoughts towards such commissions in RTP when he was given the task of refurbishing the Moorish designs in 'The Cave':

That night, long after his wife and Frankie were asleep, Owen worked in the sitting-room, searching through old numbers of the Decorators' Journal and through the illustrations in other books of designs for examples of Moorish work, and making rough sketches in pencil. He did not attempt to finish anything yet: it was necessary to think first; but he roughed out the general plan, and when at last he did go to bed he could not sleep for a long time. He almost fancied he was in the drawing-room at the `Cave'. First of all it would be necessary to take down the ugly plaster centre flower with its crevices all filled up with old whitewash. The cornice was all right; it was fortunately a very simple one, with a deep cove and without many enrichments. Then, when the walls and the ceiling had been properly prepared, the ornamentation would be proceeded with. The walls, divided into panels and arches containing painted designs and lattice-work; the panels of the door decorated in a similar manner. The mouldings of the door and window frames picked out with colours and gold so as to be in character with the other work; the cove of the cornice, a dull yellow with a bold ornament in colour - gold was not advisable in the hollow because of the unequal distribution of the light, but some of the smaller mouldings of the cornice should be gold. On the ceiling there would be one large panel covered with an appropriate design in gold and colours and surrounded by a wide margin or border. To separate this margin from the centre panel there would be a narrow border, and another border - but wider - round the outer edge of the margin, where the ceiling met the cornice. Both these borders and the margin would be covered with ornamentation in colour and gold. Great care would be necessary when deciding what parts were to be gilded because - whilst large masses of gilding are apt to look garish and in bad taste - a lot of fine gold lines are ineffective, especially on a flat surface, where they do not always catch the light. Process by process he traced the work, and saw it advancing stage by stage until, finally, the large apartment was transformed and glorified. And then in the midst of the pleasure he experienced in the planning of the work there came the fear that perhaps they would not have it done at all. The question, what personal advantage would he gain never once occurred to Owen. He simply wanted to do the work; and he saw so fully occupied with thinking and planning how it was to be done that the question of profit was crowded out. But although this question of what profit could be made out of the work never occurred to Owen, it would in due course by fully considered by Mr Rushton. In fact, it was the only thing about the work that Mr Rushton would think of at all: how much money could be made out of it. This is what is meant by the oft-quoted saying, `The men work with their hands - the master works with his brains.' (RTP 122-123)

Robert treasured above all a folio of William Morris designs. Morris had been producing his work since Robert was a boy and clearly influenced him. His importance to Robert grew as Morris embraced Socialism.

The result at St Andrew's was a mosaic of designs in formal panels up to 20 feet high and 40 feet around the chancel walls with the Lord's Prayer and the Apostles' Creed picked out in many different scripts, all topped with large scrolls crying 'Holy, Holy, Holy.' The welter of different designs and styles undoubtedly clashed, but did not appear to be out of place in the Edwardian fashions for church decoration.

It certainly went down well with the clergy and on its completion the vicar, the Reverend Henry W. Jeaves, presented Robert with a testimonial and the generous, for the times, sum of £5.

Tressell mural panel, saved from the wreckage of St Andrew's Church

But was it high art? The vicar who whitewashed over it in the 1960s did not think so. (3) And Robert dismissed it as "unimportant", believing that it was the work itself which was important. And, as Ball pointed out, the lack of insight into fine paintings or high art in RTP is a curious omission, while Robert's reported comments on great masters or the likes of Morris were either practical for his trade or because of the latter's belief that an artist should make the world a better place. A possible exception to the rule is Robert's detailed account of Owen's decorations for the Moorish drawing room, but that is largely technical rather than appreciative of higher meaning. "I don't think that he had any real originality," said Ball, "or even any interest in the art of painting as a means of revolutionary experiment and discovery. He was essentially conservative in his work, I believe, because for all his delight in his skill, painting was not his true means of expression."

That, of course, proved to be his talent for the written word. But, as befits a Renaissance-style working man, he had other talents.

One was an aptitude for designing and modelling flying machines. Aircraft were then in their infancy and friends remember that he started creating models in 1902, just before the first flight of the Wright brothers. Kathleen recalled that the whole family, Adelaide excepted, were "all mad on flying." Gower said that Robert read everything in the local library on the subject. And Walsh said he "was convinced of the utility of heavier-than-air machines long before they were invented and spent much of his time making aeroplane models." During the first decade of the century it was a national craze, with would-be inventors seeking lucrative prizes for practical designs.

In 1901-02, during his first year in Hastings, Robert completed an essay, *The Evolution of the Airship*, which he illustrated with his own drawings and designs, and which remains the only manuscript of his which survives apart from RTP. The article demonstrates Robert's growing confidence in his writing abilities and a seriousness of intent which contrasts with the whimsical sketches he is reported to have written in South Africa. The piece is hard-headed, shows no trace of pacifism and illustrates his interest of the practical fusion of mechanical techniques and intellectual vision. He also saw a vision of the future which was all too soon to approach reality.

He opened: "The most powerful navy that could be built, the strongest fortifications that the wit of man could devise, or the most numerous and efficient army in the world, would be comparatively helpless and at the mercy of the nation possessing a fleet of airships so designed as to be capable of carrying quantities of high explosives, and really under the control of those who manned them. Is the possibility of the construction of such an aerial fleet altogether remote - or is it on the eve of realisation?"

Robert then rattled through the history of those who had tried to construction airships and flying machines since the Middle Ages when "it was a very perilous business to attempt anything of the kind ...because of the dangers attending the experiments were supplemented by the additional risk of being burnt at the stake or boiled in oil for witchcraft, for in those days anyone who accomplished anything out of the common was often suspected of dealing in magic and of being able to perform his feats of skill chiefly through the secret aid of the Evil One."

Robert chronicled with some delight such failed experiments as dew in a giant hollow sphere meant to be drawn up into the sky by the sun's rays, and a 1670 construction of four balloons made of sheet copper each enclosing a vacuum and propelled by a sail and oars. Robert wrote of many other schemes, "some ingenious, some ridiculous", until the birth of real ballooning in the late 18th century through the use of hot air and gas controlled by valves. During Robert's own lifetime advances were made in dirigible balloons capable of being steered rather than at the mercy of winds. Prophetically, Robert noted that "Germany takes a keen interest in aerial navigation" throughout the latter decades of the 19th century, with experiments reaching a turning point in 1900 with the construction of the "monster" airship by Count Zeppelin. In the months preceding Robert's articles there were further breakthroughs and a British airship was being built but had not been completed at the time of his writing.

Robert concluded that "it has been demonstrated beyond question that it is possible to construct dirigible balloons which can be driven in any desired direction on calm days or on days when only moderate winds prevail, and it should be remembered that these favourable conditions exist on a very large proportion of the days of the year. Further, even under unfavourable conditions it is possible to control an airship to the extent of considerable lateral deviation from the direction of a strong wind, and to make circular movements. That an airship can be controlled to this extent is undoubtedly better than an ordinary spherical balloon which cannot be controlled at all except as regards its vertical direction." (3)

By 1905 he decided to build one of his own, a scale model six feet long. Gower helped him with the soldering and by running errands. It had a scaled engine which drove three-bladed propellers, had a large rudder and appeared from the front as the prow of an ocean-going ship. It had a crew of small Dutch wooden dolls and Robert decorated it with the rising sun on stern and rudder, along with its name *Martian*. The model was covered in aluminium paint, with more decorations picked out in red, green and gold, including the Irish harp.

No-one knows if it ever flew, but Robert had some hopes that it could make his fortune. He wrote to the War Office, influential people and newspapers in a bid to get his design adopted, all without result. He submitted the drawings to the *Daily Mail* 1907 model aircraft competition, but was rejected. After spending two years or so taking up space in his room, Robert finally lost heart and "took a hammer and smashed it all to pieces," according to Gower.

Robert's workmates knew that he was better-educated than most of them and, indeed, many of their employers, but few knew of his capacity for languages. Kathleen recorded that, with English included, he could speak seven languages. His French was fluent but he also had varying degrees of German, Gaelic, Spanish, Italian and "real Dutch, not Afrikaans."

Ball wrote: "I am not surprised that a man who ...had mastered a half-dozen skilled arts and crafts and was soon writing pieces for publication should find the life of a house-painter in Hastings galling; I am only more mystified as to his motives for remaining in the trade and the overbearing circumstances which prevented a man who was well read and could speak several languages from getting some kind of teaching or professional appointment even in those days of limited opportunity. But both Kathleen and his niece say he deliberately chose to become a worker." (5)

RELIGION

"disciples of the meek and lowly"

Robert may have liked the opportunities and bonuses which working in churches gave him, but he was himself an atheist. With his insight into the thinking of Frank Owen, his alter ego, he was scathing about the hypocrisies of "decent" church-going folk who accepted and exploited poverty on their doorstep. On Owen's neighbours he wrote:

"But although the hearts of these disciples of the meek and lowly Jewish carpenter were filled with uncharitableness, they were powerless to do much harm. The landlord regarded their opinion with indifference. All he cared about was the money: although he also was a sincere Christian, he would not have hesitated to let the top flat to Satan himself, providing he was certain of receiving the rent regularly.
"The only one upon whom the Christians were able to inflict any suffering was the child. At first when he used to go out into the street to play, the other children, acting on their parents' instructions, refused to associate with him, or taunted him with their parents' poverty. Occasionally he came home heartbroken and in tears because he had been excluded from some game." (RTP 77)

It is also clear that he had little time for what he regarded as the absurdities of organised religion. While working in St Andrew's he was continually pestered by the verger, who tried to convert him. Work was frequently interrupted by arguments, one reason why Robert often worked on late into the night, both to catch up and to work in peace. Ball wrote: "It was an imposition on the part of the verger and it put Robert at great disadvantage, as indeed it would put any man questioned about his religious and political views at his place of work."

Gower recalled: "Robert did not attend church. He once called me to his front window to observe a man going to church, a business-man with whom he was acquainted, the Bible carried ostentatiously under the arm, umbrella and tall hat complete, and wearing an air of devout respectability. The sight was too much for Noonan. He rolled up with merriment." Robert also once told him: "That's be the time when you can go to the station and take a ticket to Jerusalem – the heavenly one."

Yet, as we have seen, one of Robert's frequent callers for conversation and sociability was the Catholic priest Father O'Callaghan after Kathleen had gone to her convent school. There is no reference at all to theological arguments, so it is a fair bet that they talked late into the night about Ireland, for which they both had sentimental attachments, and politics. Robert's facilities for languages, including Gaelic, and his love of literature, would also have drawn the two men together. Ball wrote: "We can assume the priest was a man of liberal views. Robert would never have made a friend of a religious bigot. There is nothing to suggest that there was any deeper ideological or personal meaning to their relationship." In 1905 Father O'Callaghan was transferred to the Church of Our Lady of Mount Carmel in New York. (1)

It is easy to imagine the two unlikely friends debating passages from the Bible, and how they were interpreted. Robert made clear his belief that such scripture had been twisted out of all meaning:

For instance, these `disciples' assure us that when Jesus said, `Resist not evil', `If a man smite thee upon he right cheek turn unto him also the left', He really meant 'Turn on to him a Maxim gun; disembowel him with a bayonet or batter in his skull with the butt end of a rifle!' When He said, `If one take thy coat, give him thy cloak also,' the `Christians' say that what He really meant was: `If one take thy coat, give him six months' hard labour. A few of the followers of Jesus admit that He really did mean just what He said, but they say that the world would never be able to go on if they followed out His teachings! That is true. It is probably the effect that Jesus intended His teachings to produce. It is altogether improbable that He wished the world to continue along its present lines. But, if these pretended followers really think - as they say that they do - that the teachings of Jesus are ridiculous and impracticable, why continue the hypocritical farce of calling themselves `Christians' when they don't really believe in or follow Him at all?

As Jesus himself pointed out, there's no sense in calling Him `Lord, Lord' when they do not the things that He said. (RTP 221-222)

In another chapter Robert considered the existence of God, with a predictable conclusion: *But supposing that bodily death was not the end. Suppose there was some kind of a God? If there were, it wasn't unreasonable to think that the Being who was capable of creating such a world as this and who seemed so callously indifferent to the unhappiness of His creatures, would also be capable of devising and creating the other Hell that most people believed in. (RTP 229)*

Robert went on: *Looking out into the unfathomable infinity of space, Owen wondered what manner of Being or Power it was that had originated and sustained all this? Considered as an explanation of the existence of the universe, the orthodox Christian religion was too absurd to merit a second thought. But then, every other conceivable hypothesis was also - ultimately - unsatisfactory and even ridiculous. To believe that the universe as it is now has existed from all eternity without any Cause is surely ridiculous. But to say that it was created by a Being who existed without a Cause from all eternity is equally ridiculous. In fact, it was only postponing the difficulty one stage. Evolution was not more satisfactory, because although it was undoubtedly true as far as it went, it only went part of the way, leaving the great question still unanswered by assuming the existence - in the beginning - of the elements of matter, without a cause! The question remained unanswered because it was unanswerable. Regarding this problem man was but -*

`An infant crying in the night,
An infant crying for the light
And with no language but a cry.'

All the same, it did not follow, because one could not explain the mystery oneself, that it was right to try to believe an unreasonable explanation offered by someone else. (RTP 229-230)

Robert was most strident in his contempt for the clergy and the congregation at the fictionalised Shining Light Chapel. He described the Reverend Belcher in terms of a balloon constantly leaking gas:

He was a very fat man ...arrayed in a long garment of costly black cloth, a sort of frock coat, and by the rotundity of his figure he seemed to be one of those accustomed to sit in the chief places at feasts.
"The long garment before-mentioned was unbuttoned and through the opening there protruded a vast expanse of waistcoat and trousers, distended almost to bursting by the huge globe of flesh they contained. A

gold watch-chain with a locket extended partly across the visible portion of the envelope of the globe... If he had removed the long garment, this individual would have resembled a balloon: the feet representing the car and the small head that surmounted the globe, the safety valve; as it was it did actually serve the purpose of a safety valve, the owner being, in consequence of gross overfeeding and lack of natural exercise, afflicted with chronic flatulence, which manifested itself in frequent belchings forth through the mouth of the foul gases generated in the stomach by the decomposition of the foods with which it was generally loaded." (RTP 169-170)

Robert, with a sense of outrage born of a practice common amongst Hastings chapels of the time and beyond, described how this over-stuffed cleric exhorted his poorer parishioners and their children to subscribe to chapel repairs, saying: *If your friends are very poor and unable to give a large donation at one time, a good plan would be to arrange to call upon them every Saturday afternoon with your card to collect their donations. (RTP 171)*

At the same time, Robert revealed, the chapel authorities had spent part of the money already raised to send Belcher, their Shepherd,, to the south of France for a month because he suffered not from any malady but was run down, "*and rumour had it that this condition had been brought about by the rigorous asceticism of his life and his intense devotion to the arduous labours of his holy calling." (RTP 168)*

Robert is equally sarcastic about his temporary stand-in, the Reverend John Starr, a young, slender man whose *air of refinement and culture were in striking contrast to the coarse appearance of the other adults in the room: the vulgar, ignorant, uncultivated crowd of profit-mongers and hucksters in front of him... There was nothing in his appearance to give anyone even an inkling of the truth, which was: that he was there for the purpose of bolstering up the characters of the despicable crew of sweaters and slave-drivers who paid his wages. (RTP173-174)*

For saying a few words to a Sunday school meeting, Starr was paid £4 and 4 shillings from the chapel funds, roughly a month's wage for a skilled artisan, Robert noted, adding: *It was not a large sum considering the great services rendered by Mr Starr, but, small as it was, it is to be feared that many worldly, unconverted persons will think that it was far too much to pay for a Few Words, even such wise words as Mr John Starr's admittedly always were. But the Labourer is worthy of his hire." (RTP 176)*

Greed and corruption amongst those who claimed higher moral authority than their poor flock always served to outrage Robert and deepen his contempt for religion in general and chapel congregations in particular. That is shown when Nora Owen explains the fraudulent nature of organised religion to her son:

"Well, the vicar goes about telling the Idlers that it's quite right for them to do nothing, and that God meant them to have nearly everything that is made by those who work. In fact he tells them that God made the poor for the use of the rich. Then he goes to the workers and tells them that God meant them to work very hard and to give all the good things that they make to those who do nothing, and that they should be very thankful to God and to the idlers for being allowed to have even the very worst food to eat and the rags and broken boots to wear. He also tells them that they mustn't grumble, or be discontented because they're poor in this world, but that they must wait till they're dead, and then God will reward them by letting them go to a place called heaven." (RTP 81)

Robert wrote in his preface that "it will be evident that no attack is made upon sincere religions..." (RTP 14) But the book is full of anger at religion being used as one of many tools to suppress and con the working classes to the enrichment of the better-off. The villains, as Robert saw it, were both male and female. Robert describes in detail the extremely modest home of Ruth Easton and lingers on an unopened, and clearly never read, inscribed with the message:

'To dear Ruth, from her loving friend Mrs Starvem with the prayer that God's work may be her guide and that Jesus may be her very own Saviour.'
Robert continued:

Mrs Starvem was Ruth's former mistress, and this had been her parting gift when Ruth left to get married. It was supposed to be a keepsake, but as Ruth never opened the book and never willingly allowed her thoughts to dwell upon the scenes of which it reminded her, she had forgotten the existence of Mrs Starvem almost as completely as that well-to-do and pious lady had forgotten hers.

For Ruth, the memory of the time she spent in the house of 'her loving friend' was the reverse of pleasant. It comprised a series of recollections of petty tyrannies, insults and indignities. Six years of cruelly excessive work, beginning every morning two or three hours before the rest of the household were awake and ceasing only when she went exhausted to bed, late at night.

She had been what is called a 'slavey' but if she had been really a slave her owner would have had some regard for her health and welfare: her 'loving friend' had had none. Mrs Starvem's only thought had been to get out of Ruth the greatest possible amount of labour and to give her as little as possible in return.

When Ruth looked back upon that dreadful time she saw it, as one might say, surrounded by a halo of religion. She never passed by a chapel or heard the name of God, or the singing of a hymn, without thinking of her former mistress. To have looked into this Bible would have reminded her of Mrs Starvem; that was one of the reasons why the book reposed, unopened and unread, a mere ornament on the table in the bay window. (RTP 50-51)

The RTP is scattered with scathing references to the clergy. In one he describes a fine sunny day with the seaside promenade packed with the well-to-do: *Mingling with and part of this crowd were a number of well-fed individuals dressed in long garments of black cloth of the finest texture, and broad-brimmed soft felt hats. Most of these persons had gold rings on their soft white fingers and glove-like kid or calfskin boots on their feet. They belonged to the great army of imposters who obtain an easy living by taking advantage of the ignorance and simplicity of their fellow-men, and pretending to be the 'followers' and 'servants' of the lowly Carpenter of Nazareth - the Man of Sorrows, who had not where to lay His head."*

Robert's ingrained atheism made clear during a dialogue between Owen and Slyme, the professed devout Christian.

"If Gord didn't create the world, 'ow did it come 'ere?" demanded Slyme. "I know no more about it than you do," replied Owen. "That is - I know nothing. The only difference between us is that you think you know. You think that you know that God made the universe; how long it took Him to do it; why He made it; how long it's been in existence and how it will finally pass away. You also imagine that you know that we shall live after we're dead; where we shall go, and the kind of existence we shall have. In fact, in

the excess of your 'humility', you think you know all about it. But really you know no more of these things than any other human being does: that is, you know nothing." (RTP 142)

Later, when Slyme says that his heart tells him that he has felt happiness and the peace that passes all understanding since he became a committed Christian, Owen replies: "You've got some title to call yourself a Christian haven't you? As for the happiness that passes all understanding, it certainly passes my understanding how you can be happy when you believe that millions of people are being tortured in Hell; and it also passes my understanding why you are not ashamed of yourself for being happy under such circumstances." (RTP 143)

Robert knew, however, that apart from hypocrites like Crass, many working men held to a vague but decent sense of Christianity. Philpot is applauded by all but Slyme when he says: "I don't see as it matters a dam wot a man believes, as long as you don't do no 'arm to nobody. If you see a poor b—r wot's down on 'is luck, give 'im a 'elpin' 'and. Even if you ain't got no money you can say a kind word. If a man does 'is work and looks arter 'is 'ome and 'is young 'uns, and does a good turn to a fellow creature when 'e can, I reckon 'e stands as much chance of getting into 'eaven – if there is sich a place – as some of these 'ere Bible-busters, whether 'e ever goes to church or chapel or not." (RTP 144)

Robert, through Owen, constantly stressed, often to deaf ears, that working men did not have to go to church to demonstrate their moral superiority to the bosses and their acolytes who were frequent visitors. Jack Mitchell, in his 1969 analytical study, wrote: "So in Owen the workers can clearly see how superior their moral nature is to that on the bosses; he bears out their claim to the title of Humanity." (2)

A well-known scene in RTP describes two students disrupting an evangelical meeting by offering a preacher a phial of poison and challenging him to drink it to test his belief in miracles while themselves expressing their scientific belief in an antidote. It is based on an actual event in which Robert himself was the protagonist.

Every Sunday night amid the pleasure boats, fishing luggers and trawlers, rowing boats and yachts, religious meetings would be held on the beach shingle. They were rumbustious affairs drawing sight-seers as well as the devout. Among the preachers was a Mr Hubbard who spouted biblical fire and brimstone and attacked not just the Godless but also every other form of Christianity who deviated in any way from Holy Scripture. The Salvation Army band constantly tried to drown out his words and his meetings would often end in total disarray, but that never deterred him.

One of Robert's workmates, Sellens, told Ball years later: "I remember Bob once telling me how he enjoyed himself at Mr Hubbard, the beach preacher's, meeting. You know, of course, Mr Hubbard, the preacher, who attacked nearly all religious bodies. He was bitter against Atheists and Agnostics. He declared one evening that he believed every word in the Bible to be true. Bob challenged Mr Hubbard stating that he could prove that Mr Hubbard did not believe the Bible. Mr Hubbard accepted Bob's challenge. Both were present at the appointed time. Mr Hubbard was asked to read a certain part of the Bible (Mark 16: 17-18), this he did. In it, it stated that those who trusted God could drink poison and it would do them no injury. They were, of course, words to this effect, Bob then challenged him with a bottle marked 'poison.' He said, 'Now, Mr Hubbard, I have a bottle of poison enough to kill several people. If you drink this and it does you no harm we shall know that the Bible is true and that you are indeed a prophet sent by God.'

"Mr Hubbard hesitated, protested, and the crowd of religious opponents, Catholics, Anglo-Catholics, who were always bitter against him, cried out - drink it, Hubbard, drink up, drink up! hoping apparently to get rid of a pest to them. Hubbard refused to drink. Bob then stated that though Mr Hubbard could not trust the Bible, he himself could trust science which Hubbard condemned, whereupon Bob drank the contents of the bottle followed immediately by a drink from another which Bob said was an antidote invented by science. The fact was both bottles contained only water or harmless fluid."

Robert went home that night and told Kathleen he regretted tricking the "poor chap." Kathleen told Ball: "Just think how wonderful it would have been for the preacher if he had drunk the 'poison'." (3)

The fictionalised version, with Misery/Hunter one of his opponents, puts clearly Robert's logical, sustained and well-argued heckle:

By the time the singing was over a considerable crowd had gathered, and then one of the evangelists, the same man who had given out the hymn, stepped into the middle of the ring. He had evidently been offended by the unseemly conduct of the two well-dressed young men, for after a preliminary glance round upon the crowd, he fixed his gaze upon the pair, and immediately launched out upon a long tirade against what he called `Infidelity'. Then, having heartily denounced all those who - as he put it - `refused' to believe, he proceeded to ridicule those half-and-half believers, who, while professing to believe the Bible, rejected the doctrine of Hell. That the existence of a place of eternal torture is taught in the Bible, he tried to prove by a long succession of texts. As he proceeded he became very excited, and the contemptuous laughter of the two unbelievers seemed to make him worse. He shouted and raved, literally foaming at the mouth and glaring in a frenzied manner around upon the faces of the crowd. `There is a Hell!' he shouted. `And understand this clearly - "The wicked shall be turned into hell" - "He that believeth not shall be damned."'
`Well, then, you'll stand a very good chance of being damned also,' exclaimed one of the two young men.
`'Ow do you make it out?' demanded the preacher, wiping the froth from his lips and the perspiration from his forehead with his handkerchief.
`Why, because you don't believe the Bible yourselves.' Nimrod and the other evangelists laughed, and looked pityingly at the young man. `Ah, my dear brother,' said Misery. `That's your delusion. I thank God I do believe it, every word!'
`Amen,' fervently ejaculated Slyme and several of the other disciples.
`Oh no, you don't,' replied the other. `And I can prove you don't.'
`Prove it, then,' said Nimrod.
`Read out the 17th and 18th verses of the XVIth chapter of Mark,' said the disturber of the meeting. The crowd began to close in on the centre, the better to hear the dispute. Misery, standing close to the lantern, found the verse mentioned and read aloud as follows:

`And these signs shall follow them that believe. In my name shall they cast out devils: they shall speak with new tongues. They shall take up serpents; and if they drink any deadly thing it shall not hurt them: they shall lay hands on the sick, and they shall recover.'

`Well, you can't heal the sick, neither can you speak new languages or cast out devils: but perhaps you can drink deadly things without suffering harm.' The speaker here suddenly drew from his waistcoat pocket a small glass bottle and held it out towards Misery, who shrank from it with horror as he continued: `I have here a most deadly poison. There is in this bottle sufficient strychnine to kill a dozen unbelievers. Drink it! And if it doesn't harm you, we'll know that you really are a believer and that what you believe is the truth!'

`Ear, 'ear!' said the Semi-drunk, who had listened to the progress of the argument with great interest. `Ear, 'ear! That's fair enough. Git it acrost yer chest.'

Some of the people in the crowd began to laugh, and voices were heard from several quarters calling upon Misery to drink the strychnine. `Now, if you'll allow me, I'll explain to you what that there verse means,' said Hunter. `If you read it carefully - WITH the context -' `I don't want you to tell me what it means,' interrupted the other. `I am able to read for myself. Whatever you may say, or pretend to think it means, I know what it says.'

`Hear, Hear,' shouted several voices, and angry cries of `Why don't you drink the poison?' began to be heard from the outskirts of the crowd. `Are you going to drink it or not?' demanded the man with the bottle. `No! I'm not such a fool!' retorted Misery, fiercely, and a loud shout of laughter broke from the crowd.'
`P'haps some of the other "believers" would like to,' said the young man sneeringly, looking round upon the disciples. As no one seemed desirous of availing himself of this offer, the man returned the bottle regretfully to his pocket.

`I suppose,' said Misery, regarding the owner of the strychnine with a sneer, `I suppose you're one of them there hired critics wot's goin' about the country doin' the Devil's work?' (RTP 232-234)

In RTP Owen rescues a starving kitten to take home to his son and, as he picked it up and put it inside his coat, the little outcast began to purr.

This incident served to turn his thoughts into another channel. If, as so many people pretended to believe, there was an infinitely loving God, how was it that this helpless creature that He had made was condemned to suffer? It had never done any harm, and was in no sense responsible for the fact that it existed. Was God unaware of the miseries of His creatures? If so, then He was not all-knowing. Was God aware of their sufferings, but unable to help *them? Then He was not all-powerful. Had He the power but not the will to make His creatures happy? Then He was not good. No; it was impossible to believe in the existence of an individual, infinite God.. In fact, no one did so believe; and least of all those who pretended for various reasons to be the disciples and followers of Christ. The anti-Christs who went about singing hymns, making long prayers and crying Lord, Lord, but never doing the things which He said, who were known by their words to be unbelievers and infidels, unfaithful to the Master they pretended to serve, their lives being passed in deliberate and systematic disregard of His teachings and Commandments. It was not necessary to call in the evidence of science, or to refer to the supposed inconsistencies, impossibilities, contradictions and absurdities contained in the Bible, in order to prove there was no truth in the Christian religion. All that was necessary was to look at the conduct of the individuals who were its votaries.*

Mitchell said: "Tressell's picture of religion in the RTP is, even for its own day, one-sided, simplified, somewhat sectarian. In fact there is no example of 'sincere religion' shown to offset the main attack. This element of militant anti-official-Christianity was very marked in the old British radical and socialist movement. In spite of this I believe that Tressell's portrait of official religion remains a valid and important integral part of his total picture." (4)

But politically Robert had just cause for railing against the clergy. In 1906 the Hastings authorities, after much debate and a great deal of resistance, introduced school breakfasts for the poorest pupils of skimmed milk and bread and margarine in recognition of the real level of poverty in the town. The school board, dominated by the Church of England, fought that provision tooth and nail. To them it was an assault on their stranglehold not just of working adults, but their children as well. The Reverend Durnford sent a resolution from both Hastings and Rye constituency Conservatives urging them to vote down a provisions of meals in elementary schools bill which would have seen such horrors imposed nationally. His argument was that the alleviation of poverty must be the sole concern of local school boards - and therefore the Church - rather than the central board of education. Such a move, he argued, would centralise the education, nutrition, health and hygiene of the children of the working class.

This was a national issue. The Canon of Winchester, the Reverend R.F. Hessey, published his pamphlet *Socialism*, in which he wrote: "They are clamouring for the Old Age Pension of five shillings all round with no distinction whatsoever, and for the feeding of all children at school." He quoted an alleged conversation between a mother and a clergyman's wife in which the mother thanked God that her brood had grown up before school meals were thought of because "my husband cared for his children and nothing but that made him spare a penny from the drink." (5)

Such mixtures of pomposity and condescension were manna to Robert who delighted in exposing their greedy core. But he knew from his own experience that hymns were an integral part of the working man's entertainment at work and at home, not just in church. The RTP hymns are sung by working hands several times, including the following:

Work, for the night is coming,
Work through the morning hours;
Work, while the dew is sparkling,
Work 'mid springing flowers;
Work, when the day grows brighter,
Work, in the glowing sun;
Work, for the night is coming,
When man's work is done. (RTP 219)

DRINK

"for the good of the house"

Throughout his life in Hastings Robert expounded and expanded his thoughts in local pubs. Robert was no drunk, but neither was he anti-drink. He may have believed that "parsons and publicans are the enemy of the working man" but he despised the temperance movement as another capitalist con, and he never begrudged hard-working men their small extravagances once food was placed on the family table. Furthermore, in that era more than at any time since - regulated licensing laws were introduced during the First World War and never fully rescinded - the pub was a place for discussion and political debate as well as entertainment, alcohol and relief from the rigours of the day.

Even academics and campaigners who wanted stricter controls accepted that drink could be both an evil and a comfort. Charles Booth, whose research was hugely influential, wrote: "A most horrible and true picture may be drawn of the trade in drink, of the wickedness and misery that goes with it. So horrible that one cannot wonder that some eyes are blinded to all else, and there is a cry of away with this accursed abomination. There is, however, much more to be said. Anyone who frequents public-houses knows that actual drunkenness is very much the exception." (1)

In RTP Robert accepted the conviviality that the pub gave working men: *"I feel ashamed of meself,' Philpot added in confidence to Owen, `when I think of all the money I chuck away on beer. If it wasn't for that, I shouldn't be in such a hole meself now...' `It ain't so much that I likes the beer, you know,' he continued; `it's the company. When you ain't got no 'ome, in a manner o' speakin', like me, the pub's about the only place where you can get a little enjoyment. But you ain't very welcome there unless you spends your money.'* (RTP 293) Robert drank regularly, but in moderation, and only when there was food on the family table. According to family legend he kept sober by eating raisins when drinking. (2)

The issue of alcohol and whether it was a cause or symptom of poverty was a source of constant debate throughout the Edwardian period and after and that debate is reflected in RTP's characters: Slyme the teetotal religious bigot, hypocrite and rapist; Crass who guzzles alcohol to boost his own esteem and remain the centre of attention; Philpott, the widower who drinks wherever and whenever he can to ease his desperate loneliness; Easton, who neglects his wife and child to drink with, and suck up to, the under-foreman Crass. Robert made Owen a teetotal socialist but in RTP he has no truck with the charities, churches, slum missionaries and temperance tub-thumpers who linked drink and poverty purely as cause and effect:

`There's no need for us to talk about drink or laziness,' returned Owen, impatiently, `because they have nothing to do with the matter. The question is, what is the cause of the lifelong poverty of the majority of those who are not drunkards and who DO work? Why, if all the drunkards and won't-works and unskilled or inefficient workers could be by some miracle transformed into sober, industrious and skilled workers tomorrow, it would, under the present conditions, be so much the worse for us, because there isn't enough work for all NOW and those people by increasing the competition for what work there is, would inevitably cause a reduction of wages and a greater scarcity of employment. The theories that drunkenness, laziness or inefficiency are the causes of poverty are so many devices invented and fostered by those who are selfishly interested in maintaining the present states of affairs, for the purpose of preventing us from discovering the real causes of our present condition.' (RTP 26)

In a later chapter Robert wrote: There is no more cowardly, dastardly slander than is contained in the assertion that the majority or any considerable proportion of working men neglect their families through drink. It is a condemned lie. There are some who do, but they are not even a large minority. They are few and far between, and are regarded with contempt by their fellow workmen.
It will be said that their families had to suffer for want of even the little that most of them spent in that way: but the persons that use this argument should carry it to its logical conclusion. Tea is an unnecessary and harmful drink; it has been condemned by medical men so often that to enumerate its evil qualities here would be waste of time. The same can be said of nearly all the cheap temperance drinks; they are unnecessary and harmful and cost money, and, like beer, are drunk only for pleasure.
What right has anyone to say to working men that when their work is done they should not find pleasure in drinking a glass or two of beer together in a tavern or anywhere else? Let those who would presume to condemn them

carry their argument to its logical conclusion and condemn pleasure of every kind. Let them persuade the working classes to lead still simpler lives; to drink water instead of such unwholesome things as tea, coffee, beer, lemonade and all the other harmful and unnecessary stuff. They would then be able to live ever so much more cheaply, and as wages are always and everywhere regulated by the cost of living, they would be able to work for lower pay. These people are fond of quoting the figures of the `Nation's Drink Bill,' as if all this money were spent by the working classes! But if the amount of money spent in drink by the `aristocracy', the clergy and the middle classes were deducted from the `Nation's Drink Bill', it would be seen that the amount spent per head by the working classes is not so alarming after all; and would probably not be much larger than the amount spent on drink by those who consume tea and coffee and all the other unwholesome and unnecessary `temperance' drinks.

The fact that some of Rushton's men spent about two shillings a week on drink while they were in employment was not the cause of their poverty. If they had never spent a farthing for drink, and if their wretched wages had been increased fifty percent, they would still have been in a condition of the most abject and miserable poverty, for nearly all the benefits and privileges of civilization, nearly everything that makes life worth living, would still have been beyond their reach. (RTP 426-427)

Robert also regarded temperance halls with cynicism, accusing them of both condescension and exploitation: Very frequently it happened, when only a few men were working together, that it was not convenient to make tea for breakfast or dinner, and then some of them brought tea with them ready made in bottles and drank it cold; but most of them went to the nearest pub and ate their food there with a glass of beer. Even those who would rather have had tea or coffee had beer, because if they went to a temperance restaurant or coffee tavern it generally happened that they were not treated very civilly unless they bought something to eat as well as to drink, and the tea at such places was really dearer than beer, and the latter was certainly quite as good to drink as the stewed tea or the liquid mud that was sold as coffee at cheap `Workmen's' Eating Houses. (RTP 393)

Robert described one of his regular haunts, The Cricketers opposite the old cricket ground and just a few minutes' walk from his flat in Milward Road, with a mixture of warmth, revulsion, fascination and humour: Although the house was not nearly so full as it would have been if times had been better, there was a large number of people there, for the `Cricketers' was one of the most popular houses in the town. Another thing that helped to make them busy was the fact that two other public houses in the vicinity had recently been closed up. There were people in all the compartments. Some of the seats in the public bar were occupied by women, some young and accompanied by their husbands, some old and evidently sodden with drink. In one corner of the public bar, drinking beer or gin with a number of young fellows, were three young girls who worked at a steam laundry in the neighbourhood. Two large, fat, gipsy-looking women: evidently hawkers, for on the floor beside them were two baskets containing bundles of flowers - chrysanthemums and Michaelmas daisies. There were also two very plainly and shabbily dressed women about thirty-five years of age, who were always to be found there on Saturday nights, drinking with any man who was willing to pay for them. The behaviour of these two women was very quiet and their manners unobtrusive. They seemed to realize that they were there only on sufferance, and their demeanour was shamefaced and humble.

The majority of the guests were standing. The floor was sprinkled with sawdust which served to soak up the beer that slopped out of the glasses of those whose hands were too unsteady to hold them upright. The air was foul with the smell of beer, spirits and tobacco smoke, and the uproar was deafening, for nearly everyone was talking at the same time, their voices clashing discordantly with the strains of the Polyphone, which was playing `The Garden of Your Heart'. In one corner a group of men convulsed with laughter at the details of a dirty story related by one of their number. Several impatient customers were banging the bottoms of their empty glasses or pewters on the counter and shouting their orders for more beer. Oaths, curses and obscene expressions resounded on every hand, coming almost as frequently from the women as the men. And over all the rattle of money, the ringing of the cash register. The clinking and rattling of the glasses and pewter pots as they were being washed, and the gurgling noise made by the beer as it poured into the drinking vessels from the taps of the beer engine, whose handles were almost incessantly manipulated by the barman, the Old Dear and the glittering landlady, whose silken blouse, bejewelled hair, ears, neck and fingers scintillated gloriously in the blaze of the gaslight. (RTP 242)

During Robert's time in Hastings it was the Cricketers Hotel, and the landlady was a Mrs Horley. (3) During the 1950s it was turned into a basic pub, and is now a club. The cricket ground where W.G. Grace scored 210 during one annual festival is now a shopping centre.

Other pubs he is known to have frequented, some still surviving, were the Cambridge near the town centre where the trades council later met for many years, the Imperial in Queen's Road which he decorated, the Bodega by the Memorial, the Golden Cross in Havelock Road which was a port of call for rail incomers, the Nag's Head in Gensing Road, The Clarence Hotel behind the town hall which hosted meetings of the trades council, and the Fountain on Grosvenor Crescent heading towards Bexhill. In such places he honed his oratory and practiced his love of diagrams to make relatively uneducated men grasp a pertinent point. In cosy pubs and uproarious bars he also found more evidence that men were exploited in even the most convivial surroundings.

In his chapter *'The Filling of the Tank"* Robert didn't bother disguising the Cricketers, the landlord or the clientele, divided into saloon and public bar customers: *The landlord, a well-fed, prosperous-looking individual in white shirt-sleeves, and a bright maroon fancy waistcoat with a massive gold watch-chain and a diamond ring, was conversing in an affable, friendly way with one of his regular customers, who was sitting on the end of the seat close by the counter, a shabbily-dressed, bleary-eyed, degraded, beer-sodden, trembling wretch, who spent the greater part of every day, and all his money in this bar. (RTP 183)*

Robert describes the wretch as a former carpenter who effectively lived off his older wife, the landlady of a third-rate lodging-house, spending her money on beer and earning extra pints by sweeping sawdust off the pub floor: *He was a very good customer; not only did he spend whatever money he could get hold of himself, but he was the cause of other people spending money, for he was acquainted with most of the other regular customers who , knowing of his impecunious condition, often stood him a drink 'for the good of the house.' (Ibid)*

Robert contrasted the tolerance shown the wretch with the treatment of a semi-drunk house-painter who began to dance when a penny was put in the polyphone, an early jukebox. He is curtly told to stop and compounds his behaviour by almost beating the wretch at a game of throwing rings at a board. The landlord insults him and tells him he has been in the bar long enough. *This was true. The man had been there long enough to spend every*

*penny he had been possessed of when he first came in: he had no money
left now, a fact that the observant and experienced landlord had divined
some time ago." (RTP 189)*

When the man refuses to leave before he has finished his half pint, the
landlord summons a burly employee who clutched him by the collar,
dragged him violently to the door and *shot him into the middle of the road,
where he fell in a heap almost under the wheels of a brewer's dray that
happened to be passing."* (RTP 191)   Robert mentally collected such
everyday but telling scenes, initially not knowing how he could use them
save to make points in conversation.

The Cricketers took an even darker tone when Robert describes how Ruth
Easton, at the insistence of her husband the Mr and Mrs Crass, becomes
inebriated prior to her seduction or rape:

*The scene was so novel and strange to Ruth that she felt dazed and
bewildered. Previous to her marriage she had been a total abstainer, but
since then she had occasionally taken a glass of beer with Easton for
company's sake with their Sunday dinner at home; but it was generally
Easton who went out and bought the beer in a jug. Once or twice she had
bought it herself at an Off Licence beer-shop near where they lived, but she
had never before been in a public house to drink. She was so confused and
ill at ease that she scarcely heard or understood Mrs Crass, who talked
incessantly, principally about their other residents in North Street where
they both resided; and about Mr Crass. She also promised Ruth to introduce
her presently - if he came in, as he was almost certain to do - to Mr Partaker,
one of her two lodgers a most superior young man, who had been with them
now for over three years and would not leave on any account. In fact, he
had been their lodger in their old house, and when they moved he came
with them to North Street, although it was farther away from his place of
business than their former residence. Mrs Crass talked a lot more of the
same sort of stuff, to which Ruth listened like one in a dream, and answered
with an occasional yes or no. (RTP 243)*

Robert continued: *The liquor was by this time beginning to have some effect
upon Ruth: she felt dizzy and confused. Whenever it was necessary to reply
to Mrs Crass's talk she found some difficulty in articulating the words and
she knew she was not answering very intelligently. Even when Mrs Crass
introduced her to the interesting Mr Partaker, who arrived about this time,*

she was scarcely able to collect herself sufficiently to decline that fascinating gentleman's invitation to have another drink with himself and Mrs Crass.

After a time a kind of terror took possession of her, and she resolved that if Easton would not come when he had finished the game he was playing, she would go home without him. (RTP 244)

But Robert was tolerant of working men who enjoyed a drink or seven, as seen in his chapter on the annual works 'beano', which will be considered later.

Robert's view that alcohol was an irrelevant distraction from the real causes of poverty was anathema to the Edwardian Establishment, but he was not alone in expressing it. In February 1909 the celebrated Socialist and passionate teetotaller Herbert Burrows spoke in Hastings Public Hall, saying "...there was a question which the Liberal Government might have dealt with which is more important than the Licencing Bill. The question of Unemployment was infinitely more important (applause)." In response to questions he said that the best temperance reform would be the improvement of the homes and social conditions of the people, (Loud applause). (4)

ELECTION

"monopolists of wisdom"

Robert was not converted to socialism overnight; it had been a long process starting with his republican instincts. His niece, a committed Christian who had little time for her uncle's memory, told Ball: "I saw little of him but I knew his extreme socialist opinions. He had always been extremely vehement and very, very bitter. We believed this to be partly temperamental (self-willed, headstrong, idealistic, highly-principled, etc.) and partly the disappointment and disillusionment of his early life, though of course his intellectual power and strong sympathies would naturally incline him to socialism." (1)

Robert first became active with local socialists in September 1906, when he and the by now ex-apprentice William Gower joined others in The Cricketers to discuss the formation of a Hastings branch of the Social Democratic Foundation, an ardently anti-capitalist organisation. That preliminary meeting was followed the following month by a formal session at the Beehive tea rooms close to the Prince Albert memorial in the centre of town chaired by a Mr F. Owen, possibly the source of Robert's choice of names for his RTP hero. Subscriptions were set at two pence per week. Local firebrand Alf Cobb was also present at the inaugural meeting, along with Frank Willard, a campaigner for educational reform. The spark for the inauguration of the SDF, and Robert's membership, had been a hard-fought election.

The preceding decades had been turbulent ones for the socialist, Labour and trade union movements, and both successes and failures inspired Robert to get actively involved.

In 1880 the Democratic Federation was founded to pursue a class struggle and in 1884 this became the SDF. It was inspired by the writings of Karl Marx as adapted by the Englishman H.M. Hyndman. William Morris and Walter Crane joined, as well as Marx's daughter Eleanor, although Morris and others left in 1887 to form the Socialist League. Running alongside those bodies was the Fabian Society lead by George Bernard Shaw and Beatrice and Sidney Webb whose aim was to achieve socialism through lawful, peaceful and gradual means. Robert was not attracted to the latter. In 1888 Keir Hardie formed the Scottish Labour Party and then, in 1893, the Independent Labour Party (ILP). Hardie was the son of a ship carpenter and a domestic worker who at the age of seven was employed as a ship messenger before going down the Lanarkshire pits. In 1881 he had led the first strike in that coalfield. Hardie saw the ILP as essentially a pressure group on behalf of working men – a view he held as late as 1905 – and like many other contemporaries did not see the full implications of the wider male franchise. By the turn of the century the majority of voters were working class. (2)

Faced with such a plethora of organisations committed to supporting their members, the trades unions resisted any idea of political campaigning until 1899 when the Trades Union Congress passed a resolution, drafted in the ILP office, calling for a special conference of all working class organisations. That met in February 1900 and the Labour Representation Committee began recruiting "affiliations" to the prototype Labour party. The SDF walked out, condemning it as "in no way consciously socialist and as a result likely to be an obstacle and not an aid to Socialism."

Through the latter part of that internal strife, Robert voraciously read the writings of William Morris and was clearly greatly influenced by them because they have clear echoes in both the structure and detail of the RTP. In the manifesto of the Socialist League Morris had written: "The profit-grinding system is maintained by competition, or veiled war, not only between the conflicting classes, but also within the classes themselves. The remedy that we propose for this failure of our civilisation ...is that this must be altered from the foundation: the land, the capital, the machinery, factories, workshops, stores, means of transit, mines, banking, all means of production and distribution of wealth, must be declared and treated as the common property of all." (3)

Hastings and St Leonards had a strong recent history of producing independent-minded socialists. Toby King, a 22-stone giant took part in radical demonstrations for several decades, an unmistakeable figure in a white ten-gallon hat covered in rosettes. From his house near Hollington Church-in-the-Wood he taught working men to read and write. He propped up his own specially-designed coffin in his living room and would stand within it as he spoke of the vanity of a humanity on earth for only a short time. He forbade his children to salute or curtsey to the "finer" townspeople, as was required of them by society. He travelled to Ireland and wrote on its woes. During the campaign for House of Lord reform he drove a wagon with donkeys in the back, each wearing a coronet, with working men harnessed between the shafts. He died in 1899 before Robert arrived, but Robert certainly knew many of his pupils.

Edward Cruttenden became a close friend of Robert's. Cruttenden would cycle to Eastbourne to speak with the veteran South Coast socialist George Meek and other activists. Meek said that Cruttenden "kept the socialist flag flying for many years in Hastings." He was partially responsible for setting up the local trades council in 1894 and his daughters recalled waving the Red Flag at SDF meetings. (4)

There were other notable contemporaries. Alf Cobb, the son of a London docker, earned a living in Hastings as a draper's shop assistant and later a fruiterer. He became secretary of the local SDF branch and was eventually elected to the borough council in 1921, aged 40. He features later in this book. Fred Philcox was branch secretary of the National Society of Painters and of the National Federation of Building Trades Operatives and helped build up membership to equal that of Brighton, a town with four times the population. And railway driver Alf 'Razor' Leonard was chairman of the Hastings trades council for 21 years, and for 28 years chairman of the regional division of the railway workers' union ASLEF. A charismatic and popular leader, he dominated Hastings socialism for decades until his death in 1963. (5)

George Hicks, in his preface to the 1927 edition of the RTP, wrote of the rich panorama of early socialists who became Robert's friends and comrades. The former general secretary of the Amalgamated Union of Building Trade Workers, said: "Those early agitators and propagandist of the SDP and ILP working amongst their fellows carrying on in the shadow of victimisation and dismissal from their employment endeavouring to make those with whom they came in contact see the necessity of organisation and economic and political enlightenment, must have been heroes indeed possessed of lion-hearted courage and faith that conquers."

By the time Robert arrived in Hastings the traditional two-party system between the Conservatives and the Liberals was fracturing from within and challenged from without. The Liberal-owned *Hastings Weekly Mail* gleefully reported the November 1907 council elections in which its party took control of the borough. The victory, it editorialised, was "a sweeping condemnation of Tory municipal policy ...Hastings is disgusted with municipal mismanagement, muddling to extravagance. For a long number of years our Corporation has been ruled by expensive Tory partisans." (6) But the Liberals, locally and nationally, were divided over Irish home rule and tariff reforms, the Conservatives by internal divisions of their own. The emergence of a Labour party and a continuing bloc of Irish Nationalist MPs threatened to bring that two-party system down.

A general election was called for January 15 1906. By then the majority of the male population of Hastings had had the vote for just 20 years and this election, as Ball noted, was to bring Robert "into direct contact with the political movements and personalities in the town, and with local socialists."

By that election the Labour party had almost a million affiliated members nationwide and was the only organization capable of taking on the might of the established parties. However, Robert was unimpressed. Ball wrote that "it was the visionary socialists - many of whom remained suspicious of Labour's essentially reformist policy - who had brought the new fervour to the political scene which was attracting more and more people from the working classes, as well as leading intellectuals and even honest fugitives from the upper classes to the hope of a completely new society. It was this vision which involved and absorbed Robert, and it was to him at once an ideal and rational solution, which he was amazed that humanity did not recognize." (7)

The election campaign began in the cold winter of 1905. It was between the sitting Liberal MP, Freeman Freeman-Thomas, who had taken the seat in 1900, and Conservative challenger William Harvey Du Cros. Both were rich men and local notables. Freeman-Thomas was the son-in-law of local magnate Lord Brassey, who had made a fortune from building railways, and had interests in the motor trade and insurance. Du Cros was of Dublin landed gentry, although when he married he was a lowly book-keeper earning £140 a year. Yet he became chairman of a pneumatic tyre and bicycle company and later, with his son Arthur, had founded the pneumatic tyre industry, capitalising on the inventiveness of John Boyd Dunlop.

Harvey Du Cros MP

Robert put his overview in the mouth of the apprentice Bert White, displaying his 'Pandorama' to children at a Christmas party: `'Ere we 'ave another election scene. At each side we see the two candidates the same as in the last pitcher. In the middle of the road we see a man lying on the ground, covered with blood, with a lot of Liberal and Tory working men kickin' 'im, jumpin' on 'im, and stampin' on 'is face with their 'obnailed boots. The bloke on the ground is a Socialist, and the reason why they're kickin' 'is face in is because 'e said that the only difference between Slumrent and Mandriver was that they was both alike.' (RTP 305)*

The electorate of Hastings were by 1906 even more deeply divided between rich and poor than when Robert had arrived. Purchasing power amongst ordinary people had plummeted, while business profits had soared. The rich paid little direct taxation, while indirect taxes on everyday goods fell heaviest on the poor. The wages of working men varied from the 18 shillings earned by a tram conductor to 20 shillings for a large section of wage-earners to 30 shillings for the most skilled. But skilled work was scarce and most worked for between 56 and 70 hours a week. Women were paid much less and child labour remained rife. Ball interviewed one local man whose father, a carter, was paid 15 shillings a week, of which he paid three shillings and sixpence in cottage rent, occasionally augmented by a share of the carcasses of drowned sheep pulled out of nearby marshes. The poorest families survived periods of penury on bread and hot water with salt and pepper to add flavour. In the poor area of Ore life expectancy was 43.

Ball wrote: "Ragged, barefooted, rickety children walked the streets in the bleak winter weather and groups of down-at-heel and dejected-looking unemployed haunted the street corners. People (in Ore) were used to the sight of a file of old women hobbling through the streets to collect their weekly bread ration at the Workhouse." (8) That institution had 390 inmates, hundreds more received some charity relief and at the time of the election there were 147 vagrants registered in the town. Robert noted that in the frontiers of South Africa no white people lived in such poverty.

In the RTP Robert described *"those unfortunate outcasts of society - tramps and destitutes, drunken loafers. If the self-righteous hypocrites who despise these poor wretches had been subjected to the same conditions, the majority of them would have become the same as these. "Haggard and pale, shabbily or raggedly dressed, their boots broken and down at heel, they slouched past. Some of them stared about with a dazed or half-wild expression, but most of them walked with downcast eyes or staring blankly straight in front of them. They appeared utterly broken-spirited, hopeless and ashamed... (RTP 288)*

A page earlier he described the better-off promenading as *richly dressed and bejewelled loafers, whose countenances in many instances bore unmistakable signs of drunkenness and gluttony. Some of the females had tried to conceal the ravages of vice and dissipation by coating their faces with powder and paint... (RTP 287)*

The *Primitive Methodist Magazine* editorialised: "The country was never so wealthy and never so poor as now."

The election was hard fought, with both candidates speaking of the evils of socialism, although they faced no such candidate. Both, however, paid lip service to the trades council which represented 800 local workers, a source of votes which could prove crucial. Du Cros addressed meetings of postmen, but the trades council elected to back the Liberal. (9)

The principle issue which divided the two men was tariff reforms and built-in preference for Imperial imports introduced by Joseph Chamberlain which amounted to trade protectionism rather than the Liberal position of free trade.

In RTP's fictionalised contest, the Liberal is supported by the "great" Sir Featherstone Blood:

He referred to Land Taxes and Death Duties which would provide money to build battleships to protect the property of the rich, and provide Work for the poor. Another tax was to provide a nice, smooth road for the rich to ride upon in motor cars - and to provide Work for the poor. Another tax would be used for Development, which would also make Work for the poor. And so on. A great point was made of the fact that the rich were actually to be made to pay something towards the cost of their road themselves! But nothing was said about how they would get the money to do it. No reference was made to how the workers would be sweated and driven and starved to earn Dividends and Rent and Interest and Profits to put into the pockets of the rich before the latter would be able to pay for anything at all.

These are the things, Gentlemen, that we propose to do for you, and, at the rate of progress which we propose to adopt, I say without fear or contradiction, that within the next Five Hundred years we shall so reform social conditions in this country, that the working classes will be able to enjoy some of the benefits of civilization. (RTP 536-7)

The guest speaker's name gives a clear indication that Robert was actually referring to the Liberal premier Asquith. In 1893 Asquith, as Home Secretary, authorised the deployment of troops against striking miners in

Featherstone, Yorkshire. The troops opened fire, killing two and wounding many more.

Dirty tricks, scare stories, sensationalism and corrupt practices flourished during the Liberal-Conservative fight. The Liberals attached a white cloth to a High Street wall and showed film slides with anti-Tory song lyrics, encouraging the crowd to sing along to "Stamp, Stamp, Stamp on Protectionism." Mrs Freeman Freeman-Thomas was drawn through the streets in a carriage pulled by white horses, while their young son Gerard stood with his father on public platforms. The Liberal campaign ended in a 5,000-strong procession with banners, torches and pans of coloured fire. A brass band of 54 instruments marched behind the candidate while the participants sang to the patriotic tune 'Tramp, Tramp, Tramp the Boys are Marching':

Vote! Vote! Vote for Freeman-Thomas!
We'll hang old Du Cros upon a tree!
Freeman-Thomas is our man,
And we'll have him if we can,
Then we'll always have the biggest loaf for tea.

Du Cros, however, had prepared his ground well. For a year his Conservative lieutenants had toured local pubs buying free beer. The candidate had shared £50 among slate clubs and financed tea parties for schoolchildren and the elderly. He promised jobs in his London factory for the unemployed. Babies were kissed by his "lady-wife." Thugs disrupted Liberal meetings and a Liberal councillor claimed that "scoundrels" had been imported from London to do that job.

Robert looked on with a mixture of disgust and fascination: *Both sides imported gangs of hired orators who held forth every night at the corners of the principle streets, and on the open spaces from portable platforms, and from motor cars and lorries. The Tories said that the Liberal party in the House of Commons was composed principally of scoundrels and fools, the Liberals said that the Tory party were fools and scoundrels. A host of richly dressed canvassers descended ...in carriages and motor cars, and begged for votes from the poverty-stricken working men who lived there. (RTP 532)*

Robert described a violent clash, almost certainly observed during the 1906 campaign, when a Liberal procession stumbled on another meeting close to the Grand Parade:

These were the Tories and they became so infuriated at the sound of the Liberal songs and by the sight of the banners, that they abandoned their meeting and charged the processionists. A free fight ensued. Both sides fought like savages, but as the Liberals were outnumbered by about three to one, they were driven off the field with great slaughter; most of the torch poles were taken from them and the banner was torn to ribbons. Then the Tories went back to the Fountain carrying the captured torches, and singing... 'Has anyone seen a Lib'ral Flag?
"*While the Tories resumed their meeting, the Liberals rallied in one of the back streets. Messengers were sent in various directions for reinforcements, and about half an hour afterwards they emerged from their retreat and swooped down upon the Tory meeting. They overturned the platform, recaptured their torches, tore the enemy's banner to tatters and drove them from their position. Then the Liberals in their turn paraded the streets singing 'Has anyone seen a Tory Flag?' (RTP 536)*

The contest was a real cliff-hanger, and RTP reflected real life with rumours sweeping back and forth in the days and hours up to the count. Freeman-Thomas told one meeting: "Only last week there was a certain suspicion among Liberals that the Tories were catching up." On the eve of poll the Old Town Liberals began to celebrate victory after another rumour that the Tories had lost. The cricket ground beneath the town hall balcony was opened to the public for the reading of the result.

Yet another rumour swept the assembled crowd that the Liberals had won by 600 votes, but that was quickly dispelled when the results were read from the town hall's ornate stone balcony. The Tory candidate, Du Cros, had won the seat by 4,348 votes to 3,935 He shook hands with the defeated Liberal, a scene repeated in RTP by opposing candidates Sir Graball and Adam Sweater. The local papers reported that both candidates and their top supporters sat together that night at a table for 40 in the Jenny Lind public house in the Old Town. The King and Queen were toasted, music was played and "the greater part of the evening was spent in harmony. Probably deliberately, in the RTP, Robert reversed the winner and loser, signalling that there was nothing to choose between them.

Freeman-Thomas went on to win and hold Bodmin for a brief period. In 1910 he was made a baronet in 1910, a Viscount in 1924, and Earl in 1931 and Marquess of Willingdon in 1936. During that period of social elevation he was successively governor of Bombay and then of Madras, Governor-General of Canada and Viceroy of India from 1931 to 1936. He was appointed Lord Warden of the Cinque Ports until his death in 1942.

A Du Cros election poster in All Saints Street

Hastings and neighbouring Rye were the only Conservative gains at that election, their party was turned out of government and a new one formed by the Liberals. The *Hastings Mail*, always loyal to the Liberals, was outraged by the local outcome: "Our feeling is summed up in one word – disgust, disgust at the ludicrous position in which our town is placed in view of the overwhelming in the country against Mr Balfour. Hastings Tories fought a political fight in 1900 and were worsted; they knew that their only chance to retrieve that disaster was to introduce a millionaire. He came, and aided by powerful combinations, strange artifice, peculiar methods, his capital triumphed." (10)

In the days after the election Liberals spluttered ineffectually. On the Sunday the Reverend John Bailey told a public meeting in Robertson Street that he blamed townspeople for supporting "ancient, fossilised and encrusted Toryism in this age of progress and liberty." He went on: "I thought in my simplicity that the day was gone, even in Hastings, for the descendants of heroes and martyrs to allow themselves to be bought and sold like dumb, driven cattle. I would not believe that men could be so idiotic or ignorant as to be led astray by false promises or delusive hopes. I was mistaken. I knew that there were some fools in Hastings, but I was unaware that they were so numerous. Poor, deluded, benighted, infatuated and demented Hastings." (11) The cattle metaphor was used several times by Robert.

Nationally, the Liberals appear to have harnessed the swelling working-class vote with promises of social reform, some of which, it has to be admitted, was delivered. Defeated Tory premier A.J. Balfour saw this as a sinister development. He wrote to Lord Balfour: "If I read the signs aright what has occurred is nothing whatever to do with any of the things we have been squabbling over the last few years ...what is going on here is the faint echo of the same movement which has produced massacres in St Petersburg, riots in Vienna and Socialist processions in Berlin."

To some degree Robert agreed, but from the opposite perspective: *Unconsciously each of the two parties put in some splendid work for Socialism, in so much that each of them thoroughly exposed the hypocrisy of the other. If the people had only had the sense, they might have seen that the quarrel between the Liberal and Tory leaders was merely a quarrel between thieves over the spoil; but unfortunately most of the people had not the sense to perceive this. They were blinded by bigoted devotion to their parties, and - inflamed with maniacal enthusiasm - thought nothing but carrying their flags to victory. (RTP 539)*

He added: *Truly do the wolves have an easy prey* (RTP 550)

THE BIRTH OF A BOOK

"not a treatise or essay"

1906 had seen a hard-fought Parliamentary election in Hastings and Robert's enrolment in active local politics. The year also saw him losing his job, moving his home and starting to write the book for which he is remembered.

Former employees of Burton's told Fred Ball that Robert was a "hot-tempered man" who got himself into a severe argument with the boss at a house in Trinity Street which the firm was renovating. The boss, Mr Burton, complained that the work was taking too long. Robert argued back and Burton called him a "blackguard" who spent most of his time spouting Red views. Robert, incensed, threatened to "knock his bloody head off" and there is some suggestion he may actually have hit him. He stormed out, turning the key in the lock on the outside, leaving Burton trapped inside. Possibly Burton's embarrassment saved Robert from criminal prosecution. (1)

Robert drifted between short-term work for various firms, but ended up as an employee of Adam's and Jarrett's which had showrooms in Norman Road, St Leonards, and workshops in Alfred Street. Given the circumstances in which he had left Burton's, and his reputation as a firebrand, it is a testament to Robert's skills that another major boss took him on.

At around that time Robert, Kathleen Adelaide and her son Arthur left 115 Milward Road and moved twice to temporary apartments in Warrior Square and St John's Road, St Leonards, although the exact addresses are lost.

Robert was by now heavily involved in the new SDF branch. He, as we have seen, had little faith in more mainstream Labour movements or, it appears, with the trade union movement. There is no record of Robert being active, or joining, any trade union branch in Hastings. He was put off by the union movement's reluctance to embrace radical socialism, but he also knew that the nature of the building and decorating trade is notoriously difficult to unionise, never mind radicalise. He had become a member of the of the painters' union in London but Raymond Postgate, in *The Builders' History*, wrote that "the deadness of the union so depressed him that he did not re-enrol in Hastings as a member but put all his strength in agitating for the SDF." (2)

Disgust with the gullibility of the voters and the hypocrisies of the two-party system saw a limited renaissance of socialism in Hastings. The local National Democratic League, inaugurated by shopkeeper Frank Willard, had been set up to provide an umbrella group for Radical Liberals, Labourites and socialists was dominated by Liberals and collapsed under its own ineffectiveness. The Labour Representation Committee struggled on but was irrelevant given the growth of the Independent Labour Party. Robert, a radical socialist, had little time for any of the above and was encouraged to attend those first inaugural meetings of the Social Democratic Federation. Several further meetings at the Beehive tea rooms, named after the first Labour journal, led to its first public meeting at the Fishmarket, addressed by George Meek. The *Hastings Observer* and the *Hastings Weekly Mail and Times* opened ferocious anti-socialist campaigns.

But it was not only the supporters of capitalism and the status quo who opposed the SDF. Several union branches voted not to support "Marxist" candidates at any level, and the trades council left the Labour Representation Committee after a vote of 630 to 35, while the SDF remained.

The trades council appeared to have lost all sense of politics. At the November municipal elections it issued a questionnaire to candidates asking whether they were for Sunday trading, evening council meetings, direct employment on corporation contracts, perks enjoyed by corporation employees and additional town baths. As a result of the replies, it recommended its members to support three Conservatives, three Liberals and one Independent Conservative. (3)

There were further divisions over the prominence in the SDF of activist Alf Cobb, who was separated from his wife and living with another woman whom he later married. A meeting of the SDF was convened at Phelps

coffee house and the majority agreed that "his living with this lady should not bar him from serving the cause." But many disagreed and quit the SDF to form the Hastings branch of the Independent Labour Party. They included Frank Willard.

Cobb – who features later in this book and is pictured here – and Willard had clashed from the start. Willard, irascible but able and committed, was an ardent Christian-Socialist who believed that radical politics should come from a moral high ground. Cobb's messier brand of socialism, although not as radical as Robert's, grated, as did his messier private life. Willard was also authoritarian and held high political ambitions. In acrimonious exchanges Cobb accused him of trying to wreck the SDF branch because members had tried to curb his autocratic attitude, of approaching Tory and Liberal candidates' committees and of supporting affluent businesses involved in municipal trading.

The feud became very public, and in January 1907 focused on a march of the unemployed organised by Willard's supporter James Thompson. They continued every day that week, as the *Observer* duly reported: "In order to relieve their distress to some extent some hundreds of the unemployed of Hastings have paraded the town during the week and raised a large quantity of money, which had been distributed amongst the men with satisfactory results." (4) The *Hastings Mail* wrote: "No doubt some people thought that if they were to continue they would drive residents away from the town." (5)

The processions began at 10.30 on the Tuesday morning, and the men mustered fours-abreast from Station Road before marching behind a small brass band. On subsequent days they mustered at the Drill Hall, Middle Street and Wellington Place and marched silently along the promenade in a bid to prick the consciences of the fashionable folk parading there. Each day's take worked out at between 1s 5d and 1s 10d a man. But little came from the rich, and most of the coins came from the less well-off and those approaching the poverty line themselves. Showers of pennies were dropped by servants from the upper windows of the grander houses on the route. Many of the hundreds who watched the procession were themselves unemployed or in urgent need, or too proud to ask for aid. Local socialists, including Alf Cobb, disapproved of "begging marches", believing that the workers needed work, not charity. (6)

But Willard wrote: "Comrade Thompson has also organised several street processions and has thereby raised over £170, which has gone to relieve pressing cases. Last Thursday the men marched a mile and a half through the snow to the workhouse (where a meeting of the Guardians was taking place) headed by a brass band. Comrade Thompson laid before the board the position claiming work for the 800 unemployed men of the town... The result has been to convince the most sceptical that we are affected by unemployment." (7).

Robert captured the scene, and added his own interpretation: *The processions of unemployed continued every day, and the money they begged from the public was divided equally amongst those who took part. Sometimes it amounted to one and sixpence each, sometimes it was a little more and sometimes a little less. These men presented a terrible spectacle as they slunk through the dreary streets, through the rain or the snow, with the slush soaking into their broken boots, and, worse still, with the bitterly cold east wind penetrating their rotten clothing and freezing their famished bodies.*

The majority of the skilled workers still held aloof from these processions, although their haggard faces bore involuntary testimony to their sufferings. Although privation reigned supreme in their desolate homes, where there was often neither food nor light nor fire, they were too 'proud' to parade *their misery before each other or the world. They secretly sold or pawned their clothing and their furniture and lived in semi-starvation on the proceeds, and on credit, but they would not beg. Many of them even echoed the sentiments of those who had written to the papers, and with a strange lack of class-sympathy blamed those who took part in the processions. They said it was that sort of thing that drove the `better class' away, injured the town, and caused all the poverty and unemployment. However, some of them accepted charity in other ways; district visitors distributed tickets for coal and groceries. Not that that sort of thing made much difference; there was usually a great deal of fuss and advice, many quotations of Scripture, and very little groceries. And even what there was generally went to the least-deserving people, because the only way to obtain any of this sort of `charity' is by hypocritically pretending to be religious: and the greater the hypocrite, the greater the quantity of coal and groceries. These `charitable' people went into the wretched homes of the poor and - in effect - said: `Abandon every particle of self- respect: cringe and fawn: come to church: bow down and grovel to us, and in return we'll give you a ticket that you can take to a certain shop and exchange for a shillingsworth of groceries. And, if you're very servile and humble we may give you another one next week.' (RTP 335-336)*

Nevertheless, the unemployed marches gave Robert a taste for public demonstration, but Cobb was stinging in his criticism.

James Thompson, the prime organiser of the unemployed marches, challenged Cobb. Before leaving the branch along with Willard to join the ILP, Thompson said: "I am, glad to say that as a result of our parades the matter of find work has been pushed forward and today, in several hundred homes there are fires in the grates and at least something on the table, where had the matter been left to the SDF I would hide my head in shame at my branch's inactivity instead of trying to cover up its deficiencies by paltry excuses." (8)

Hastings now had three socialist parties, all selling and distributing different weekly newspapers – *The Clarion* for both radical socialists and Labourites, the *Labour Leader* for the ILP and *Justice* for the SDF. *The Clarion* was the most visible on the streets, its van a common sight in the town, with guest speakers including the highly articulate Thomas Kennedy. 1907 saw, Hopper wrote, "the growth of the entire movement in the Hastings area... But it was also a year of factionalism that saw the founding of the ILP, two trades council candidates at the municipal elections, and a vibrant but marginalised SDF group." (9)

In public, as far as we know, Robert kept out of the in-fighting and feuds which were a scourge of the Left for generations. But he, a militant socialist, stayed with the SDF.

Willard, Thompson and the local ILP branch continued the unemployment marches but in smaller forms, better disciplined and more rigidly controlled. Agreement was reached with the Chief Constable that "rapscallions" could not join them, that the marches should not be frequent, and that they could not, as before, join the Sunday congregation at Christ Church. Smoking was banned.

But such compliance did not prevent the police turning away a group of Midlands hunger marchers who dragged a van full of progressive literature along the south coast towns in August 1908. Officers halted them at the borough boundary at Bulverhythe. There was a three-hour stand-off, with marchers branding the police 'blacklegs', before the interlopers camped for the night off Sedlescombe Road before continuing their journey, skirting Hasting, to Winchelsea and Rye. (10)

Visiting Socialists were attacked by mobs of working men and there were attempts to overturn the *Clarion* van, often with near-fatal results, as Robert described: *As it was quite evident that the crowd meant mischief - many of them had their pockets filled with stones and were armed with sticks - several of the Socialists were in favour of going to meet the van to endeavour to persuade those in charge from coming, and with that object they withdrew from the crowd, which was already regarding them with menacing looks, and went down the road in the direction from which the van was expected to come. They had not gone very far, however, before the people, divining what they were going to do, began to follow them and while they were hesitating what course to pursue, the Socialist van, escorted by five or six men on bicycles, appeared round the corner at the bottom of the hill. As soon as the crowd saw it, they gave an exultant cheer, or, rather, yell, and began running down the hilt to meet it, and in a few minutes it was surrounded by a howling mob. The van was drawn by two horses; there was a door and a small platform at the back and over this was a sign with white letters on a red ground: `Socialism, the only hope of the Workers.'* (RTP 430-431)

Robert witnessed much violence during that period and, given his volatile nature, probably suffered some himself. In the book Owen tries to address an unruly crowd but is drowned out: Owen made no attempt to reply, *and the manner of the crowd became every moment more threatening. It was evident that several of them found it difficult to refrain from attacking him. It was a splendid opportunity of doing a little fighting without running any risks. This fellow was all by himself, and did not appear to be much of a man even at that. Those in the middle were encouraged by shouts from others in the crowd, who urged them to `Go for him' and at last - almost at the instant of Barrington's arrival - one of the heroes, unable to contain himself any longer, lifted a heavy stick and struck Owen savagely across the face. The sight of the blood maddened the others, and in an instant everyone who could get within striking distance joined furiously in the onslaught, reaching eagerly over each other's shoulders, showering blows upon him with sticks and fists, and before Barrington could reach his side, they had Owen down on the ground, and had begun to use their boots upon him. Barrington felt like a wild beast himself, as he fiercely fought his way through the crowd, spuming them to right and left with fists and elbows. He reached the centre in time to seize the uplifted arm of the man who had led the attack and wrenching the stick from his hand, he felled him to the ground with a single blow. The remainder shrank back, and meantime the crowd was augmented by others who came running up.* (RTP 548)

The year saw several attempts within ILP and other connected organisations to get into bed with the Liberals. But personal antagonisms, political rivalries and a lack of united purpose defeated all such bids in Hastings and across the country. The *Observer* crowed: "The Labourists and Liberals of Hastings are following in the footsteps of their colleagues by quarrelling with each other." (11)

Hastings now had several socialist, trade union and Labour groups, none of whom could agree. Splits over policy, personalities and tactics continued to create division, diverting the struggle against any common enemy. The SDF evolved, during Robert's time at least, and Ball reckoned that "the local situation played a part in determining how Robert was to portray the role of socialism and socialists in his book."

Robert certainly played a full role in raising public awareness of the SDF during a period when another recession had hit the building trade and unemployment was reaching its highest levels for 20 years. Peak wrote:

"His South African experience in politics and trade unionism would have given him a wider and deeper understanding of the need for a radical movement than that of most Hastings political newcomers." (12) But his campaigning was limited by his illness, his erratic income and his role as a single parent. His political agitation was largely confined to propaganda and face-to-face debate.

With the established politicians helped by the newspapers whipping up sentiment against socialism, such activities were often clandestine. Many meetings were held in the Central Hall, Middle Street, later to become one of the town's first cinemas, booked in the name of other, more anodyne bodies. George Gallop, an SDP founder-member, recalled how members would avoid arriving in bunches and, if they saw each other heading in the same direction, would take different routes. "If we both arrived at the same time, one used to go in and the other walk on a bit, then turn around and come back in. If there was a speaker arriving from London for a meeting, we used to meet him from the train to act as a bodyguard in case of trouble. Branch meetings were kept secret after a time as there would have been trouble as the town was all Tories and Liberals."

The local police would intimidate people by taking the names of all who attended SDP meetings. PC Burr, who later became branch secretary of the Municipal Employees' Association, confirmed that lists of attendees would be posted up at all police stations. Such tactics helped swell the blacklists of employers' associations who refused employment to anyone named.

The SDF was also under pressure from the growing Parliamentary Labour movement which felt that to get elected they must take account of all shades of trade union, religious and non-socialist opinion. The SDF comprised mainly of a hard core of militant socialists. Robert was amongst them.

Others were Edward Cruttenden, his wife Phoebe and their daughter Rose, described as "very gentle, compassionate people." When George Meek was blacklisted in January 1907 he decided to go walkabout to find work. The Cruttendens gave him three shillings, put him up for the night, and he set off on a weary slog to Ashford. Robert was a frequent visitor to the Cruttenden home at 16 Wellington Square, and Kathleen became friends with their children. Rose Cruttenden recalled meetings at their home and afterwards, "we frequently used to sing songs from the Socialist Song Book.

My elder sister playing the piano. In fact our house was known as 'Liberty Hall.'" (13)

Robert, whether in or out of work himself, devoted much of his spare time helping the unemployed, going on marches, painting banners, joining every protest, carrying collecting tins and presenting petitions to the borough council. But often his most effective and long-remembered help was individual acts of kindness and generosity. John Whitelock, a friend, said: "He would never watch anyone go without if he had anything and would help workmates laid off or having a rough time." Kathleen said: "He was the kind of man who would give away the clothes off his back." Gower said that the RTP passage in which Owen walks across town drenched to the skin to tell a sacked workmate of a job he had heard about was "typical of Bob." (14)

Robert wrote on numerous occasions, according to friends and family, to the local newspapers, but always anonymously to avoid local blacklists. No certain examples survive, but one, written to the *Observer* by 'WAGE SLAVE, St Leonards, is a contender due to both its style and content: "Sir – Your correspondent 'Working Man' is no doubt right in attributing a lot of the present distress to the late disgraceful War. But, 'the poor we have always with us' and in my opinion, the main cause of poverty is that the workers receive such a small share of the wealth that they produce.

"We have lately had in this town an example. Certain persons have argued that while something over twenty shillings was enough for a labourer employed by the Council, sixteen or more pounds is not too much for a gentleman retained by the same Council. Rather different this is to the Socialist motto, 'From each according to his ability, to each according to his needs.' Of course very impracticable, Mr Editor, but after all, the gentleman only has one stomach.

"The fact is, the workers are robbed from the cradle to their grave. When fully employed, the majority only earn a subsistence wage, then considering they are unemployed as an average four months out of twelve, the wonder is that the distress is not more acute.

"Limitation of families, total abstinence, vegetarianism and several other isms are recommended, and no doubt enable individuals to live on less, but were these quack remedies to be universally adopted, they would soon lose their efficiency, as the average wage certainly tends to subside. That is to say, were the workers able to live on rice, they would only receive rice pay, or, better still, could they exist on grass, they would have been turned out to pasture with the other asses long ago.

"Instead of this, to improve their position and raise the standard of living, they must be educated up to the idea that the best is only good enough for the most useful class, the workers. Nature made a mistake at the start. There should have been two race of mankind, one as we know him today, the other as an automaton, without any of the senses that would make him wish to be something more than a mere machine, and certainly not the power to vote. See the difference they would make to the dear disinterested Liberal and Tory gentlemen; what lies and humbug it would save them.

"But, as your correspondent shows, they are beginning to open their eyes, and it will not be long before they understand that the only remedy is Socialism, which says that the workers should receive the full result of their labour, to obtain which the land and instruments of production must belong to: and be worked by, the state (i.e. the people) for the benefit of all, instead of as now, for the few." (15)

Despite the burgeoning socialist activity in Hastings, the Tories continued to make ground. Their opposition was fragmented and constantly squabbling. Between the 1906 election and the November 1907 council elections, in which the Conservative defeated two Labour candidates in St Clements and Upper St Marys, Robert decided that his value lay outside mainstream politicking. No doubt disappointed at the failure of local radical movements to organise themselves into a coherent unit and put aside petty difference, he decided to pull together all his thoughts, experience and plans for the future.

Peak wrote that Robert took that decision after witnessing "the rise in poverty and despair in Hastings, and the dramatic but ineffectual fightback by socialist and Labour campaigners – while the Tories and bosses increased their voting box support from the ragged trousered philanthropists." (16) Ball wrote: "He found only partial fulfilment in his work for the SDP branch, although this was vital to him in many ways, but his were not the talents of the public leader and organizer such as Cobb, and he could not fully express himself or work to his capacity simply as a party member. He had to do more."

By 1906-07 he had a wealth of notes and there is strong evidence, largely from Kathleen, that it was around then that he decided to put them together into book form. The question was what form it would take? Many of his workmates thought only that Robert was keeping a daily diary. And publisher Grant Richards said in a Press handout: "It seems that when the work was started the author had no intention of writing a book but had in mind the writing of a series of pamphlets. It was only when the book was begun that he found itself turning into a novel under his hand." (17)

Ball wrote:" The history of trades and crafts, and of the domestic lives of those who work in them, have been almost entirely neglected and the workers as human beings have received scant recognition in our literature. Robert recognised the importance of correcting this, and of giving the workers a sense of identity and a perspective on his position in society without which he was literally unconscious." (18)

He must have known that a learned tract from the likes of him would never be published and even if it was would disappear amongst the miasma of similar publications. And, more to the point, it would never be read by his workmates, their families or the working population he wanted to attract. Since the huge expansion of literacy the previous century, working people devoured newspapers, magazines, penny dreadfuls and, above all else, novels, whether they be serialised or sold in cheap versions by publishers keen to build up a mass market for their own ends.

Robert had always been a prolific note-taker and Kathleen's childhood recollections, and those of his friends picture him writing obsessively between bouts of drawing and designing. His notes ranged from extracts from books and newspaper article to depictions of scenes he had witnessed and conversations he had overheard. The real-life scenes depicted in RTP cover several years. He had already developed the habit of working late into the night scouring illustrated books for design ideas, copying them and adapting them. He had already developed a keen eye for detail, humour, compassion and anger in the written word. It is quite easy to see how he switched his late-night labours, in part at least, to a manuscript. He had a wealth of material, funny and tragic, from the men he worked with and the families he lived amongst. He had heroes, plenty of villains, the pathetic and the desperate, and an ear for language. He decided to use such talents in the form of fiction taken from real life.

Robert later gave a good insight into his motives when he wrote unsuccessfully to publishers enclosing his manuscript several years later:

"The action of the story covers a period of only a little over twelve months, but in order that the picture might be complete it was necessary to describe how the workers are circumstanced at all periods of their lives, from the cradle to the grave. Therefore the characters include women and children, a young boy - the apprentice - some improvers, journeymen in the prime of life, and worn-out old men.

"I designed to show the conditions resulting from poverty and unemployment: to expose the futility of the measures taken to deal with them and to indicate what I believe to be the only real remedy, namely - Socialism. I intended to explain what Socialists understand by the word 'Poverty': to define the Socialist theory of the causes of poverty, and to explain how Socialists propose to abolish poverty.

"It may be objected that, considering the number of books dealing with these subjects already existing, such a work as this was un-called for. The answer is that not only are the majority of people opposed to Socialism, but a very brief conversation with an average anti-socialist is sufficient to show that he does not know what Socialism means. The same is true of all the anti-socialist writers and the 'great statesmen' who make anti-socialist speeches: unless we believe that they are all deliberate liars and impostors, who to serve their own interests labour to mislead other people, we must conclude that they do not understand Socialism. There is no other possible explanation of the extraordinary things they write and say. The thing they cry out against is not Socialism but a phantom of their own imagining.

"Another answer is that the book is not a treatise or essay, but a novel. My main object was to write a readable story full of human interest and based on the happenings of everyday life, the subject of Socialism being treated incidentally.

"This was the task I set myself. To what extent I have succeeded is for others to say; but whatever their verdict, the work possesses at least one merit - that of being true. I have invented nothing. There are no scenes or incidents in the story that I have not either witnessed myself or had conclusive evidence of. As far as I dared I let the characters express themselves in their own sort of language and consequently some passages may be considered objectionable. At the same time I believe that - because it is true - the book is not without its humorous side.

"The scenes and characters are typical of every town in the South of England and they will be readily recognized by those concerned. If the book is published I think it will appeal to a very large number of readers. Because it is true it will probably be denounced as a libel on the working classes and their employers, and upon the religious-professing section of the community. But I believe it will be acknowledged as true by most of those who are compelled to spend their lives amid the surroundings it describes, and it will be evident that no attack is made upon sincere religion." (RTP 13-14)

But such limited aims, although admirable in themselves, hardly do justice to the breadth of the final manuscript. Or its length.

To many, including Ball, Robert came to realise that his true talent lay in writing. He took joy in the written word, not just the views and sentiments expressed in them. He was also driven by fear of dying penniless and leaving no legacy to his daughter. Gower recalled him saying in desperation: "I'll have to make some money or I'll die in the workhouse." He genuinely believed that he could spread the socialist message whilst saving his family from penury. He set to work organising his material into a coherent form.

His first task was to devise a central character, based on himself, but not too closely. Robert was too secretive a person to give too much away. It is interesting to see how Robert described the background of Frank Owen, overlapping his own experiences with inventions he deemed necessary for plot purposes. It provided some clues to his own past, but not too many:

Frank Owen was the son of a journeyman carpenter who had died of consumption when the boy was only five years old. After that his mother earned a scanty living as a needle-woman. When Frank was thirteen he went to work for a master decorator who was a man of a type that has now almost disappeared, being not merely an employer but a craftsman of a high order.

He was an old man when Frank Owen went to work for him. At one time he had had a good business in the town, and used to boast that he had always done good work, had found pleasure in doing it and had been well paid for it. But of late years the number of his customers had dwindled considerably, for there had arisen a new generation which cared nothing about craftsmanship or art, and everything for cheapness and profit. From this man and by laborious study and practice in his spare time, aided by a certain measure of natural ability, the boy acquired a knowledge of decorative painting and design, and graining and signwriting.

Frank's mother died when he was twenty-four, and a year afterwards he married the daughter of a fellow workman. In those days trade was fairly good and although there was not much demand for the more artistic kinds of work, still the fact that he was capable of doing them, if required, made it comparatively easy for him to obtain employment. Owen and his wife were very happy. They had one child - a boy - and for some years all went well. But gradually this state of things altered: broadly speaking, the change came slowly and imperceptibly, although there were occasional sudden fluctuations.

Even in summer he could not always find work: and in winter it was almost impossible to get a job of any sort. At last, about twelve months before the date that this story opens, he determined to leave his wife and child at home and go to try his fortune in London. When he got employment he would send for them. (RTP 65)

Robert already had a wealth of material from his work in Hastings. His new job at Adam's and Jarrett's would provide him with an awful lot more.

THE PROFESSOR

"not quite of them but wholly with them"

Robert's strong opinions, and his willingness to share them with all and sundry, were well known in Hastings and St Leonards, as were his learned tone and ability to quote all manner of sources. For years he was affectionately known by his workmates as "The Professor."

Gower recalled that he would often give an air of intellectual superiority, whatever the audience. "In conversations at work, Robert was usually affable and friendly but if roused could launch a stream of bitter invective, sometimes against social evils or, if called for, against an antagonist personally." He was a master of the pointed questions, put quietly and with the façade of courtesy, and Ball listed some of those put frequently to those who advocated the status quo: "You agree then that your children are not good enough for a better standard of living? Do you agree that your children are not fit to be properly educated? Can you tell me *why* your children should have shoes on their feet? What makes you think you are *entitled* to food and clothing?"

But it was the lectures he delivered, at home, on the way to and from work, and at work during tea breaks, which earned him his nickname. He would illustrate them with chalk or drawings or any props which came to hand. It is easy to hear Robert delivering his "great money trick" oration which he put into Owen's mouth. It is perhaps the most famous section of the RTP and deserves to be reproduced here in full:

"Money is the real cause of poverty," said Owen.

"Prove it," repeated Crass.

"Money is the cause of poverty because it is the device by which those who are too lazy to work are enabled to rob the workers of the fruits of their labour."

"Prove it," said Crass.

Owen slowly folded up the piece of newspaper he had been reading and put it into his pocket.

"'All right,' he replied. 'I'll show you how the Great Money Trick is worked.'"

Owen opened his dinner basket and took from it two slices of bread but as these were not sufficient, he requested that anyone who had some bread left would give it to him. They gave him several pieces, which he placed in a heap on a clean piece of paper, and, having borrowed the pocket knives they used to cut and eat their dinners with from Easton, Harlow and Philpot, he addressed them as follows:

"These pieces of bread represent the raw materials which exist naturally in and on the earth for the use of mankind; they were not made by any human being, but were created by the Great Spirit for the benefit and sustenance of all, the same as were the air and the light of the sun."

"You're about as fair-speakin' a man as I've met for some time," said Harlow, winking at the others.

"Yes, mate," said Philpot. "Anyone would agree to that much! It's as clear as mud."

"Now," continued Owen, "I am a capitalist; or, rather, I represent the landlord and capitalist class. That is to say, all these raw materials belong to me. It does not matter for our present argument how I obtained possession of them, or whether I have any real right to them; the only thing that matters now is the admitted fact that all the raw materials which are necessary for the production of the necessaries of life are now the property of the Landlord and Capitalist class. I am that class: all these raw materials belong to me."

"Good enough!" agreed Philpot.

"Now you three represent the Working Class: you have nothing - and for my part, although I have all these raw materials, they are of no use to me - what I need is - the things that can be made out of these raw materials by Work: but as I am too lazy to work myself, I have invented the Money Trick to make you work for me. But first I must explain that I possess something else beside the raw materials. These three knives represent - all the machinery of production; the factories, tools, railways, and so forth, without which the necessaries of life cannot be produced in abundance. And these three coins' - taking three halfpennies from his pocket - 'represent my Money Capital."

"But before we go any further," said Owen, interrupting himself, "it is most important that you remember that I am not supposed to be merely "a" *capitalist. I represent the whole Capitalist Class. You are not supposed to be just three workers - you represent the whole Working Class."*

"All right, all right," said Crass, impatiently, "we all understand that. Git on with it."

Owen proceeded to cut up one of the slices of bread into a number of little square blocks.

"These represent the things which are produced by labour, aided by machinery, from the raw materials. We will suppose that three of these blocks represent - a week's work. We will suppose that a week's work is worth - one pound: and we will suppose that each of these ha'pennies is a sovereign. We'd be able to do the trick better if we had real sovereigns, but I forgot to bring any with me."

"I'd lend you some," said Philpot, regretfully, "but I left me purse on our grand pianner."

As by a strange coincidence nobody happened to have any gold with them, it was decided to make shift with the halfpence.

"Now this is the way the trick works"

"Before you goes on with it," interrupted Philpot, apprehensively, "don't you think we'd better have someone to keep watch at the gate in case a Slop comes along? We don't want to get runned in, you know."

"I don't think there's any need for that," replied Owen, "there's only one slop who'd interfere with us for playing this game, and that's Police Constable Socialism."

"Never mind about Socialism," said Crass, irritably. "Get along with the bloody trick."

Owen now addressed himself to the working classes as represented by Philpot, Harlow and Easton.

"You say that you are all in need of employment, and as I am the kind-hearted capitalist class I am going to invest all my money in various industries, so as to give you Plenty of Work. I shall pay each of you one pound per week, and a week's work is - you must each produce three of these square blocks. For doing this work you will each receive your wages; the money will be your own, to do as you like with, and the things you produce will of course be mine, to do as I like with. You will each take one

of these machines and as soon as you have done a week's work, you shall have your money.'

The Working Classes accordingly set to work, and the Capitalist class sat down and watched them. As soon as they had finished, they passed the nine little blocks to Owen, who placed them on a piece of paper by his side and paid the workers their wages.

"These blocks represent the necessaries of life. You can't live without some of these things, but as they belong to me, you will have to buy them from me: my price for these blocks is - one pound each."

As the working classes were in need of the necessaries of life and as they could not eat, drink or wear the useless money, they were compelled to agree to the kind Capitalist's terms. They each bought back and at once consumed one- third of the produce of their labour. The capitalist class also devoured two of the square blocks, and so the net result of the week's work was that the kind capitalist had consumed two pounds worth of the things produced by the labour of the others, and reckoning the squares at their market value of one pound each, he had more than doubled his capital, for he still possessed the three pounds in money and in addition four pounds worth of goods. As for the working classes, Philpot, Harlow and Easton, having each consumed the pound's worth of necessaries they had bought with their wages, they were again in precisely the same condition as when they started work - they had nothing.

This process was repeated several times: for each week's work the producers were paid their wages. They kept on working and spending all their earnings. The kindhearted capitalist consumed twice as much as any one of them and his pile of wealth continually increased. In a little while - reckoning the little squares at their market I value of one pound each - he was worth about one hundred pounds, and the working classes were still in the same condition as when they began, and were still tearing into their work as if their lives depended upon it.

After a while the rest of the crowd began to laugh, and their merriment increased when the kindhearted capitalist, just after having sold a pound's worth of necessaries to each of his workers, suddenly took their tools - the Machinery of Production - the knives away from them, and informed them that as owing to Over Production all his store-houses were glutted with the necessaries of life, he had decided to close down the works.

"Well, and what the bloody 'ell are we to do now?" demanded Philpot.

"That's not my business," replied the kindhearted capitalist. "I've paid you your wages, and provided you with Plenty of Work for a long time past. I have no more work for you to do at present. Come round again in a few months' time and I'll see what I can do for you."

"But what about the necessaries of life?" demanded Harlow. "We must have something to eat."

"Of course you must," replied the capitalist, affably; "and I shall be very pleased to sell you some."

"But we ain't got no bloody money!"

"Well, you can't expect me to give you my goods for nothing! You didn't work for me for nothing, you know. I paid you for your work and you should have saved something: you should have been thrifty like me. Look how I have got on by being thrifty!"

The unemployed looked blankly at each other, but the rest of the crowd only laughed; and then the three unemployed began to abuse the kindhearted Capitalist, demanding that he should give them some of the necessaries of life that he had piled up in his warehouses, or to be allowed to work and produce some more for their own needs; and even threatened to take some of the things by force if he did not comply with their demands. But the kindhearted Capitalist told them not to be insolent, and spoke to them about honesty, and said if they were not careful he would have their faces battered in for them by the police, or if necessary he would call out the military and have them shot down like dogs, the same as he had done before at Featherstone and Belfast.

"Of course," continued the kindhearted capitalist, "if it were not for foreign competition I should be able to sell these things that you have made, and then I should be able to give you Plenty of Work again: but until I have used them myself, you will have to remain idle." (RTP 211-214)

Another famous section shows how Robert, in the guise of Owen, would keep it up while working:

"When there's no work," Owen went on, taking another dip of paint as he spoke and starting on one of the lower panels of the door, 'when there's no work, you will either starve or get into debt. When - as at present - there is a little work, you will live in a state of semi-starvation. When times are what you call "good", you will work for twelve or fourteen hours a day and - if you're very lucky - occasionally all night. The extra money you then earn will

go to pay your debts so that you may be able to get credit again when there's no work.'

Easton put some putty in a crack in the skirting.

"In consequence of living in this manner, you will die at least twenty years sooner than is natural, or, should you have an unusually strong constitution and live after you cease to be able to work, you will be put into a kind of jail and treated like a criminal for the remainder of your life."

Having faced up the cracks, Easton resumed the painting of the skirting.

"If it were proposed to make a law that all working men and women were to be put to death - smothered, or hung, or poisoned, or put into a lethal chamber - as soon as they reached the age of fifty years, there is not the slightest doubt that you would join in the uproar of protest that would ensue. Yet you submit tamely to have your life shortened by slow starvation, overwork, lack of proper boots and clothing, and through having often to turn out and go to work when you are so ill that you ought to be in bed receiving medical care."

Robert's strategy for educating and converting his colleagues was full-blooded and full-frontal. First, as in *The Great Money Trick*, he would explain the clear faults, inconsistencies and injustices of capitalism as an economic system.

Secondly, he would use diagrams, as in *The Oblong* chapter, to describe the social structures of capitalist society. Here he was clearly influenced by William Morris's *"Useful Work versus Useless Toil"* published in 1884. Robert would draw an elongated rectangle and divided it into five. In the first column he put "tramps, beggars, society people, the aristocracy, great landowners and all those possessed of inherited wealth", in the second "exploiters of labour, thieves, swindlers, pickpockets, burglars, bishops, financiers, shareholders and ministers of religion"; in the third "all those engaged in unnecessary work," in the fourth "all those engaged in necessary work – the production of the benefits of civilisation," and in the fifth, the "unemployed." He then used blacked-in blocks to show how the fourth category, the producers of wealth, shared a fraction of the proceeds enjoyed by the first two. (*RTP 272*)

And thirdly he would explain the meaning of socialism and how it could be brought to Britain. For this, in RTP, he used as a mouthpiece George Barrington, with Owen another facet of Robert's own character –

Barrington is a quiet socialist with a mysterious, affluent family background.

In *The Great Oration* Barrington describes at great length how capitalism had turned artisans into paupers created the conditions for ignorance and starvation amongst the poor. He set out his socialist stall: *"It is not a wild dream of Superhuman Unselfishness. No-one will be asked to sacrifice himself for the benefit of others or to love his neighbours better than himself as is the case in the present system which demands that the majority shall unselfishly be content to labour and live in wretchedness for the benefit of a few. There is no such principle of Philanthropy in Socialism, which simply means that even as all industries are now owned by shareholders, and organised and directed by committees and officers elected by the shareholders, so shall they in future belong to the State, that is, the whole people – and they shall be organised and directed by committees and officers elected by the community.*

"Under existing circumstances the community is exposed to the danger of being invaded and robbed and massacred by some foreign power. Therefore the community has organised and owns and controls an Army and Navy to protect it from that danger. Under existing circumstances the community is menaced by another equally great danger – the people are mentally and physically degenerating from lack of proper food and clothing. Socialists say that the community should undertake and organise the business of producing and distributing all these things; that the State should be the only employer of labour and should own all the factories, mills, mines, farms, railways, fishing fleets, sheep farms, poultry farms and cattle ranches.

"Under existing circumstances the community is degenerating mentally and physically because the majority cannot afford decent homes to live in. Socialists say that the community should take in hand the business of providing proper houses for all its members, that the State should be the only landlord, that all the land and all the houses should belong to the whole people...

"We must do this if we are to keep our old place in the van of human progress. A nation of ignorant, unintelligent, half-starved, broken-spirited degenerates cannot hope to lead humanity in its never-ceasing march onwards to the conquest of the future." (RTP 476)

Robert used national earnings figures calculated by economists Griffin, Levi and Mulholland to show that "the British Isles do not belong to the British people." And the influence of Michael Davitt and the Land League is clear:

They must live on the land: and that's the beginning of the trouble; because - under the present system - the majority of the people have really no right to be in the country at all! Under the present system the country belongs to a few - those who are here represented by this small black square. If it would pay them to do so, and if they felt so disposed, these few people have a perfect right - under the present system - to order everyone else to clear out!   But they don't do that, they allow the majority to remain in the land on one condition - that is, they must pay rent to the few for the privilege of being permitted to live in the land of their birth. The amount of rent demanded by those who own this country is so large that, in order to pay it, the greater number of the majority have often to deprive themselves and their children, not only of the comforts, but even the necessaries of life. In the case of the working classes the rent absorbs at the lowest possible estimate, about one-third of their total earnings, for it must be remembered that the rent is an expense that goes on all the time, whether they are employed or not. If they get into arrears when out of work, they have to pay double when they get employment again. The majority work hard and live in poverty in order that the minority may live in luxury without working at all, and as the majority are mostly fools, they not only agree to pass their lives in incessant slavery and want, in order to pay this rent to those who own the country, but they say it is quite right that they should have to do so, and are very grateful to the little minority for allowing them to remain in the country at all.' (RTP 150-151)

Robert's personal credo, summed up and pared down, was: "No man shall profit from another's loss and we shall no longer be masters and servants but brothers, free men and friends. A state wherein it will be possible to put into practice the teachings of Him whom so many pretend to follow. A society which will have justice and co-operation for its foundations and International Brotherhood and love for its law."

To some Robert's hectoring may have become tiresome, as illustrated in the following heckles: `*Bloody rot! Wonder wot the bloody 'ell 'e thinks 'e is? A sort of schoolmaster?' (RTP150)*

But such was Robert's popularity that his workmates generally responded with good humour which he illustrated in the run-up to *The Great Money Trick*:

'Hooray!' shouted Philpot, leading off with a cheer which the others took up. 'The Professor 'as arrived and will now proceed to say a few remarks.'
A roar of merriment greeted this sally.
'Let's 'ave our bloody dinner first, for Christ's sake,' appealed Harlow with mock despair. As Owen, having filled his cup with tea, sat down in his usual place, Philpot rose solemnly to his feet, and, looking around the company, said: 'Gentlemen, with your kind permission, as soon as the Professor 'as finished 'is dinner 'e will deliver 'is well-known lecture, entitled: "Money the Principal Cause of being 'ard up", proving as money ain't no good to nobody. At the hend of the lecture a collection will be took up to provide the lecturer with a little encouragement.'" (RTP 210)

But behind such good nature, Robert must have felt a growing frustration at the failure of most of his workmates to grasp the essentials of what he believed to be the blindingly obvious strengths and justice of socialism. From such inability to understand what Robert believed to be the true nature of society – that the poor gave to the rich – it is easy to see where he got the term "philanthropists" for his title.

In arguments with his supposed "betters" Robert could be vehement, calling such people "bloody hypocrites." But with his workmates he was more tolerant. Ball wrote: "With working-men who showed any interest in reading and improving their knowledge he would discuss at length all kinds of subjects, always treating knowledge as belonging to all by right, and trying to instil that sense of human dignity and social consciousness which he so passionately pleads for in book." *(1)* Noakes also recalled getting ribbed by workmates for his membership of the Artillery Volunteers, whereas Robert always expressed interest in the technologies of warfare and what it was like going to camp, even though he hated militarism.

But what Robert hated most of all was how bosses exploited the fear of unemployment to divide and rule their workforce. Jobs were scarce and trade unionism weak in the Hastings area during a slump in the building trade. Each workforce was riddled with professed Tories and boss's narks, exemplified by Crass and Slyme. They were easily identifiable, but what also grated were the tactics of ordinary men desperate to hold onto their jobs or perks at the expensed of their mates. Another contemporary interviewed by Ball, Mr Sellens, said: "I did not last long at Adam's and Jarrett's. The painters tried to make it appear that I was of little use, afraid I might work one of them out of their job. One of the foremen put me on a job, let Jarrett see me on it, then when he was gone took me off it, but arranged for me to be back on it just before Jarrett came back. Jarrett, of course, thought I was on that job all the time. The painters were all fighting each other and not the boss."

Another factor playing into the hands of the employers was the working man's fear of immigration and technological change, exacerbated by poor education and ignorance. In RTP Robert quotes Sawkins: *"Why even 'ere in Mugsborough we're overrun with 'em! Nearly all the waiters and the cook at the Grand hotel where we was working last month were foreigners,"* Philpot chips in: *"And then thers all them Hitalian horgin grinders, an' the blokes wot sell 'ot chestnuts: an' wen I was goin' 'ome last night I see a lot of them Frenchies sellin' hunions, an' a little wile afterwards I met two more of 'em coming up the street with a bear."* (RTP 22)

In the chapter *The Exterminating Machines* Robert displayed an example of Edwardian Luddism:

'I don't see no sense in always grumbling,' Crass proceeded. "These things can't be altered. You can't expect there can be plenty of work for everyone with all this 'ere labour savin' machinery what's been invented.' 'Of course,' said Harlow, 'the people what used to be employed on the work what's now being done by machinery, has to find something else to do. Some of 'em goes to our trade, for instance: the result is there's too many at it, and there ain't enough work to keep 'em all goin'. 'Yes,' cried Crass eagerly, 'That's just what I say. Machinery's the real cause of all the poverty.' (RTP 101)

Robert, as we have seen, was heavily influenced by William Morris and read everything he wrote which was available to him. It is easy to hear Robert's own developing style of oratory and prose in the following passage: "Now this view of Socialism which I hold today, and hope to die holding, is what I began with...

"Apart from the desire to produce beautiful things, the leading passion of my life has been and is hatred of modern civilisation. What shall I say of it now, when the words are put into my mouth, my hope of its destruction – what shall I say of its supplanting by Socialism?

"What shall I say concerning its mastery of and its waste of mechanical power, its commonwealth so poor, its enemies of the commonwealth so rich, its stupendous organisation – for the misery of life! Its contempt of simple pleasures which everyone could enjoy but for its folly? Its eyeless vulgarity which has destroyed art, the one certain solace of labour? All this I felt then as now, but I did not know why it was so. The hope of the past times was gone, the struggles of mankind for many ages had produced nothing but this sordid, aimless, ugly confusion; the immediate future seemed to me likely to intensify all the present evils by sweeping away the last survivals of the days before the dull squalor of civilisation had settled down on the world...

"So there I was in for a fine pessimistic end of life, if it had not somehow dawned on me that amidst all this filth of civilisation the seeds of a great change, what we others call social-Revolution, were beginning to germinate. The whole face of things was changed to me by the discovery, and all I had to do then in order to become a Socialist was to hook myself onto the practical movement..." (2)

Many people, at the time and since, have asked why Robert, with his broad knowledge and intellect, did not become a teacher. They forget that he had no formal academic qualifications and he was not temperamentally suited to the sort of rigid institutions where they could be gained. His background and attitudes meant that in Edwardian England there were few such institutions which would take him. He was a relatively young family man who wished to use whatever talents he had to support his dependants. There is also some evidence to support his niece's assertion, given to Ball, that he went into the painting and decorating business to "crusade" for socialism. Certainly the lack of intellectual rigour involved in his job meant he had some time to focus on developing his own political and social credo.

Trade unionism and mainstream Labour parties were too "soft" for him, and Robert felt more frustrations at the lack of progress made by the SDF branch and the inertia and fatalism of those with whom he worked. His understanding of a working man's life devoid of aspirations also produced sympathy rather than anger. Ball put the slow transformation from teacher to scribe most succinctly:

"In his workmates he saw men like himself for whom there was no escape. Yet they had a way of coming to terms with their situation without becoming wholly contaminated. And they had a strange ability not to become so dispirited as they ought. This gave him a deeper understanding of the working classes, opened his eyes to their deep roots and their resilience which he almost unconsciously portrays all through the book, even when most exasperated about them, indeed perhaps in that very exasperation itself. And gradually his own circumstances made him realise that he had little more chance of 'escape' than they had and this gave him a feeling of total involvement. He was hardly any longer a man outside looking in, although this was a feeling he never completely overcame because this is not a matter of will but nurture. He was not quite of them but wholly with them." *(3)*

Gradually his lectures tailed off and he spent more time on his book. But life went on and Robert, although occasional despondent and disillusioned, and often ill, embraced it.

PLAY AND POLITICS

"Why put idiots into insane asylums?"

Edwardian pastimes, even for those who could not afford lavish expenditure, were many and varied and Robert's zest for life ensured that he played them with gusto.

Kathleen recalled her father being shocked by the price she had paid for dancing shoes. "According to his explanation it was a lot to pay for 'one night's wear,'" she said. If he wore out a pair of shoes in a night he must have danced more than I ever would!

"We used to play cricket and hockey at St Helen's, Robert liked cricket – and I played tennis at various places. I remember a group of us, possibly part of our class, going to Battle, I don't remember how, and we were met there. I'm not sure of all the conveyances but a couple of girls and myself drove off in a dog-cart. I don't know whether it was Telham or not but I think it was a large white house two storeys high, I would think, with lovely grounds. It was a garden party. Sometimes the girls used to cycle out there to play tennis and to walk around the garden." (1)

Robert was also a keen cyclist and no doubt got a good deal from his landlord, cycle-shop owner Charles Beney. With Gower and others he would range far across East Sussex. Gower said that the countryside "delighted and restored" his older friend. Cycling down Westfield Lane, Robert said: "This is better than washing off ceilings." It was like a weight had been lifted from his shoulders and his natural enthusiasm was most evident.

Walking and cycling Robert would talk non-stop about everything around him and Gower said he received a better education on such rambles than he ever did at school. At Brede church Robert pointed to Dean Swift's cradle and said: "This should be in Ireland." That sparked another intense monologue on the injustices in Ireland and the case for independence. On another trip to Old Roar on the outskirts of the town Gower took his famous photograph of Robert, who said as he fiddled with the camera: "Look out or you''ll finish up being hung in the Tate Gallery." *(2)*

His passion for cycling and socialism merged around 1908 with membership of the Clarion Cycling Scouts with which he would travel the county spreading the word at rural Sunday meetings.

Robert's socialism did not stop him coming up with ideas for commercial enterprises to provide a route for himself and his family out of poverty. He saw no contradictions in that, and sometimes the two could be combined. Gower said: "About this time he conceived the project of carrying entertainment and enlightenment to the people of Brede, Westfield and country districts around. I had a lecture lantern and we hired a set of slides called 'A Trip Round the World,' including scenes from the Great San Francisco earthquake of 1906." Robert was to provide the accompanying lecture while Gower operated the lantern. They called themselves The South Coast Amusement Company and obtained permission from the Brede village schoolmaster to use the schoolroom. They had handbills printed and distributed them to schoolchildren. Robert arranged for several local firms to defray expenses by introducing advertising slides. A local music-seller agreed to supply a phonograph and records in return for free advertising. Tickets were to be sold at the door for sixpence for the best seats and three pence for the rest.

On the appointed day Gower cycled to meet Robert at 241 London Road and got soaked in the pouring rain. Robert was staring out of the window in a deep depression. "Look at that lot," he said, referring to the weather, "I don't think we can go." Gower replied: "But we must go ...we can't back out now."

Robert was persuaded to put aside his fears for the state of his lungs and they set off in mid-winter rain to cycle the six miles with their gear. Gower recalled: "We were wet through when we arrived. The schoolmaster, Mr Harvey, gave us some tea and we dried out a little and then got ready for the lecture." As they prepared for the show they discovered that the music-seller had forgotten to include the phonograph needles in his package. That setback seemed the last straw until the pair realised they had a full house, with more coming by the moment despite the atrocious weather. Entertainment was in short supply in the outlying villages and families would put up with discomfort for a show.

Gower took the ticket money and the audience waited without the introductory music that had been planned. Robert took the stand by the screen and began his lecture, using a pointer borrowed from the school master. His boots squelched with every movement, but Robert was soon in his element. "If the audience was not entertained, they were certainly instructed that evening," Gower said.

Inevitably, between exotic scenes, Robert could not resist injecting some socialist theory which, according to Gower, the audience took "wonderfully well." They were used to dry sermons from vicars rather than Robert's rumbustious style and found it a refreshing change. Also, Ball speculated, Brede and the nearby villages had been at the forefront of the Captain Swing riots 70 years earlier in which agricultural labourers had revolted and the Brede parish poor law overseer had been trundled down the hill in a wheel-barrow, making the villagers no strangers to a rough-and-ready form of socialist action.

Whatever the cause, Robert held them in rapt attention and it was past 11 o'clock before the lecture ended and the last slide shown.

Robert and Gower packed up and set off for home on their cycles. But progress was painfully slow as Robert had to frequently stop to get his breath back on the many hills approach the Ridge which surrounds Hastings in a semi-circle. When Robert arrived home after midnight he was exhausted. He told Gower: "That journey nearly killed me."

Gower added: "Next day poor Robert was laid up and the South Coast Amusement Company ceased to exist. We didn't make any profit anyhow." (3)

Sometime later Robert and Gower had one of their few rows when Robert called on him in a state of "great enthusiasm." "Bill," he said, "I've got an idea. Let's hire the St Leonards Pier Hall and show Moving Pictures!" Gower, fed up with schemes which never turned a profit, said he could not "entertain" that. Robert exploded, but quickly calmed down and then for weeks pressed his case. Lack of enthusiasm from his friend, and lack of money to invest in the enterprise, led Robert to reluctantly drop the plan. Later Gower admitted that he was wrong when an entrepreneur went ahead and opened the pier hall for the showing of early movies. Kathleen remembered going to see some of them: "I don't remember the names of films – a St Bernard dog racing all over the countryside after a stolen baby – that kind of thing."

She did, however, remember being taken by her father to see plays and concerts, including *The Bohemian Girl, Les Cloches de Corneville* and *Madame Butterfly*, and to productions by the D'Oyly Carte opera company which performed in Hastings for a week every year.

Singing, whether hymns or popular tunes, were also a staple of both public and home entertainment in those days. Hastings and St Leonards boasted music pavilions on both its piers, the Royal Assembly Rooms in George Street, the Public Hall and the Gaiety Theatre (later a cinema) in the town centre, Burton's Assembly Rooms in St Leonards, the Palace of Varieties on Marine Parade and the Royal Concert and Opera House in Warrior Square.

In RTP Robert quoted the titles of numerous music hall favourites which are still known today, including *Two Lovely Black Eyes, Down at the Old Bull and Bush* and *For He's A jolly Good Fellow*. Fairground organs were used at Sunday charity concerts to belt out such songs as *Put Me amongst the Girls and Has Anyone Seen a German Band?* Boer War songs such as *Goodbye, Dolly Grey* were also hugely popular. *(4)*

More contentious, to Robert, were the songs hijacked by the Tories and Liberals to rally support while advocating the status quo. Chief amongst those was *Work, Boys, Work*, sung to the tune of *Tramp, Tramp, Tramp, the Boys are Marching*, the anthem of tariff reformers:

`Now I'm not a wealthy man,*
But I lives upon a plan
Wot will render me as 'appy as a King;
An' if you will allow, I'll sing it to you now,
For time you know is always on the wing.

Work, boys, work and be contented
So long as you've enough to buy a meal.
For if you will but try, you'll be wealthy - bye and bye -
If you'll only put yer shoulder to the wheel.'

Another favourite Tory song was:

His clothes may be ragged, his hands may be soiled.
But where's the disgrace if for bread he has toiled.

His 'art is in the right place, deny it no one can
The backbone of Old England is the honest workin' man.'

As well as traditional hymns, RTP refers to those of Dwight Lyman Moody and Ira David Sankey, two American evangelist preachers whose song books had been popular in England throughout the latter half of the 19th century and into the 20th. The book quotes in some form or another, at least eight of their hymns, including:

Trim your feeble lamp, my brother,
Some poor seaman tempest-tost,
Trying now to make the harbour,
In the darkness may be lost.
Let the lower lights be burning;
Send a gleam across the wave!
Some poor fainting, struggling seaman
You may rescue, you may save. (RTP 215)

In the book, however, the words are put in the vernacular and nasal twang of three unemployed men imitating the whine of street-singers.

Songs and music are quoted throughout the book. But when still living in Milward Road with Adelaide and Arthur, Robert refused Kathleen her request to learn to play the piano. "My aunt told me my mother had played and it made him sad to see a woman at the piano," Kathleen said.

And that raises the tricky issue of sex. None of his workmates and wider circle of friends and comrades could remember any romantic assignations during the time that Robert lived in Muggsborough. He was not a church-goer, could not find solace in religion, was not a drunk, and could only find comfort in family, the written word and his own sacred cause of socialism. That is not usually enough for a man barely 40.

Robert had married, fathered a child, and had almost remarried in South Africa. Kathleen said: "When I was little, before I was six, apparently there was someone I think he was thinking of marrying but she wanted him to get rid of me and so he didn't accept her." In Hastings he, according to Kathleen, "started talking about this girl he saw in the tram and all of a sudden he didn't talk about her any more. At the time I thought I was going to have a stepmother. And then I asked about her and apparently he had heard her talk and that finished him. It was probably her voice, I have the same trait – I can listen to the most absolute drivel if the voice producing it is lovely in tone and expression, whereas if a voice is unpleasant or strident I just cannot bear to hear what is said, from listening to the voice, no matter how interesting or informative the subject may be." (5)

It cannot have been voices which apparently kept Robert celibate. Fred Ball, who spoke at length to Kathleen and some of Robert's best mates, believes he still held a torch for his now dead wife. "He may have continued, as many people do, to live in the aura of his first marriage," Ball wrote. Nevertheless Ball was puzzled, saying: "I find it difficult to understand why, if his wife meant so much to him, why he didn't celebrate her memory with his daughter." Kathleen agreed, up to a point: "There was never any question of my mother being impossible; on the contrary. I was brought up a Roman Catholic, probably in accordance with my mother's wishes. Once when I asked Robert what she looked like he said I was very like her. Was that why he was so fond of me? I think he never spoke of her because his feelings were too deep." (6)

On the other hand, Kathleen acknowledged that perhaps he had no need of a women's company, he was ill, worked long hours and had limited opportunities to meet unattached females. He was also an honourable man who would not have taken advantage of others, particularly the "fairer sex." There is also speculation that his poor health held him back. He would have believed that it would have been unfair on a woman to form a relationship which might not last, and he also may have feared infecting a lover with tuberculosis. There is no suggestion that he was homosexual, and in RTP he, while reticent about the sexual act and over-romantic about women in general, clearly shows the married state between a man and a woman as "natural." In chapter 25 he speaks of the "unnatural" life of the bachelor.

At work the drudgery was not entirely unremitting. Robert wrote: "*Now and then a transient gleam of sunshine penetrated the gloom in which the lives of the philanthropists were passed. The cheerless monotony was sometimes enlivened by a little innocent merriment. Every now and then there was a funeral which took Misery and Crass away for the whole afternoon, and although they always tried to keep the dates secret, the men generally knew when they were gone.*

"Sometimes the people in whose houses they were working regaled them with tea, bread and butter, cake or other light refreshments, and occasionally even with beer – very different stuff from the petrifying liquid they bought at the Cricketers at twopence a pint. At other places, where the people of the house were not so generously disposed, the servants made up for it, and entertained them in a similar manner without the knowledge of their masters and mistresses. Even when the mistresses were too cunning to permit this, they were seldom able to prevent the men from embracing the domestics, who for their part were quite often willing to be embraced; it was an agreeable episode that helped to vary the monotony of their lives, and there was no harm done." (RTP 435)

The highlight of the year was the annual "Beano" a trip into the countryside for a slap-up meal with the bosses. The men paid their share. Adams and Jarrett possibly cancelled theirs, although one was booked in 1908, but the previous firms Robert worked for maintained the tradition. It is no accident that Robert devoted one of the longer chapters in RTP to such an occasion. It gave him free rein to express subversive humour, show his ear for dialogue, and mine a political goldfield of satire. The destination venue is in the book called the *Queen Elizabeth* inn. In reality it was The *St John's Cross Inn* on the Battle Road just outside Robertsbridge, which Robert first visited on August 15 1906. Built in 1511 it was named after the banner of St John the Baptist as the hamlet was a marshalling point for the Crusades. It still stands there.

The carriages, or brakes, picked up the men outside the Cricketers at one pm on a Saturday.

There were four brakes altogether - three large ones for the men and one small one for the accommodation of Mr Rushton and a few of his personal friends... Most of the chaps were smoking twopenny cigars, and had one or two drinks with each other to try to cheer themselves up before they started, but all the same it was a melancholy procession that wended its way up the hill to Windley. To judge from the mournful expression on the long face of Misery, who sat on the box beside the driver of the first large brake, and the downcast appearance of the majority of the men, one might have thought that it was a funeral rather than a pleasure party, or that they were a contingent of lost souls being conducted to the banks of the Styx. The man who from time to time sounded the coachman's horn might have passed as the angel sounding the last trump, and the fumes of the cigars were typical of the smoke of their torment, which ascendeth up for ever and ever." (RTP 436)

Brief halts were made along the way to pick up more men, and there were two stops outside country inns, although most of the men stayed on board, having spent all their money on the Beano ticket.

They reached the long-desired Queen Elizabeth at twenty minutes to four, and were immediately ushered into a large room where a round table and two long ones were set for dinner - and they were set in a manner worthy of the reputation of the house.
The cloths that covered the tables and the serviettes, arranged fanwise in the drinking glasses, were literally as white as snow, and about a dozen knives and forks and spoons were laid for each person. Down the centre of the table glasses of delicious yellow custard and cut-glass dishes of glistening red and golden jelly alternated with vases of sweet-smelling flowers. The floor of the dining-room was covered with oilcloth - red flowers on a pale yellow ground; the pattern was worn off in places, but it was all very clean and shining. Whether one looked at the walls with the old-fashioned varnished oak paper, or at the glossy piano standing across the corner near the white-curtained window, at the shining oak chairs or through the open casement doors that led into the shady garden beyond, the dominating impression one received was that everything was exquisitely clean.
The landlord announced that dinner would be served in ten minutes, and while they were waiting some of them indulged in a drink at the bar - just as an appetizer - whilst the others strolled in the garden or, by the landlord's invitation, looked over the house. Amongst other places, they glanced into the kitchen, where the landlady was superintending the preparation of the feast, and in this place, with its whitewashed walls and tiled floor, as in every other part of the house, the same absolute cleanliness reigned supreme.
`It's a bit differint from the Royal Caff, where we got the sack, ain't it?' remarked the Semi-drunk to Bill Bates as they made their way to the dining-room in response to the announcement that dinner was ready...
The dinner was all that could be desired; it was almost as good as the kind of dinner that is enjoyed every day by those persons who are too lazy to work but are cunning enough to make others work for them. There was soup, several entrees, roast beef, boiled mutton, roast turkey, roast goose, ham, cabbage, peas, beans and sweets galore, plum pudding,

custard, jelly, fruit tarts, bread and cheese and as much beer or lemonade as they liked to pay for, the drinks being an extra; and afterwards the waiters brought in cups of coffee for those who desired it. Everything was up to the knocker, and although they were somewhat bewildered by the multitude of knives and forks, they all, with one or two exceptions, rose to the occasion and enjoyed themselves famously. The excellent decorum observed being marred only by one or two regrettable incidents. The first of these occurred almost as soon as they sat down, when Ned Dawson who, although a big strong fellow, was not able to stand much beer, not being used to it, was taken ill and had to be escorted from the room by his mate Bundy and another man. They left him somewhere outside and he came back again about ten minutes afterwards, much better but looking rather pale, and took his seat with the others.   *The turkeys, the roast beef and the boiled mutton, the peas and beans and the cabbage, disappeared with astonishing rapidity, which was not to be wondered at, for they were all very hungry from the long drive, and nearly everyone made a point of having at least one helping of everything there was to be had. Some of them went in for two lots of soup. Then for the next course, boiled mutton and ham or turkey: then some roast beef and goose. Then a little more boiled mutton with a little roast beef. Each of the three boys devoured several times his own weight of everything, to say nothing of numerous bottles of lemonade and champagne ginger beer. There was enough and to spare of everything to eat, the beer was of the best, and all the time, amid the rattle of the crockery and the knives and forks, the proceedings were enlivened by many jests and flashes of wit that continuously kept the table in a roar. (RTP 439-441)*

Once the dinner was over Cross made his financial statement as Beano secretary. Thirty-seven men had paid five shillings each, totalling £9 5s. It was agreed that three boys should only pay half price, taking the cost to £9 12/6d. The boss. Rushton, had contributed £1 10s and Mr Sweater £1. Three other clients, Lettuim, Didlum, Grinder and Toonarf each chipped in 10 shillings. All were cheered. Other firms in the area, after much chivvying, took the total to £17. From that was deducted 2/6d a head for the meal and the same for transport. The balance, as was the custom, was shared amongst the workforce, and that came to 3 shillings for the men and £1/4d for the boys. The cash was distributed by Slyme and his cronies. In reality, as Robert made clear with his detailed accounting, the men had virtually paid for their own meal, with the bosses and their clients paying – just one day a year – for the transport. The landlord then made his profit from the drinks once the share-out was complete.

"Then Mr Rushton requested the landlord to serve drinks and cigars all round. Some had cigarettes and the teetotallers had lemonade or ginger beer. Those who did not smoke themselves took the cigar all the same and gave it to someone else who did. When all were supplied there suddenly arose loud cries of `Order!' and it was seen that Hunter was upon his feet.

"As soon as silence was obtained, Misery said that he believed that everyone there present would agree with him, when he said that they should not let the occasion pass without drinking the 'ealth of their esteemed and respected employer, Mr Rushton. (Hear, hear.) Some of them had worked for Mr Rushton on and off for many years, and as far as THEY was concerned it was not necessary for him (Hunter) to say much in praise of Mr Rushton. (Hear, hear.) They knew Mr Rushton as well as he did himself and to know him was to esteem him. (Cheers.) As for the new hands, although they did not know Mr Rushton as well as the old hands did, he felt sure that they would agree that as no one could wish for a better master. (Loud applause.) He had much pleasure in asking them to drink Mr Rushton's health. Everyone rose.

"`Musical honours, chaps,' shouted Crass, waving his glass and leading off the singing which was immediately joined in with great enthusiasm by most of the men, the Semi-drunk conducting the music with a table knife:

For he's a jolly good fellow,
For he's a jolly good fellow,
For he's a jolly good fel-ell-O,
And so say all of us,
So 'ip, 'ip, 'ip, 'ooray!
So 'ip, 'ip, 'ip, 'ooray!" (RTP 442-443)

While most joined in, there were a few expressions of contempt and uneasiness amongst the men's faces. That changed as more drinks were served and Nimrod toasted the guests of honour from the business community who had contributed towards the expenses, and there was another chorus.

To judge from the manner in which they sang the chorus and cheered, it was quite evident that most of the hands did agree. When they left off,

Grinder rose to reply on behalf of those included in the toast. He said that it gave them much pleasure to be there and take part in such pleasant proceedings and they were glad to think that they had been able to help to bring it about. It was very gratifying to see the good feeling that existed between Mr Rushton and his workmen, which was as it should be, because masters and men was really fellow workers - the masters did the brain work, the men the 'and work. They was both workers, and their interests was the same. He liked to see men doing their best for their master and knowing that their master was doing his best for them, that he was not only a master, but a friend. That was what he (Grinder) liked to see - master and men pulling together - doing their best, and realizing that their interests was identical. (Cheers.) If only all masters and men would do this they would find that everything would go on all right, there would be more work and less poverty. Let the men do their best for their masters, and the masters do their best for their men, and they would find that that was the true solution of the social problem, and not the silly nonsense that was talked by people what went about with red flags. (Cheers and laughter.) Most of those fellows were chaps who was too lazy to work for their livin'. (Hear, hear.) They could take it from him that, if ever the Socialists got the upper hand there would just be a few of the hartful dodgers who would get all the cream, and there would be nothing left but 'ard work for the rest. (Hear. hear.) That's wot hall those hagitators was after: they wanted them (his hearers) to work and keep 'em in idleness. (Hear, hear.)   (RTP 445-446)

Some of the audience challenged any socialists to respond, and most expected wen to do so. In fact it was the mysterious and intellectual George Barrington who responded after more goading from Grinder. He delivered a passionate rebuttal, opening with:

`We are here today as friends and want to forget our differences and enjoy ourselves for a few hours. But after what Mr Grinder has said I am quite ready to reply to him to the best of my ability.*

`The fact that I am a Socialist and that I am here today as one of Mr Rushton's employees should be an answer to the charge that Socialists are too lazy to work for their living. And as to taking advantage of the ignorance and simplicity of working men and trying to mislead them with nonsensical claptrap...,*

If Mr Grinder had ever tried, he would know that manual workers have to concentrate their minds and their attention on their work or they would not be able to do it at all. His talk about employers being not only the masters but the "friends" of their workmen is also mere claptrap because he knows as well as we do, that no matter how good or benevolent an employer may be, no matter how much he might desire to give his men good conditions, it is impossible for him to do so, because he has to compete against other employers who do not do that. It is the bad employer - the sweating, slave-driving employer - who sets the pace and the others have to adopt the same methods - very often against their inclinations - or they would not be able to compete with him. If any employer today were to resolve to pay his workmen not less wages than he would be able to live upon in comfort himself, that he would not require them to do more work in a day than he himself would like to perform every day of his own life, Mr Grinder knows as well as we do that such an employer would be bankrupt in a month; because he would not be able to get any work except by taking it at the same price as the sweaters and the slave-drivers."(RTP 447-448)

Barrington's monologue was a prelude to his Great Oration in the following chapter, both of which spoke with Robert's clear voice.

In the book the speech is cut short, to much applause, as the men get on with the serious business of drinking, singing and playing cricket. They were entertained by a party of female glee singers and a fight was narrowly avoided when one of the girls was insulted. At 7.30 the brakes were loaded up for the return journey.

"They called at all the taverns on the road, and by the time they reached the Blue Lion half of them were three sheets in the wind, and five or six were very drunk, including the driver of Crass's brake and the man with the bugle. The latter was so far gone that they had to let him lie down in the bottom of the carriage amongst their feet, where he fell asleep, while the others amused themselves by blowing weird shrieks out of the horn.

"There was an automatic penny-in-the-slot piano at the Blue Lion and as that was the last house of the road they made a rather long stop there, playing hooks and rings, shove-ha'penny, drinking, singing, dancing and finally quarrelling." (RTP 454)

They finally arrived home at midnight, worse for wear, after many rows, mishaps and near-crashes. Robert was not judgemental of his workmates, but such events made him more than ever contemptuous of those that exploited them.

SWEATER AND OTHER BOSSES

"The idear! Sitting down in my time!"

Robert was used to petty tyrants in the Hastings building and decorating trade and Adams and Jarrett provided more examples.

The firm, the basis of Makehaste and Sloggem in RTP, had been created by Alfred Adams, a general builder, and Boaz Jarrett of Silverhill in 1905. Until then Adams had been operating a gas-fitting business at Gensing Road and a decorating concern in Alfred Street. Together they set up a combined building and decorating outfit which could compete with Burton's. That may have been why Robert, a skilled artisan who had fallen out with Burton, was hired.

The company had its showrooms near Warrior Square in Norman Road, with two workshops close to Christ Church, a long walk downhill from Robert's flat. They were notoriously poor payers, even by the standards of the place and age. Wages could be as low as 5d an hour for the least skilled, rising to 8d for the most. Two pence were deducted from each week's wage in insure the firm against accidents. If anyone complained they got the deducted 2d back along with instant dismissal. Hours were from six am to 5.30 pm and there were no holidays, including Bank holidays. Anyone who was sick had to re-apply for their jobs and they rarely succeeded.

The building trades unions, amongst the most militant in the mid-19th century, had also become the most conservative and toothless. Between 1875 and 1900 there had been marked improvements in pay and conditions but the new century saw that go into reverse. In Hastings and across the south east they were seriously undermined by casual labour and non-unionists. Postgate wrote: "Wage cuts were enforced; almost every union submitted to some deterioration, either of conditions or pay, and the disorganisation of the union machinery permitted the Master Builders to select their time and place for their attacks, with the effect that the burden of the bad trade was almost entirely shifted onto the operatives." (1)

Robert's expertise again saw him being paid slightly above the normal rates when there was sign-writing, graining or gilding, but at other times he was put on basic painting as a "plain-layer-on."

The foreman, who had joined the firm from an ironmonger's, provided more of the composite for Misery, or Hunter, or Nimrod in RTP. A workmate of Robert's, Mr Noakes, told Ball: "This man, like Misery, was a Chapel-man, and always wanted to rush everything. There was a non-smoking rule on the firm and he would go around sniffing for smokers and would instantly dismiss anyone he caught. Men used to lie down on the floor in empty houses and smoke up the chimney. At the Convent in Magdalen Road one day he comes in suddenly and a chap smothered the cigarette he was smoking by putting the lighted end into his mouth. I have seen men burn their mouths when doing this. Men were not even allowed to smoke when pushing a hand-cart." (2)

Robert describes Misery approaching a work site behind high hedges: *"Then he carefully crept along until he came to the gate-post, and bending down, he cautiously peeped around to see if he could detect anyone idling, or talking, or smoking."* RTP 37)

Misery, like his other incarnations, reported directly to the boss, Mr Rushton, and was himself responsible for the roughest jobs. If anything went wrong he could be made the scapegoat, and the boss regarded any break for any reason to be shirking. That is vividly illustrated by the description of the paint-boy Bert White, who struggles to push a heavily-laded cart up London Road, known in the book as The Long Hill:

"The cart became heavier and heavier. After a while it seemed to the boy as if there was someone at the front of it trying to push him back down the hill. This was such a funny idea that for a moment he felt inclined to laugh, but the inclination went almost as soon as it came and was replaced by the dread that he would not be able to hold out long enough to reach the lamp-post, after all. Clenching his teeth, he made a tremendous effort and staggered forward two or three more steps, and then – the cart stopped. He struggled with it despairingly for a few seconds, but all the strength had suddenly gone out of him: his legs felt so weak that he nearly collapsed on the ground, and the cart began to move backwards down the hill. He was

just able to stick to it and guide it so that it ran into and rested against the kerb, and there he stood holding it in a half-dazed way, very pale, saturated with perspiration, and trembling. His legs in particular shook so much that he felt that unless he could sit down for a little, he would fall down."

After a few moments rest the boy was about to resume when a harsh voice said:

"'How much longer are you going to sit there?
"Bert started up guiltily, and found himself confronted by Mr Rushton, who was regarding him with an angry frown, whilst close by towered the colossal figure of the obese Sweater, the expression on his greasy countenance betokening the pain he experienced on beholding such an appalling example of juvenile depravity.
"'What do you mean by sich conduct?' demanded Rushton, indignantly. 'The idear of sitting there like that when most likely the men are waiting for those things.'

The lad, "parched with terror," cannot reply.

"'You know, that's not the way to get on in life, my boy,' observed Sweater lifting his forefinger and shaking his head reproachfully.
'Get along with you at once," Rushton said roughly. 'I'm surprised at yer! The idear! Sitting down in my time.'" (RTP 114-116)

The treatment of young boys at Adam's and Jarrett's infuriated Robert. Another incident from his tenure there, which was fully written up in RTP, was recalled by former workmates.

On a day in which they witnessed his volcanic temper on the side of right, Robert returned to the paint-shop and found the apprentice painter cleaning pots in freezing conditions. It was "as chilly as a tomb" but the boy, though trembling with cold, was too frightened to light a fire because it was forbidden by the firm. "We'll see about that," said Robert, who collected old splintered wood, doused the pile with turpentine and set a roaring fire. He then stormed into the boss's office, shaking with rage, and said that if he ever again found the lad in such conditions he would report the firm to the Royal Society for the Prevention of Cruelty to Children. In real-life, repeated in the book but attested to by workmates, he bellowed:

"The place is not good enough for a stable. I give you fair warning. I know enough about you to put you where you deserve to be…" Robert was out of breath, coughing from the depths of his weak lungs and panting with rage when he made the threats, wheeled on his heels and stalked out. When he got home he told Kathleen: "I nearly got the sack today." (3)

In RTP he described his fears that he had gone too far. But it is another testament to Robert's value as an artisan, together with a recognition that he would carry out his threat, that he escaped dismissal.

Robert's talents, his obvious intelligence and his experience were indeed recognised by bosses and he was on several occasions offered the chance to become a foreman himself, or at least to take charge of some of Misery's tasks. He turned them down despite the offers of higher pay. He was not a "master's man" and his workmates respected that. Above all, he did not want to become the creature he most despised.

Robert's work on the homes of the rich and unscrupulous also gave him an insight into how such men had made their money. One such was Adam Sweater, probably based on Charles Eaton, a prosperous draper and Hastings Mayor in 1904. (4) His associate was Stanley T. Weston whose firm Paine, Rogers and Co., had a virtual monopoly on the towns wholesale and retail trade, provided a convenient template for another RTP boss, Amos Grinder. (5) In one RTP passage Robert slashed away their man's façade of benevolent respectability. It is rarely quoted but, for me, represents the anger with which Robert turned to the pen:

Mr Sweater was the managing director and principal shareholder of a large drapery business in which he had amassed a considerable fortune. This was not very surprising, considering that he paid none of his workpeople fair wages and many of them no wages at all. He employed a great number of girls and young women who were supposed to be learning dressmaking, mantle-making or millinery. These were all indentured apprentices, some of whom had paid premiums of from five to ten pounds. They were `bound' for three years. For the first two years they received no wages: the third year they got a shilling or eightpence a week. At the end of the third year they usually got the sack, unless they were willing to stay on as improvers at from three shillings to four and sixpence per week.
They worked from half past eight in the morning till eight at night, with an interval of an hour for dinner, and at half past four they ceased work for

fifteen minutes for tea. This was provided by the firm - half a pint for each girl, but they had to bring their own milk and sugar and bread and butter. Few of the girls ever learned their trades thoroughly. Some were taught to make sleeves; others cuffs or button-holes, and so on. The result was that in a short time each one became very expert and quick at one thing; and although their proficiency in this one thing would never enable them to earn a decent living, it enabled Mr Sweater to make money during the period of their apprenticeship, and that was all he cared about. Occasionally a girl of intelligence and spirit would insist on the fulfilment of the terms of her indentures, and sometimes the parents would protest. If this were persisted in those girls got on better: but even these were turned to good account by the wily Sweater, who induced the best of them to remain after their time was up by paying them what appeared - by contrast with the others girls' money - good wages, sometimes even seven or eight shillings a week! and liberal promises of future advancement. These girls then became a sort of reserve who could be called up to crush any manifestation of discontent on the part of the leading hands.

The greater number of the girls, however, submitted tamely to the conditions imposed upon them. They were too young to realize the wrong that was being done them. As for their parents, it never occurred to them to doubt the sincerity of so good a man as Mr Sweater, who was always prominent in every good and charitable work.
At the expiration of the girl's apprenticeship, if the parents complained of her want of proficiency, the pious Sweater would attribute it to idleness or incapacity, and as the people were generally poor he seldom or never had any trouble with them. This was how he fulfilled the unctuous promise made to the confiding parents at the time the girl was handed over to his tender mercy - that he would `make a woman of her'.
This method of obtaining labour by false pretences and without payment, which enabled him to produce costly articles for a mere fraction of the price for which they were eventually sold, was adopted in other departments of his business. He procured shop assistants of both sexes on the same terms. A youth was indentured, usually for five years, to be `Made a Man of and `Turned out fit to take a Position in any House'. If possible, a premium, five, ten, or twenty pounds - according to their circumstances - would be extracted from the parents. For the first three years, no wages: after that, perhaps two or three shillings a week.
At the end of the five years the work of `Making a Man of him' would be completed. Mr Sweater would then congratulate him and assure him that

he was qualified to assume a 'position' in any House but regret that there was no longer any room for him in his. Business was so bad. Still, if the Man wished he might stay on until he secured a better 'position' and, as a matter of generosity, although he did not really need the Man's services, he would pay him ten shillings per week! Provided he was not addicted to drinking, smoking, gambling or the Stock Exchange, or going to theatres, the young man's future was thus assured. Even if he were unsuccessful in his efforts to obtain another position he could save a portion of his salary and eventually commence business on his own account.

However, the branch of Mr Sweater's business to which it is desired to especially direct the reader's attention was the Homeworkers Department. He employed a large number of women making ladies' blouses, fancy aprons and children's pinafores. Most of these articles were disposed of wholesale in London and elsewhere, but some were retailed at 'Sweaters' Emporium' in Mugsborough and at the firm's other retail establishments throughout the county. Many of the women workers were widows with children, who were glad to obtain any employment that did not take them away from their homes and families.

The blouses were paid for at the rate of from two shillings to five shillings a dozen, the women having to provide their own machine and cotton, besides calling for and delivering the work. These poor women were able to clear from six to eight shillings a week: and to earn even that they had to work almost incessantly for fourteen or sixteen hours a day. There was no time for cooling and very little to cook, for they lived principally on bread and margarine and tea. Their homes were squalid, their children half-starved and raggedly clothed in grotesque garments hastily fashioned out of the cast-off clothes of charitable neighbours...

By these and similar means Adam Sweater had contrived to lay up for himself a large amount of treasure upon earth, besides attaining undoubted respectability; for that he was respectable no one questioned. He went to chapel twice every Sunday, his obese figure arrayed in costly apparel, consisting - with other things - of grey trousers, a long garment called a frock-coat, a tall silk hat, a quantity of jewellery and a morocco-bound gilt-edged Bible. He was an official of some sort of the Shining Light Chapel. His name appeared in nearly every published list of charitable subscriptions. No starving wretch had ever appealed to him in vain for a penny soup ticket. (RTP 195-198)

RTP is punctuated by scenes in which men at work took as much comfort as the could in breaks, dipping their mugs into pails of tea and eating bread and butter "disinfected" by pickled cabbage, and Robert's appreciation of rough-and-ready comradeship is apparent.

Noakes said of the company: "Their operations extended all over the town. At all hours of the day and night they could be seen carrying ladders, planks, pots of paint, pails of whitewash, earthenware chimney pots, drainpipes, lengths of guttering, closet pans, grates, bundles of wallpaper, buckets of paste, sacks of cement, and loads of brick s and mortar." (6) All of which had to be transported across hilly Hastings in handcarts.

Robert is believed to have painted a large advertisement for Adams and Jarrett on the side of its London Road building, fragments of which survived until 2006 when it was painted over. He is known to have painted another large company advertisement on the end of a house in Perth Road, Silverhill, which was visible until the 1960s Other work that Robert is believed to have done in St Leonards (although some may have been done for his previous two employers), include a scenic wall at the Buchanan Hospital, the Presbyterian Church of St Columbia on Warrior Square which was destroyed in World War Two, the Post Office in King's Road, possibly St john's Church, Hollington, and No 10 Stockleigh Road. (7)

The work was not just gruelling and uncomfortable, it could be dangerous. Robert pointed out that ladders propped up from pavements were at the mercy of boisterous children, errand boys, fat people, superstitious people, nursemaids wheeling prams whilst reading halfpenny papers detailing the love lives of the famous, the blind and ungainly people with large feet. Cost cutting had its risk for the workforce. Painting a turret or spire on some Gothic properties involved men standing on the third rung from the top, clutching whatever they could, while others steadied the ladder at the bottom.

It was cheaper to do it this way than to rig up a proper scaffold, which would have entailed perhaps two hours' work for two or three men. Of course it was very dangerous, but that did not matter at all, because even if the man fell it would make no difference to the firm - all the men were

Tressell's end wall in Perth Road, Silverhill

Insured and somehow or other, although they frequently had narrow escapes, they did not often come to grief. (RTP 401)

Unstable loads on carts, rotten floorboards and beams, burning-off lamps, sharp tools, noxious fumes, toxic chemicals, white lead, the elements and heavy materials all added to the risk. Foremen were not entirely immune. Robert's fictionalised workforce were delighted when Misery was off for three weeks after coming off his bicycle while racing to catch any workers leaving early for dinner.

Tressell's end wall in Perth Road, Silverhill

But fatalities, although not common, were not that rare either. In RTP the elderly Philpot is crushed by an exceptionally long 65-foot ladder which he and his mates were trying to manoeuvre into position to paint high gables: *The three men found the weight so overpowering, that once or twice they were compelled to relax their efforts for a few seconds, and at those times the rope had to carry the whole weight of the ladder; and the part of the rope that had to bear the greatest strain was the part that chanced to be at the angle of the brickwork at the side of the window. And presently it happened that one of the frayed and worn places that Dawson had remarked about was just at the angle during one of those momentary pauses. On one end there hung the ponderous ladder, straining the frayed rope against the corner of the brickwork and the sharp edge of the stone sill, at the other end were Dawson and Sawkins pulling with all their strength, and in that instant the rope snapped like a piece of thread. One end remained in the hands of Sawkins and Dawson, who reeled backwards into the room, and the other end flew up into the air, writhing like the lash of a gigantic whip. For a moment the heavy ladder swayed from side to side: Barrington, standing underneath, with his hands raised above his head grasping one of the rungs, struggled desperately to hold it up. At his right stood Bundy, also with arms upraised holding the side; and on the left, between the ladder and the wall, was Philpot.*

For a brief space they strove fiercely to support the overpowering weight, but Philpot had no strength, and the ladder, swaying over to the left, crashed down, crushing him upon the ground and against the wall of the house. He fell face downwards, with the ladder across his shoulders; the side that had the iron bands twisted round it fell across the back of his neck, forcing his face against the bricks at the base of the wall. He uttered no cry and was quite still, with blood streaming from the cuts on his face and trickling from his ears. Philpot was dead. (RTP 551)

His insurance money went to his landlady, an old lady of whom he was fond, as he had no known relatives. The company foremen persuaded her to give them the task of arranging the funeral and the making of the coffin, for which they received handsome commissions, but on the way the body was stolen by the rival undertaker Snatchem. The foremen snatched it back. An inquest recorded a verdict of accidental death and, despite evidence that the rope hauling up the long ladder was known to have been frayed, no blame was attached to the company.

More outrages were committed under the Adam's and Jarrett's regime, but Noakes, like other former lad apprentices interviewed by Ball, remembered fondly Robert's kindness to them and his whimsical humour. Noakes recalled working with him on high ladders within the Presbyterian Church of St Columbia where Robert was putting the finishing touches to some murals. He asked the youngster to hand him a sign-writer's straight-edge which he then swung like a pendulum in front of his face. "I was nearly hypnotised and would have fallen off the steps but Bob put out a hand and stopped me," Noakes said. (8)

His humour was more barbed with bosses. One morning Robert turned up late for work because of a sleepless night coughing. The boss, Jarrett, was waiting for him and told him he should have arrived at six am. Robert replied: "But you don't have to pay me for the lost time, do you?" Jarrett walked away without a word.

Robert's spirit was not just apparent at work. When Kathleen slipped on a sloping pavement outside the local police station, he stormed in and complained that several people had injured themselves on that same spot. Kathleen said: "Perhaps he got mad, like he did about Bert working in the cold paint-shop, and created a scene, but whatever he did or said, the pavement there was scored and so made safer for poor pedestrians." *(9)*

For Robert it was a small victory. Bigger ones would remain outside his grasp.

FATHER AND DAUGHTER ALONE

"Put your light out."

Late in 1907 or early 1908 Robert and Kathleen moved to rooms at 241 London Road, St Leonards. They went alone.

His relationship with Adelaide appears to have broken down. Although always affectionate in a brotherly and sisterly way, their differences in outlook were too broad for such intimate living conditions. Kathleen never saw her aunt again, or her other aunt Ellie who had visited from Liverpool in 1901 but who never returned.

Kathleen had never regarded Adelaide as a mother, saying: "She never forgave me for that first meeting at Cape Town, which was very foolish for a grown woman, and every now and then she would throw it up at me. But she was very good in lots of ways. I was always well dressed as she used to make most of my clothes but apparently she used to spank me because I can remember the children saying to me: 'Your aunt beats you, doesn't she?'"

Of the split Kathleen said: "Adelaide like the rest of the family did not approve of Robert's social 'descent' and possibly she came to the end of her tether and may have returned to the family.

"I don't remember them after Warrior Square except for seeing Arthur walking in crocodile with the choir boys on the way to church – all the boys in Eton suits and mortar-boards. I don't remember missing either of them or how the break came. I was always shy and retiring and with my nose in a book most of the time – I do not even remember my friends of my own age. There was a difference of age between Arthur and myself. I think Dad treated us both the same. Arthur called Dad 'Uncle Robert.' I think Arthur looked upon him as a father and that would be the relationship between them." *(1)*

Given his loving attitude to both children, Robert must have missed Arthur terribly. Maybe that is why he gave his fictional alter ego, Owen, a son rather than a daughter. Arthur was nine when he left, the same age as the fictional Frankie.

Robert and Kathleen's rooms – not a self-contained flat – were at the top of a five-storey house. There was a front living room where Robert wrote and designed, and two small bedrooms. The shared bathroom was three floors below. Robert's book may have been conceived in Milward Road, but it was here that he wrote the bulk of it.

The ground floor was taken by a cycle-shop, the Adna Cycle Depot, owned and run by their landlord, Charles Alfred Beney. He and Robert became firm friends as did Kathleen and Mrs Beney who was 12 years older than her, and 10 years younger than her husband. Kathleen said: "Mr and Mrs Beney were very nice people. Their little boy was about five years old and used to be in and out of our rooms. At one time I was 'engaged' to him – with a rubber ring out of a pop bottle, one of those that used to have marbles in the top. There was also a baby who I used to take out. Dad liked the Beneys and it was Mrs Beney who cooked the dinner on the occasion Dad asked my cousin Paul round." *(2)*

Kathleen also became friends with another lodger, Kitty Saunders, nick-named Gypsy, who was also close to Mrs Beney. It appears to have been a very happy, friendly household. That must have helped ease the trauma of single parenthood.

Len Green, whose father worked with Robert, remembered him as a "very happy man." He recalled: 'Our family always called him 'Dolphus', he had a very hearty laugh but would put his hand on his chest and I asked him once what was the matter and he said: 'I am 'one lung' in Chinese." The Green family invited Robert (and presumably Kathleen, although green could not recall her) to join them on Christmas Day 1907. "We knew he had nowhere else to go," said Green in 1968. "He danced with my sisters while the youngest, who became blind later on, played the piano for them... He always saw the funny side of things and was a jolly little chap, always laughing and singing." (3)

Kathleen had done well in her studies at St Andrew's Church of England elementary school and was top of her class. She rushed home to tell her father "I beat them all!" Robert told her curtly that was because she had enjoyed more advantages over her classmates.

Such snubs were rare, however, and Robert always encouraged Kathleen to broaden her studies well beyond those required at school. She took his advice, and friends recalled that she was always reading when they visited. Her friend Rose Cruttenden said that she even took a book to picnics and on one occasion sat reading while the rest collected blackberries. Robert believed that education was as necessary for women as for men, and he feared deeply for Kathleen's future if he succumbed to his ill health. He saw education as a way out of dire straits, particularly for following generations.

Robert's encouragement had paternal limits. Kathleen said: "I used to like to read in bed and would go on reading late and Dad would call up to me.
'Katie, is your light out?'
'No, Dad.'
'Put it out at once.'
'Oh, can't I finish this chapter?'
'Put your light out.'
'Alright.'
"And I put out my light, but darn it all it was such an exciting book that I couldn't sleep and I put on the light again and he came up and found out and thought I had lied to him before and there were ructions." (4)

Kathleen said that her father read "everything but rubbish" and was surprised by her own ability to read "the utmost trash as well as what was worthwhile."

Her studies paid off and in 1908 Kathleen received a bursary to enrol in the St Helen's pupil-teacher centre, which later became St Helen's high school for girls. The bursary was repeated the following year and she appeared to be well on the way to achieving her father's ambition for her to become a teacher. She, at various stage in her teens, had other ideas and wanted to become either a nun or an actress. Robert, despite his independent thinking and advocacy of rights of self-determination for all, was still an Edwardian father and told her no daughter of his would tread the boards.

Kathleen's pupil-teacher school was a long way from home and her father commissioned a new bicycle for her from Beney. Both were exasperated by her dare-devil riding. She said: "One time I was coming home from school the wheel of my bike got caught in the tram-lines on a hill not far from home. I was thrown and my handle-bars bent and I had to wheel it home. I don't think I was hurt but when I took it to the shop and told him what had happened, Mr Beney said, 'You know they say that there's a special providence that looks after children and fools, and you're not a child Katie!'

Robert also rebuked her once for singing a risque song called "teasing, teasing, I was only teasing you." Kathleen was now 16 and Robert must have had the same fears all loving fathers do when their daughter reaches mid-teens.

A schoolmaster friend, whom Robert converted from Toryism to socialism, wrote in her autograph book *The Golliwog Rhyme*:

A Golliwog was she of powder, paint and scent,
Who spake sweet words to all and none were meant,
She praised her sister's dress; said 'twas lovely style,
And then behind her back smiled a sarcastic smile.
God save us from all such; speed the day when we
False Gods dethrone, no more to reign,
Our own true selves may be.

Kathleen tried her best to be of use around the home to ease the pressure on her father, but she was hopeless at cooking as Aunt Adelaide had never taught her. Kathleen tried to make her father culinary treats but they were invariably a disaster. She once made rice pudding for him but the only flavouring she could find was oil of cloves bought for a toothache. She added a drop or two. "It was so awful that I couldn't even eat it to save my face."

She told Ball that she remembered until she was 17 meeting her father in a very small restaurant, possibly Pallett's eating house at 97 Bohemia Road, each day for their evening meal. "I suppose I must have made sandwiches for me to take for lunch to school and him for his lunch at work," she said. "I shiver to think what kind of lunch he had. After I was 17 I cooked our meals during the holidays and these were not very successful. I remember making a stew one time and thinking it was very successful. But when I suggested making it again, Dad said, 'Oh no.' I said, 'Well I thought you liked it,' and he said, 'Well I didn't want to hurt your feelings.'" (5)

Robert continued to struggle to make ends meet while ensuring that Kathleen had all she needed to complete her education. Their friend Edward Cruttenden said: "Robert had just enough goods and chattels to enable him and his little girl to get along."

Socialist politics continued to be fractious in Hastings, and Robert continued incorporating elements in his manuscript. In October 1907 Mr Potter of the ILP gave a lecture in the Fishmarket which was remarkably similar to *The Great Money Trick* in the novel: "Mr Potter produced a diagram showing the annual proportionate distribution of the national wealth. After placing before the gathering figures showing the taxation of luxuries he appealed to the working men to send to Parliament not those who shackled them with taxation, but those who represented the Labour Party." (6)

The Hastings ILP drew large audiences at meetings to hear such speakers as Arthur Hardy of Brighton and Paul Campbell of Walthamstow, and there was continuing friction with the SDF, which became the SDP in 1908. By August 1909 the ILP accused the SDP of holding rival meetings at the same time as that to reduce turnout. "Matters are getting lively her," the ILP reported. (7) The SDP reported back: "Our Fishmarket pitch beling in the possession of the ILP, we had to satisfy ourselves with one meeting at the Yachts." (8)

Such squabbles were overshadowed by a crackdown on all socialist and radical factions by the council, armed with new by-laws curbing public demonstrations. These were ostensibly intended to "control flower sellers, vagrant musicians and others termed undesirable..." (9) but were used to tackle dissent and events which might disturb the genteel and privileged. The council decreed that public meetings should be restricted to eight pitches along the vicinity of the three-mile promenade. But, as Cobb pointed out, that two in West St Leonards were remote and "inconvenient," three were below the tidewater mark and others were hard to access. Two traditional sites, the Yachts in Denmark Place and the Fishmarket, were restricted. "Comrades, rally!" wrote Cobb. "Hastings for the first time calls upon the movement for aid. Now for a short but sharp fight the victory will be yours and ours." (10)

But it was not the socialist movement which came to their aid, but the Salvation Army which had also been hit by the restrictions. Together they made a fearsome, if temporary alliance, and the council was forced to withdraw. It is not known whether Robert, a fervent atheist, appreciated the irony. My guess is that he did.

THE BYELECTION

"a splendid and ideal candidate"

1908 saw Hastings embroiled in another Parliamentary election, and Robert watched sardonically from the sidelines, gathering more rich material for his book.

The sitting Tory MP, Harvey Du Cros, whom Robert had seen defeating the sitting Liberal in the 1906 general election, resigned and sparked a by-election. He cited his old doctor friend from Ireland, Sir Lambert Ormsby, who had diagnosed "ill-health and the pressure of business." Du Cros said if tariff reform was introduced his business would become easier "because the foreigner would be checked." From resignation to polling day was just eight days and Du Cros assumed it would see a natural succession.

The Conservative candidate was his son Arthur, who had been born in Dublin a year after Robert in 1871, but in very different circumstance. The *Observer* described him as coming from "good stock, being descended from a notable Huguenot family, a chip off the old block." He was a friend of the financier Ernest Terah Hooley and was a founder of the Junior Imperial League. He had risen, from an elevated start, within the family firm, and in 1901 founded the Dunlop Rubber Company, converting 400 acres of Birmingham land into Fort Dunlop for the manufacture of tyres. By 1908 the firm employed over 30,000 with factories in London, Coventry and Birmingham and had many foreign subsidiaries including rubber plantations in Malaya and Ceylon. (1) He was reportedly immensely wealth with estates in Cambridgeshire and party literature claimed he provided "a living example of what may be accomplished by perseverance combined with ability and a determination to succeed." His main home was in Edgeware, London, but he bought a house at 106 Marina, St Leonards. He was, in short, a "splendid and ideal candidate." (2)

The *Observer* reported: "Without the slightest warning Hastings finds itself plunged into all the turmoil and excitement of a Parliamentary Election. The news that Mr Harvey Du Cros had resigned his seat came upon the general public like a bolt from the blue on Monday morning. Mr Du Cros' reasons for his resignation, ill health and the pressures of business, were set forth in a letter read to a crowded and enthusiastic meeting of the Unionists in the Public Hall on Monday evening. The town seemed to become immediately flooded with motor cars, literature began to fly around and everything pointed to the fact that the Conservative organisation had been brought to a high pitch of perfection." (3)

The by-election had been called so suddenly that local Liberals were forced to send a delegation to London to find a candidate. He was Robert Vernon Harcourt, the son of the late Sir William Harcourt who had first used the phrase "We're all socialists now."

The new candidate, a former diplomat, a journalist and a playwright, was also the brother of the Liberal government's First Commissioner of Works. (4)

Under the popular blue and white colours Du Cros launched his campaign on a policy platform to uphold the constitution and the House of Lords, to maintain a united Empire and the Union of England and Ireland, to support tariff reform and imperial preference in trade, and to maintain an "invincible" Royal Navy. He also supported religious education in elementary schools and a limited form of old age pensions, although on the latter he viewed "with great alarm the extravagant – almost impossible – proposal of the Socialist party." He also opposed unrestricted immigration of those refugees whom the *Sun* described as "the undesirable outcasts of Continental nations." (5)

At his first speaking engagement in Hasting, the younger Du Cros was joined on the platform by the more experienced Colonel E. Hildred Carlile, Tory MP for Mid-Hertfordshire and a vehement Free Trader. To illustrate his opposition to tariffs he described "miles of magnificent carpet which he saw in a hotel. As he thought of the work that it had provided, his temperature went up to 212 in the shade (laughter) and he asked where it was made. 'Saxony' was the reply, and his temperature dropped to 10 degrees below zero (renewed laughter)." (6)

Another contemporary newspaper account gives a flavour of the debate between the two parties:

"The speaker for Arthur Du Cros called to the crowd: "Who kept the unemployed from starving through the winter?'

'Harvey du Cros' shouted back some women in the crowd. 'Did Freeman-Thomas do that?' asked the orator.

'No!' came the chorus.

'Will Mr Harcourt do that?'

'No!'

'And who found boots for the poor little children in the cold weather?'

And the crowd, having got the cue, rejoined: 'Harvey du Cros, God Bless him!' (7)

The Liberals chanted comic verse, including:

Llyodie George bent his bow,

Aimed at a pigeon and killed Du Cros."

The Conservative candidate suffered worse than rhyming couplets when he knocked on the door of 241 London Road while canvassing for support. Mrs Beney answered and Du Cros asked to speak to Mr Noonan. Robert was entertaining Gower and his one-time Tory schoolteacher friend Mr Turner in his rooms and told her to show the candidate in. Robert gave him a chair by the fire and told him to sit. Those present later insisted that it was one of the most uncomfortable episodes in the campaign.

Du Cros began his spiel but was stopped mid-sentence by Robert who asked him about Ireland. The Tory was flabber-ghasted, never having been questioned directly by a rough working man. He stumbled through a reply and then faced a barrage of further questions about Irish history. Robert disliked Tory Irishmen, particularly rich ones, and Du Cros fitted that bill. Gower recalled: "Bob went back hundreds of years into the history of Ireland and that's where the candidate obviously wished himself at that moment. Hard words began to flow. Du Cros's agent stood at the door rattling the handle to indicate that he should break off the engagement, and Robert rose to his feet, two hectic spots glowing on his cheeks, the sign that I had got to know so well." Kathleen recalled that during the one-sided debate her father said that the problems of Ireland would not be solved until the Irish "got rid of the priests and the whiskey." But the thrust of the tirade was most likely to have been England's occupation and denial of self-rule or independence.

Robert showed Du Cros the door and politely bade him "good day" after calling him an Irish traitor and renegade. The spark for Robert's uncharacteristic temper and lack of hospitality may have been Du Cros's condescending manner. Gower said: "I never met any man, however well-educated or high up who didn't appear intellectually inferior to Bob, even in ordinary conversation. Bob was completely at ease in any company and never addressed a 'superior' as other working-men did, but as an equal." (8)

Du Cros had a strong ally in the *Hastings and St Leonards Observer*, dubbed the *Obscurer* by Robert in RTP. Its editor, Alfred Dyer, was chairman of the local Conservative Association and was later knighted for his services. His by-election editorials did not just urge overwhelming support for du Cros, but also told readers to "Be on guard against over-confidence" and "vote early." The newspaper sold for two pence every Saturday, while the *Chronicle and Advertiser* sold on Wednesdays and Thursdays respectively. The *Hastings and St Leonards Weekly Mail and Times* supported the Liberals. Other newspapers circulating in the area were the *South Weekly News, the Sussex Daily News, the Morning Argus* and *the Evening Argus*. All broadly supported one or other of the main two parties to differing degrees but none had any sympathy for Robert's brand of socialism. It was not until October that year that his SDP branch produced a "monthly journal for working people."

It is not certain which of the scenes so vividly described in RTP had their origins in the 1908 and which in the earlier 1906 election. The depictions of thuggery and hypocrisy described in an earlier chapter could have featured in either, although the balance of probabilities is that the near-riot was in 1906. But the new contest freshened up and added to the material Robert was by now pulling together for his nearly-completed book. By now Robert despaired of the refusal of so many working men to embrace socialism, and of their gullibility in accepting the word of the ruling, privileged class.

Robert describes the candidate Adam Sweater railing against socialism, and the reaction of his mainly poor audience:

`What is this Socialism that we hear so much about, but which so few understand? What is it, and what does it mean?'

Then, raising his voice till it rang through the air and fell upon the ears of the assembled multitude like the clanging of a funeral bell, he continued:

`It is madness! Chaos! Anarchy! It means Ruin! Black Ruin for the rich, and consequently, of course, Blacker Ruin still for the poor!'

As Sweater paused, a thrill of horror ran through the meeting. Men wearing broken boots and with patches upon the seats and knees, and ragged fringes round the bottoms of the legs of their trousers, grew pale, and glanced apprehensively at each other. If ever Socialism did come to pass, they evidently thought it very probable that they would have to walk about in a sort of prehistoric highland costume, without any trousers or boots at all.

Toil-worn women, most of them dressed in other women's shabby cast-off clothing - weary, tired-looking mothers who fed their children for the most part on adulterated tea, tinned skimmed milk and bread and margarine, grew furious as they thought of the wicked Socialists who were trying to bring Ruin upon them.

It never occurred to any of these poor people that they were in a condition of Ruin, Black Ruin, already. But if Sweater had suddenly found himself reduced to the same social condition as the majority of those he addressed, there is not much doubt that he would have thought that he was in a condition of Black Ruin.

The awful silence that had fallen on the panic-stricken crowd, was presently broken by a ragged-trousered Philanthropist, who shouted out:

`We knows wot they are, sir. Most of 'em is chaps wot's got tired of workin' for their livin', so they wants us to keep 'em.'

Encouraged by numerous expressions of approval from the other Philanthropists, the man continued:

`But we ain't such fools as they thinks, and so they'll find out next Monday. Most of 'em wants 'angin', and I wouldn't mind lendin' a 'and with the rope myself.' (RTP 534-535)

After one hustings Barrington recognises a former socialist, a man with a scarred face, working for the ruling party's election machine. He challenges him:

'Even if you no longer believe in working for Socialism, there's no need to work AGAINST it. If you are not disposed to sacrifice yourself in order to do good to others, you might at least refrain from doing evil. If you don't want to help to bring about a better state of affairs, there's no reason why you should help to perpetuate the present system.'

The other man laughed bitterly. 'Oh yes, there is, and a very good reason too.'

'I don't think you could show me a reason,' said Barrington.

The man with the scar laughed again, the same unpleasant, mirthless laugh, and thrusting his hand into his trouser pocket drew it out again full of silver coins, amongst which one or two gold pieces glittered.

'That is my reason. When I devoted my life and what abilities I possess to the service of my fellow workmen; when I sought to teach them how to break their chains; when I tried to show them how they might save their children from poverty and shameful servitude, I did not want them to give me money. I did it for love. And they paid me with hatred and injury. But since I have been helping their masters to rob them, they have treated me with respect.'

Barrington made no reply and the other man, having returned the money to his pocket, indicated the crowd with a sweep of his hand.

'Look at them!' he continued with a contemptuous laugh. 'Look at them! the people you are trying to make idealists of! Look at them! Some of them howling and roaring like wild beasts, or laughing like idiots, others standing with dull and stupid faces devoid of any trace of intelligence or expression, listening to the speakers whose words convey no meaning to their stultified minds, and others with their eyes gleaming with savage hatred of their fellow men, watching eagerly for an opportunity to provoke a quarrel that they may gratify their brutal natures by striking someone - their eyes are hungry for the sight of blood! Can't you see that these people, whom you are trying to make understand your plan for the regeneration of the world, your doctrine of universal brotherhood and love are for the most part - intellectually - on level with Hottentots? The only things they feel any real interest in are beer, football, betting and - of course - one other subject. Their highest ambition is to be allowed to Work. And they desire nothing better for their children!

`They have never had an independent thought in their lives. These are the people whom you hope to inspire with lofty ideals! You might just as well try to make a gold brooch out of a lump of dung! Try to reason with them, to uplift them, to teach them the way to higher things. Devote your whole life and intelligence to the work of trying to get better conditions for them, and you will find that they themselves are the enemy you will have to fight against. They'll hate you, and, if they get the chance, they'll tear you to pieces. But if you're a sensible man you'll use whatever talents and intelligence you possess for your own benefit. Don't think about Socialism or any other "ism". Concentrate your mind on getting money - it doesn't matter how you get it, but - get it. If you can't get it honestly, get it dishonestly, but get it! it is the only thing that counts. Do as I do - rob them! exploit them! and then they'll have some respect for you.' (RTP 544-545)

Such passages still have the power to shock with their vehemence but they are a sign not so much of disillusionment with the working man on Robert's part, more a sense of regret at the lack of progress, and a growing fatigue.

The SDP, trade unions and other Labour groups leafleted election meetings tirelessly. Robert and others distributed socialist material and heckled at meetings, often putting themselves in some danger. Robert's SDP branch continued to hold their own meetings. At one outside the Royal Oak in Castle Street they were surrounded by a hostile mob who shouted and jeered and broke up the meeting. The small band of socialists were manhandled and shaken, but escaped without injury.

Robert wrote a leaflet called *Under the Red Flag* for the campaign, according to Kathleen, but no copy appears to have survived.

The metaphoric red flag continued to be waved during the campaign, but to little effect:

These Socialists held quite a lot of informal meetings on their own. Every now and then when they were giving their leaflets away, some unwary supporter of the capitalist system would start an argument, and soon a crowd would gather round and listen.

Sometimes the Socialists succeeded in arguing their opponents to an absolute standstill, for the Liberals and Tones found it impossible to deny that machinery is the cause of the overcrowded state of the labour market; that the overcrowded labour market is the cause of unemployment; that the fact of there being always an army of unemployed waiting to take other men's jobs away from them destroys the independence of those who are in employment and keeps them in subjection to their masters. They found it impossible to deny that this machinery is being used, not for the benefit of all, but to make fortunes for a few. In short, they were unable to disprove that the monopoly of the land and machinery by a comparatively few persons, is the cause of the poverty of the majority. But when these arguments that they were unable to answer were put before them and when it was pointed out that the only possible remedy was the Public Ownership and Management of the Means of production, they remained angrily silent, having no alternative plan to suggest. (RTP 539-540)

Robert was also disgusted by jingoism aroused by both main parties, the violent rhetoric between two elites with more similarities than difference, the pandering to family values, the empty election literature and the meaningless slogans and posters. One Tory poster referred to in RTP *represented the interior of a public house; in front of the bar, with a quart pot in his hand, a clay pipe in his mouth, and a load of tools on his back, stood a degraded-looking brute who represented the Tory ideal of what an Englishman should be; the letterpress on the poster said it was a man! This is the ideal of manhood that they hold up to the majority of their fellow countrymen, but privately – amongst themselves – the Tory aristocrats regard such `men' with far less respect than they do the lower animals. Horses or dogs, for instance. (RTP 543)*

Robert Du Cros's children were put on display in an open touring car festooned with placards urging people to vote for their "Daddy." Du Cros was portrayed as a local family man against a government incomer – Harcourt – from London.

Such tactics worked before the term "spin" was coined for the political forum. On March 3 Robert du Cross more than doubled his father's majority to 1,018, taking 4,495 votes to Harcourt's 3,477. Turnout was slightly down on the general election, but was still an impressive 91 per cent of the electorate. Naturally, they included trade unionists and socialist defectors. One, a gas-worker called J. Allen, told Cobb he was "tired of playing the martyr, his new occupation pays him better." (9) Such arguments are reflected in RTP when Barrington asks a former socialist why he had become a Liberal. The man had been injured when struck by a stone hurled by a working man during a socialist meeting the previous year: *"I did it for love. And they paid me with hatred and injury. But since I have been helping their masters rob them, they have treated me with respect." (RTP 544)*

On polling day, out of mischief, Robert had spread rumours that the Liberal had won. But an apprentice sign-writer at Adam's and Jarrett's, a pupil of Robert's, was told to paint a board shaped like a top hat with the Conservative colours and the election result for a hired man to walk through the town.

Despite the shortness of the campaign, the outcome produced the usual drunken street brawls, as reported locally: "A huge concourse of people, principally men, youths, boys and girls, standing in the open space cheering and counter cheering and booing and yelling defiance at each other, with now and again a scrimmage between rival bands of men who swayed backwards and forwards in a mass of wrestling humanity." (10)

Harcourt shook off defeat and only had to wait a few months to enter Parliament – he was adopted as Liberal candidate in the Montrose Burghs following the sitting Member's elevation to the peerage. He was elected on May 12 1908 and was MP for a full decade.

Kathleen remembered a rhyme her father told her during this time but did not know whether it was Robert's own composition:

There was a man who lived down our street,

Who was full of aches and pains.

He fell out of the window one day

And dashed out all his brains.

And when he found he had no brains

 He became a Member of Parliament

Where brains he did not need.

Arthur Du Cros in 1909 formed the Parliamentary aerial defence committee to ensure funding for military aircraft, perhaps the only common cause he shared with Robert. In April 1913 his magnificent home in St Leonards was burned down by suffragette militants angered at his tenacious opposition to votes for women. Newspaper accounts, probably exaggerated, put the cost at around £100,000. During the Great War he worked on an honorary basis for the munitions ministry, donated two motorised ambulance convoys and was honorary colonel of the 8th battalion of the Royal Warwickshire Regiment. In 1916 he was created a baronet. He remained MP for Hastings until 1918 and was then elected to represent Clapham, but resigned four years later.

His downfall reinforced some of the stereotypes created in RTP. Even by the lax financial laws of the day he was found to be a crook. In accounting to the tax man and company regulators, he refused to distinguish between personal and company assets, plundering the latter whenever it suited him. Company funds were blatantly diverted to prop up family investments and to employ hopeless relatives in senior positions. He became a close associate of the notorious James White, a financier with a fondness for share rigging.

Such jiggery-pokery left Dunlop close to bankruptcy in 1921. By then Du Cros had lost the confidence of his shareholders and was dismissed later that year. The last three decades of his life were spent in comfortable, if disappointing, obscurity. He died in October 1955. (10)

CROOKS, THIEVES AND COUNCILLORS

" Daylight robberies were of frequent occurrence."

During his years in Hastings Robert became increasingly close to Alf Cobb, the London docker's son who had set himself up as a draper. Cobb was also a public muckraker, exposing corrupt local practice in local government and the town's ruling business cabal. Biographer Mike Matthews wrote: "While Tresesll played only a minor role in the SDF's organisation, committing his energy to writing one of the great Socialist novels, Cobb became its inspirational leader; quickly propelled from virtual obscurity as a mysterious, unknown Londoner, living under a variety of false names, to branch secretary of the Federation. He was the automatic choice of his SDF comrades in local debate or public address." (1),

There was much to uncover and he was the biggest thorn in the borough elite's side. He was dangerous because he was so often right and because he was a marvellously witty orator and rabble-rouser. The authorities responded with surveillance and attempted repression – he was bankrupted, repeatedly hauled before the bench, imprisoned and sued for libel – but he was irrepressible. By 1908 he was secretary of Robert's renamed Social Democratic Party branch. He held meetings throughout the town and sponsored candidates in ward elections.

Cobb had arrived in Hastings a year or so before Robert, in 1900 when he was 26. Like Robert he was diminutive – five feet four inches – but he made a splash wherever he went. His entrance coincided with a slump in the Hastings tourist trade and, Matthews wrote, he "was soon to drag the backward-looking spa out of its inertia... he hit the place running, shaking the sleep-walking authorities out of their reverie (2)

Cobb's business dealings were nefarious and he initially worked under an alias. But he quickly came to the attention of the authorities. In December 1900 he was summoned to the county court after backing his horse-drawn trap into a window.

Cobb, a commercial traveller in the capital, had married the previous year and had a new-born baby when he arrived to work in a draper's shop at 50

Norman Road, St Leonards. His wife, Florence, was an aspiring actress who did not take to Hastings and the lifestyle her husband provided, and she soon left, leaving their baby daughter. Florrie Kathleen, with him.

His first connection with Robert was for inexplicably shady reasons. Cobb changed his name to A.J. Thompson to run the draper's business which was co-owned by William Laite, the Liberal editor and proprietor of the *Hastings Weekly Mail and Times*, and Frederick Burton, Robert's first boss in Hastings.

The business, built on credit, failed and Cobb was sacked. Laite went on a long sea voyage to cope with nervous exhaustion, and Burton incorporated what was left of the firm in his Queen's Road ironmonger's shop. (3)

Cobb moved in with an Old Town flower seller, Polly Bassett, a well-known firebrand, and they ran a florists' together. They were inseparable until death. During the decade's first century he worked for various firms but opened his own greengrocer's in Norman Road, taking Polly's surname to confound creditors. By 1906 he had gone bankrupt, He blamed the ruthless tactics of the town's biggest greengrocery retailer, Stanley Weston, the mayor of Hastings that year. Weston is almost certainly the model for Amos Grinder in RTP, a cunning self-made man who would shut down competitors if they refused to buy foodstuffs off him by selling below price. (4) Cobb's grocery premises were later demolished when Adams and Jarrett, Robert's last employer, took over and expanded the premises.

The collapse of his commercial aspirations saw Cobb consider emigration and a Hastings émigré offered him a job as a market gardener in British Columbia. But lack of cash for the crossing stopped him. He and Robert would certainly have talked about Canada, a land, so it seemed, where the old class rules did not apply.

It was inevitable that he and Robert would become firm friends and comrades in the SDP. Matthews reckoned that Robert and Cobb joined the local branch on the same day, but that the two friends and comrades were very different in both their outlook and forms of agitation: "Alf had been encouraged as a young man to read the works of Marx. He strongly

Right to Live unemployment rally in Wellington Square, Hastings, on 10 October 1908. The speaker has a strong resemblance to Robert Noonan, and many believe this is the only photograph of him addressing a crowd.

believed in a Socialist system wrought by social change. His political instinct adhered to the practical step-by-step objectives of the Independent Labour Party. Cobb possessed a down-to-earth pragmatic faculty. He searched relentlessly for immediate remedial measures to help his fellow working man and the mass ranks of the unemployed always conspicuous in the old economically blighted Cinque Port. He regarded Robert very much as a visionary.

"Tressell, in contrast, was more the revolutionary idealist. He dreamed of the overthrow of capitalism with a greater passion and emotional intensity. While cobb led from the front – organising branch meetings, challenging opponents to public debate, standing for municipal elections – Tressell stood aside, watching, listening and recording horror=struck and fascinated by M ugsborough's misery and degredation. Both men complemented each other." (5)

Cobb's irreverent and gleeful sallies against local dignitaries were pounced upon by Robert for his own manuscript and many of the scandals uncovered by Cobb feature in barely disguised form in the book.

Cobb referred to the chief constable's sword of office as "that cheese-cutter" and described the Workhouse Master as "that retired skilly-server." At public meetings he gave out the addresses of councillors and officials so that they could view their gardens crammed with shrubs, plants and flowers bought with ratepayers' money to stock the public Alexandria Park. They could also see drives surfaced with Corporation asphalt. His slogan was: "Many are called – but few get up."

Robert's description of the borough council and its members matched Cobb's view:

The town of Mugsborough was governed by a set of individuals called the Municipal Council. Most of these `representatives of the people' were well-to-do or retired tradesmen. In the opinion of the inhabitants of Mugsborough, the fact that a man had succeeded in accumulating money in business was a clear demonstration of his fitness to be entrusted with the business of the town.

Consequently, when that very able and successful man of business Mr George Rushton was put up for election to the Council he was returned by a large majority of the votes of the working men who thought him an ideal personage ...

These Brigands did just as they pleased. No one ever interfered with them. They never consulted the ratepayers in any way. Even at election time they did not trouble to hold meetings: each one of them just issued a kind of manifesto setting forth his many noble qualities and calling upon the people for their votes: and the latter never failed to respond. They elected the same old crew time after time....

The Brigands committed their depredations almost unhindered, for the voters were engaged in the Battle of Life. Take the public park for instance. Like so many swine around a trough - they were so busily engaged in this battle that most of them had no time to go to the park, or they might have noticed that there were not so many costly plants there as there should have been. And if they had inquired further they would have discovered that nearly all the members of the Town Council had very fine gardens. There was reason for these gardens being so grand, for the public park was systematically robbed of its best to make them so.

There was a lake in the park where large numbers of ducks and geese were kept at the ratepayers' expense. In addition to the food provided for these fowl with public money, visitors to the park used to bring them bags of biscuits and bread crusts. When the ducks and geese were nicely fattened the Brigands used to carry them off and devour them at home. When they became tired of eating duck or goose, some of the Councillors made arrangements with certain butchers and traded away the birds for meat. (RTP 194-195)

The parks and gardens scandal was one which, in real life, outraged local ratepayers. The parks superintendent, C.W. Kerswel, was found to have set aside large tracts of municipal grounds to cultivate plants and flowers for his own profit. Public employees were ordered to tend them, dig up the crops and load them into carts and delivered to the homes of eminent councillors. When the scandal broke the head gardener was scapegoated and tendered his resignation. The councillors avoided any sanctions. Alf Cobb, in a public speech, said that as long as the people of Hastings voted for such men, "they must look out for such occurrences: these individuals put up for election not to represent the ratepayers, but to get something for themselves." (6)

Robert named the most "energetic" members of the Forty Thieves as Jeremiah Didlum, a house-furnisher; Amos Grinder, who had a practical monopoly of the greengrocery trade and Adam Sweater, the chief of the band, several times Mayor and the Liberal candidate in the Parliamentary elections. The latter was Robert's top target, a rich businessman whose house he had worked in and the town's top citizen: *"A bright `honour', forsooth! to be the first citizen in a community composed for the most part of ignorant semi-imbeciles, slaves, slave-drivers and psalm-singing hypocrites. (RTP 195)*

Earlier, Robert had described Sweater as a *very tall, obese figure, with a large, fleshy, coarse-featured, clean-shaven face, and a great double chin, the complexion being of the colour and appearance of the fat of uncooked bacon. (RTP 106-107)*

An SDF rally on the beach, July 1908

Sweater, as shown in a previous chapter, was a ruthless exploiter whose sins were hidden behind church and respectability. Robert let rip, not just at such villains, but at the gullible who elected them:

Small wonder that when this good and public-spirited man offered his services to the town - free of charge - the intelligent working men of Mugsborough accepted his offer with enthusiastic applause. The fact that he had made money in business was a proof of his intellectual capacity. His much-advertised benevolence was a guarantee that his abilities would be used to further not his own private interests, but the interests of every section of the community, especially those of the working classes, of whom the majority of his constituents was composed.

As for the shopkeepers, they were all so absorbed in their own business - so busily engaged chasing their employees, adding up their accounts, and dressing themselves up in feeble imitation of the `Haristocracy' - that they were incapable of taking a really intelligent interest in anything else. They thought of the Town Council as a kind of Paradise reserved exclusively for jerry-builders and successful tradesmen. Possibly, some day, if they succeeded in making money, they might become town councillors themselves! but in the meantime public affairs were no particular concern of theirs. So some of them voted for Adam Sweater because he was a Liberal and some of them voted against him for the same `reason'

Now and then, when details of some unusually scandalous proceeding of the Council's leaked out, the townspeople - roused for a brief space from *their customary indifference - would discuss the matter in a casual, half-indignant, half-amused, helpless sort of way; but always as if it were something that did not directly concern them. It was during some such nine days' wonder that the title of `The Forty Thieves' was bestowed on the members of the Council by their semi-imbecile constituents, who, not possessing sufficient intelligence to devise means of punishing the culprits, affected to regard the manoeuvres of the Brigands as a huge joke. There was only one member of the Council who did not belong to the Band - Councillor Weakling, a retired physician; but unfortunately he also was a respectable man. When he saw something going forwards that he did not think was right, he protested and voted against it and then - he collapsed! There was nothing of the low agitator about HIM. As for the Brigands, they laughed at his protests and his vote did not matter. With this one exception, the other members of the band were very similar in character to Sweater, Rushton, Didlum and Grinder. They had all joined the Band with the same objects, self-glorification and the advancement of their private interests. These were the real reasons why they besought the ratepayers to elect them to the Council, but of course none of them ever admitted that such was the case. No! When these noble-minded altruists offered their services to the town they asked the people to believe that they were actuated by a desire to give their time and abilities for the purpose of furthering the interests of Others, which was much the same as asking them to believe that it is possible for the leopard to change his spots. Owing to the extraordinary apathy of the other inhabitants, the Brigands were able to carry out their depredations undisturbed. Daylight robberies were of frequent occurrence. (RTP 198-199)*

RTP is littered with examples of entwined business and council corruption. The misappropriation of flora to stock the gardens of councillors is repeated. And when Sweater and Rushton, both councillors, are negotiating the cost of drains from Sweater's refurbished house, there is the following exchange:

'I've been thinking over this business lately,' said Sweater, looking at Rushton with a cunning leer. `I don't see why I should have to pay for the connecting pipe. The Corporation ought to pay for that. What do you say?' Rushton laughed. `I don't see why not,' he replied.
`I think we could arrange it all right, don't you?' Sweater went on. `Anyhow, the work will have to be done, so you'd better let 'em get on with it. £55.0.0. covers both jobs, you say? `Yes.'

'Oh, all right, you get on with it and we'll see what can be done with the Corporation later on.' 'I don't suppose we'll find 'em very difficult to deal with,' said Rushton with a grin, and Sweater smiled agreement. (RTP 111)

Of course, the close relationship between businessmen-councillors did not prevent them cheating each other. In RTP Rushton estimates that Owen's work on the Cave's drawing room, including materials, will cost £15 but doesn't hesitate to charge Sweater £45.

The cheating of customers by skimping on materials, inflating costs and literally papering over deficiencies has already been described in detail. But Robert also exposed blatant theft:

Rushton and Misery robbed everybody. They made a practice of annexing every thing they could lay their hands upon, provided it could be done without danger to themselves. They never did anything of a heroic or dare-devil character: they had not the courage to break into banks or jewellers' shops in the middle of the night, or to go out picking pockets: all their robberies were of the sneak-thief order. At one house that they `did up' Misery made a big haul. He had to get up into the loft under the roof to see what was the matter with the water tank. When he got up there he found a very fine hall gas lamp made of wrought brass and copper with stained and painted glass sides. Although covered with dust, it was otherwise in perfect condition, so Misery had it taken to his own house and cleaned up and fixed in the hall.
In the same loft there were a lot of old brass picture rods and other fittings, and three very good planks, each about ten feet in length; these latter had been placed across the rafters so that one could walk easily and safely over to the tank. But Misery thought they would be very useful to the firm for whitewashing ceilings and other work, so he had them taken to the yard along with the old brass, which was worth about fourpence a pound.

There was another house that had to be painted inside: the people who used to live there had only just left: they had moved to some other town, and the house had been re-let before they vacated it.

The new tenant had agreed with the agent that the house was to be renovated throughout before he took possession.
The day after the old tenants moved away, the agent gave Rushton the key so that he could go to see what was to be done and give an estimate for the work. While Rushton and Misery were looking over the house they

discovered a large barometer hanging on the wall behind the front door: it had been overlooked by those who removed the furniture. Before returning the key to the agent, Rushton sent one of his men to the house for the barometer, which he kept in his office for a few weeks to see if there would be any inquiries about it. If there had been, it would have been easy to say that he had brought it there for safety - to take care of till he could find the owner. The people to whom it belonged thought the thing had been lost or stolen in transit, and afterwards one of the workmen who had assisted to pack and remove the furniture was dismissed from his employment on suspicion of having had something to do with its disappearance. No one ever thought of Rushton in connection with the matter, so after about a month he had it taken to his own dwelling and hung up in the hall near the carved oak marble-topped console table that he had sneaked last summer from 596 Grand Parade. And there it hangs unto this day: and close behind it, supported by cords of crimson silk, is a beautiful bevelled-edged card about a foot square, and upon this card is written, in letters of gold: `Christ is the head of this house; the unseen Guest at every meal, the silent Listener to every conversation.' And on the other side of the barometer is another card of the same kind and size which says: `As for me and my house we will serve the Lord.'

From another place they stole two large brass chandeliers. *This house had been empty for a very long time, and its owner - who did not reside in the town - wished to sell it. The agent, to improve the chances of a sale, decided to have the house overhauled and redecorated. Rushton & Co.'s tender being the lowest, they got the work. The chandeliers in the drawing-room and the dining-room were of massive brass, but they were all blackened and tarnished. Misery suggested to the agent that they could be cleaned and relacquered, which would make them equal to new: in fact, they would be better than new ones, for such things as these were not made now, and for once Misery was telling the truth. The agent agreed and the work was done: it was an extra, of course, and as the firm got twice as much for the job as they paid for having it done, they were almost satisfied. When this and all the other work was finished they sent in their account and were paid. (RTP 405-406)*

Other examples of downright theft by the bosses and foremen included the removal of shrubs and ornamental plants from the garden of an absent landlord, light fittings, venetian blinds and an elaborately carved oak table.

Such venality was dwarfed by real-life scandals involving businessmen and councillors who saw knew how to make a killing out of 'public duty.'

In April 1902 the council bought eleven and a half acres of agricultural land at Bohemia from the estate of the late Miss Brisco. Alderman Tuppenney said that something "wonderful" could be done by incorporating the land into White Rock Gardens. He said that the asking price of £20,000 was a real bargain, and another councillor assured his colleagues that on the open market the land would be worth £3,000 an acre, or almost £35,000 for the package. The land was duly bought at the asking price, but remained undeveloped. By 1908 the council decided to resell it for just £8,000. The campaigning publication *Justice* stormed: "The worthy Councillors who had some years previously waxed eloquent of the glorious advantage that they had obtained for the town, came again before the public and assured their poor silly dupes – the townspeople - that it would be in the best interests of the town..." (7)

Questions remain unanswered about the whole sorry affair: Who benefited most from the original purchase at an inflated price, and from the subsequent sale at a knock-down price? Which solicitors and land agents represented whom? Which councillors facilitated the deal in which local ratepayers lost £12,000 plus interest and associated costs? Such unanswered questions fed into the public's consciousness the belief that business benefits were a normal perk of municipal power. Robert saw it as simple crookery.

The ruthlessness amongst the business community in Hastings was exposed by a war between the new power suppliers. Robert followed the extraordinary machinations between the Electric Light Works, the Gas Company and the borough council to light streets and homes and power local industries. That sordid tale, which ran throughout Robert's stay in Hastings, involved corruption and bribery as the two power interests competed for dominance resulting in the imposition on the gas firm of an extra duty on coal, the building of a new gas-works just outside the borough boundary to avoid that tax, and the council's purchase of the electricity company at an inflated price based on the valuation of an "independent" expert.

In February 1899 the Corporation valued the privately-owned Electric Light Company at around £60,000, including assets and goodwill, and that price was agreed with the owners. When the time came for the public purchase, however, a report from a Professor Robinson commissioned by the public lighting committee assessed that actual value at £40,000. That was ignored by the council who went ahead and paid the previous owners the top whack with ratepayers' money.

Robert exposed the scam in RTP by describing how four "brigands" – Sweater, Rushton, Didlum and Grinder – major shareholders of the private electric company first considered declaring it bankrupt as losses grew due to outdated and broken machinery and competition from the gas company:

`Well, what do you propose, then?' demanded Grinder. `Reconstruct the company? Ask the shareholders for more money? Pull down the works and build fresh, and buy some new machinery? And then most likely not make a do of it after all? Not for me, old chap! I've 'ad enough. You won't catch me chuckin' good money after bad in that way.'
`Nor me neither,' said Rushton.
`Dead orf!' remarked Didlum, very decidedly.
Sweater laughed quietly. `I'm not such a fool as to suggest anything of that sort,' he said. `You seem to forget that I am one of the largest shareholders myself. No. What I propose is that we Sell Out.'
`Sell out!' replied Grinder with a contemptuous laugh in which the others joined. `Who's going to buy the shares of a concern that's practically bankrupt and never paid a dividend?' `I've tried to sell my little lot several times already,' said Didlum with a sickly smile, `but nobody won't buy 'em.'
`Who's to buy?' repeated Sweater, replying to Grinder. `The municipality of course! The ratepayers. Why shouldn't Mugsborough go in for Socialism as well as other towns?' Rushton, Didlum and Grinder fairly gasped for breath: the audacity of the chief's proposal nearly paralysed them. `I'm afraid we should never git away with it,' ejaculated Didlum, as soon as he could speak. `When the people tumbled to it, there'd be no hend of a row.' `PEOPLE! ROW!' replied Sweater, scornfully. `The majority of the people will never know anything about it! (RTP 307-308)

Robert's fiction mirrored reality and the sale went through. Eventually similar questions were raised as in the Brisco estate affair, but they remained unanswered. In 1909 *Justice* reported that company shares with a face value of £100 had, before the handover, been selling for just £7 10s in local auctioneers' and were hastily withdrawn before the public purchase. The publication said: "Negotiations were opened, which resulted in the town paying over £60,000 for the concern so that £100 shares which could not find purchasers became worth £120." (8)

Meanwhile, business was booming for the local Gas Company, and its shares remained at a high premium. To increase profits and dividends even further the board of directors decided to shift its gasworks to a new site on unoccupied sea front ground between St Leonards and Bexhill. That was outside the borough boundary and therefore avoided a coal tax. Planning permission was granted even though a gasworks was hardly an adornment to a promenade meant to attract rich visitors, and even though the privately-owned and prosperous gas company was in direct competition to the struggling, corporation-owned electric company. The reason was a simple clash of interests which went unaddressed – several councillors were both shareholders and directors of the gas company, while some were also former shareholders in the disbanded electric company.

Justice railed: "Hastings local authorities would appear rotten to the core. Where one does not find jobbery and robbery, one finds gross mismanagement. Where one does not find the latter, he will find a scandal." (9)

The electric and gas manoeuverings were boiled down into farce in RTP:

For many years these Brigands had looked with greedy eyes upon the huge profits of the Gas Company. They thought it was a beastly shame that those other bandits should be always raiding the town and getting clear away with such rich spoils.
At length - about two years ago - after much study and many private consultations, a plan of campaign was evolved; a secret council of war was held, presided over by Mr Sweater, and the Brigands formed themselves into an association called `The Mugsborough Electric Light Supply and Installation Coy. Ltd.', and bound themselves by a solemn oath to do their best to drive the Gas Works Bandits out of the town and to capture the spoils at present enjoyed by the latter for themselves. There was a large piece of ground, the property of the town, that was a suitable site for the works; so in their character of directors of the Electric Light Coy. they offered to buy this land from the Municipality - or, in other words, from themselves - for about half its value.
At the meeting of the Town Council when this offer was considered, all the members present, with the solitary exception of Dr Weakling, being

shareholders in the newly formed company, Councillor Rushton moved a resolution in favour of accepting it. He said that every encouragement should be given to the promoters of the Electric Light Coy., those public-spirited citizens who had come forward and were willing to risk their capital in an undertaking that would be a benefit to every class of residents in the town that they all loved so well. (Applause.) There could be no doubt that the introduction of the electric light would be a great addition to the attractions of Mugsborough, but there was another and more urgent reason that disposed him to do whatever he could to encourage the Company to proceed with this work. Unfortunately, as was usual at that time of the year (Mr Rushton's voice trembled with emotion) the town was full of unemployed. (The Mayor, Alderman Sweater, and all the other Councillors shook their heads sadly; they were visibly affected.) There was no doubt that the starting of that work at that time would be an inestimable boon to the working-classes. As the representative of a working-class ward he was in favour of accepting the offer of the Company. (Hear. Hear.)

Councillor Didlum seconded. In his opinion, it would be nothing short of a crime to oppose anything that would provide work for the unemployed. Councillor Weakling moved that the offer be refused. (Shame.) He admitted that the electric light would be an improvement to the town, and in view of the existing distress he would be glad to see the work started, but the price mentioned was altogether too low. It was not more than half the value of the land. (Derisive laughter.)
Councillor Grinder said he was astonished at the attitude taken up by Councillor Weakling. In his (Grinder's) opinion it was disgraceful that a member of the council should deliberately try to wreck a project which would do so much towards relieving the unemployed.
The Mayor, Alderman Sweater, said that he could not allow the amendment to be discussed until it was seconded: if there were no seconder he would put the original motion. There was no seconder, because everyone except Weakling was in favour of the resolution, which was carried amid loud cheers, and the representatives of the ratepayers proceeded to the consideration of the next business.
Councillor Didlum proposed that the duty on all coal brought into the borough be raised from two shillings to three shillings per ton. Councillor Rushton seconded. The largest consumer of coal was the Gas Coy., and, considering the great profits made by that company, they were quite justified in increasing the duty to the highest figure the Act permitted. After a feeble protest from Weakling, who said it would only increase the

price of gas and coal without interfering with the profits of the Gas Coy.,
this was also carried, and after some other business had been transacted,
the Band dispersed.

That meeting was held two years ago, and since that time the Electric Light
Works had been built and the war against the gasworks carried on
vigorously. After several encounters, in which they lost a few customers and
a portion of the public lighting, the Gasworks Bandits retreated out of the
town and entrenched themselves in a strong position beyond the borough
boundary, where they erected a number of gasometers. They were thus
enabled to pour gas into the town at long range without having to pay the
coal dues.
This masterly stratagem created something like a panic in the ranks of the
Forty Thieves. At the end of two years they found themselves exhausted
with the protracted campaign, their movements hampered by a lot of worn-
out plant and antiquated machinery, and harassed on every side by the
lower charges of the Gas Coy. They were reluctantly constrained to admit
that the attempt to undermine the Gasworks was a melancholy failure, and
that the Mugsborough Electric Light and Installation Coy. was a veritable
white elephant. They began to ask themselves what they should do with it;
and some of them even urged unconditional surrender, or an appeal to the
arbitration of the Bankruptcy Court.
In the midst of all the confusion and demoralization there was, however,
one man who did not lose his presence of mind, who in this dark hour of
disaster remained calm and immovable, and like a vast mountain of flesh
reared his head above the storm, whose mighty intellect perceived a way to
turn this apparently hopeless defeat into a glorious victory. That man was
Adam Sweater, the Chief of the Band. (RTP 199-201)

Another scandal which Robert read about shortly after his arrival
concerned the purchase of 18 acres in Elphinstone Road as the site for a
new workhouse. It cost £14,000 in 1901, plus £4,000 in fees to a prominent
local architect, but the workhouse was never built because it would "lower
the tone of the neighbourhood."

Robert scoured the local press, despite his disdain for the *Obscurer*, for
other such examples of venality. His book, his great project, took shape.

COMPLETION, REJECTION AND DECLINE

"Through the deathlike silence of the night"

Robert embarked on a frenzy of writing in what spare time he had during his fifty-six and a half hour working week. That spare time increased from Sundays and late nights as Robert grew increasingly ill and had to take more and more unpaid sick leave from Adam's and Jarrett's. His workmate, Noakes, said: "By this time he was a very sick man and couldn't do a full week and was losing a lot of time." Gower said that he looked "thinner and thinner."

Another contemporary, Mr Cradduck, joined the firm as an apprentice sign-writer and said: "Bob was very thin and looked a sick man. He used to come to work for about two days and then he would be away for two or three weeks. He always looked cold and pinched as if he needed a good meal. I was only 17 and offered myself for 2d or 3d an hour less than the rate and I said to Bob, 'Don't think I've come to cut you out of your job.' And he said, 'Don't worry about that at all, son.'" (1)

He hid most of his predicament from Kathleen, who only noticed that "he would have recurrent attacks of bronchitis and would cough and cough." Robert wrote of Owen: *As time went on the long-continued privation began to tell... He had a severe cough: his eyes became deeply sunken and of remarkable brilliancy, and his thin face was always either deathly pale or dyed with a crimson flush. (RTP 331)*

Robert was both shocked and amused by the recommended diet for consumptives – over three pints of milk throughout the day, coffee, chocolate, bread and butter, egg and bacon, fish and roast mutton, or a mutton chop with as much fat as possible, vegetables, milk pudding, two eggs or oatmeal. Robert wrote: *As far as the majority of those who suffered from consumption are concerned, the good doctor might just as well have prescribed a trip to the moon. (RTP 347)*

It is difficult to see how Robert made ends meet during those last years of regular sickness. From home he wrote showcards for shopkeepers, had letter-heads advertising his own abilities printed, and did odd jobs. No doubt he also took credit from grocers' and pawned belongings, as Owen did in the book. He also continued to write coffin-plates for Adam's and Jarrett's for piece-rate payment. The firm had the contract to provide them for all Poor Law funerals in the borough. All those who died in workhouses or were buried as paupers where entitled to a plate, but only inscribed with their name and age at death. Robert wrote of Owen's similar predicament:

Owen was alternately dejected and maddened by the knowledge of his own helplessness: when he was not doing anything for Rushton he went about the town trying to find some other work, but usually with scant success. He did some samples of showcard and window tickets and endeavoured to get some orders by canvassing the shops in the town, but this was also a failure, for these people generally had a ticket-writer to whom they usually gave their work. He did get a few trifling orders, but they were scarcely worth doing at the price he got for them. He used to feel like a criminal when he went into the shops to ask them for the work, because he realized fully that, in effect, he was saying to them: `Take your work away from the other man, and employ me.' He was so conscious of this that it gave him a shamefaced manner, which, coupled as it was with his shabby clothing, did not create a very favourable impression upon those he addressed, who usually treated him with about as much courtesy as they would have extended to any other sort of beggar. Generally, after a day's canvassing, he returned home unsuccessful and faint with hunger and fatigue. (RTP 332)

He may also occasionally have earned money for articles. Kathleen said: "When we were at 241 every now and again he would give me some money for 'riotous living' as he called it. I don't remember how much it could be – two shillings? Five? This makes me think that he must have occasionally sold articles or short stories for he would not have been able to do that out of his wages and it must have been spasmodic and not a fund he could draw on at will or he could have used it when unemployed." Kathleen may not have full recognised her father's predicament, but she was aware that times were hard: "One time when we were hard up we were having some soup. There was only enough for him so I dirtied a soup-plate and put it in the sink and saved the soup for him and when he came in he said I might have waited and had my supper with him and I said, 'Well, I was too hungry to wait', and II don't know now which would have hurt him most, the fact that I had not waited for him or that fact that I'd gone without and he'd eaten it. That was the only time I can remember being short of food." *(2)*

Despite poverty and illness, Robert was obsessed with finishing his book. Kathleen recalled that period in their London Road rooms: "...he had this large table and papers all over it and sometimes he would be writing and didn't like what he had written and he'd just screw it up and throw it aside, but you daren't go and pick it up again because it was quite possible that if you cleared up those papers and threw them out he'd want them back again. So I had to leave him to clear up his mess. I can still see the screwed-up papers lying around the floor.

"I can see that room. As you went in, right opposite the door was his bed and at the head of that on the side where the fireplace was, there were books up to the ceiling...

"I can remember Robert drinking tea – tea was his drink. He had said at one time that he could understand how difficult it was for men to give up drinking beer and stuff because if he had to give up drinking *tea*, he didn't know whether he could do it. He used to smoke but he never bought packages of cigarettes but used to buy them loose." (3)

Degrees of despair appear to have influenced his writing, and a dark anger against working men who refused to fight on behalf of themselves and, more importantly, their children:

It was a pathetic and wonderful and at the same time a despicable spectacle. Pathetic that human beings should be condemned to spend the greater part of their lives amid such surroundings, because it must be remembered that most of their time was spent on some job or other. When `The Cave' was finished they would go to some similar `job', if they were lucky enough to find one. Wonderful, because although they knew that they did more than their fair share of the great work of producing the necessaries and comforts of life, they did not think they were entitled to a fair share of the good things they helped to create! And despicable, because although they saw their children condemned to the same life of degradation, hard labour and privation, yet they refused to help to bring about a better state of affairs. Most of them thought that what had been good enough for themselves was good enough for their children.
It seemed as if they regarded their own children with a kind of contempt, as being only fit to grow up to be the servants of the children of such people as Rushton and Sweater. But it must be remembered that they had been taught self-contempt when they were children. In the so-called `Christian'

schools they attended then they were taught to `order themselves lowly and reverently towards their betters', and they were now actually sending their own children to learn the same degrading lessons in their turn! They had a vast amount of consideration for their betters, and for the children of their betters, but very little for their own children, for each other, or for themselves.

That was why they sat there in their rags and ate their coarse food, and cracked their coarser jokes, and drank the dreadful tea, and were content! So long as they had Plenty of Work and plenty of - Something - to eat, and somebody else's cast-off clothes to wear, they were content! And they were proud of it. They gloried in it. They agreed and assured each other that the good things of life were not intended for the `Likes of them', or their children. (RTP208-208

Robert's manuscript also shows increasing anger of workmates who fail to support each other, ignoring blatant injustice through fear of getting the sack. That manifested itself in grovelling to the bosses, having no sympathy for those who were dismissed, and laughing and sneering at the unfortunate: *With a few exceptions, they had an immense amount of respect for Rushton and Hunter, and very little respect or sympathy for each other.*

Exactly the same lack of feeling for each other prevailed amongst the members of all the different trades. Everybody seemed glad if anybody got into trouble for any reason whatever. There was a garden gate that had been made at the carpenter's shop: it was not very well put together, and for the usual reason; the man had not been allowed the time to do it properly. After it was fixed, one of his shopmates wrote upon it with lead pencil in big letters: `This is good work for a joiner. Order one ton of putty.' But to hear them talking in the pub of a Saturday afternoon just after pay-time one would think them the best friends and mates and the most independent spirits in the world, fellows whom it would be very dangerous to trifle with, and who would stick up for each other through thick and thin. All sorts of stories were related of the wonderful things they had done and said; of jobs they had `chucked up', and masters they had `told off': of pails of whitewash thrown over offending employers, and of horrible assaults and batteries committed upon the same. But strange to say, for some reason or other, it seldom happened that a third party ever witnessed any of these prodigies. It seemed as if a chivalrous desire to spare the feelings *of their victims had always prevented them from doing or saying anything to them in the presence of witnesses.* (RTP 417)

It remains a matter of speculation when he finished the manuscript, but it cannot have been earlier than April 1908 because he refers in a later chapter to the Territorial Force (later Army) which was created than. As Ball pointed out, however, the bulk must have been completed before the beginning of 1909 when social measures introduced by the Liberal government, including an embryonic pension, welfare state and employment exchange network, came into effect, including old age pensions, Labour exchanges, school medical inspections and the regulation of child employment outside school hours. The whole tone of the book is of the era just before such reforms. In chapter seven he quoted the *Daily Mail Yearbook* for 1907, and the main "live" political debate in RTP – tariff reform – culminated in the 1906 general election.

The best likelihood is that he finished his main draft early in 1909 and then spent a year or more amending it and then carefully writing out the completed manuscript with Kathleen's help. Robert gave a hint at what he felt on completion by describing Owen's emotions when he completed the ornate drawing room decoration at The Cave: *"Now that it was finished he felt something like one aroused from a dream to the stern realities and terrors of life."* Robert continued: *For the last month he had forgotten that he was ill; he had forgotten that when the work at `The Cave' was finished he would have to stand off with the rest of the hands. In brief, he had forgotten for the time being that, like the majority of his fellow workmen, he was on the brink of destitution, and that a few weeks of unemployment or idleness meant starvation. As far as illness was concerned, he was even worse off than most others, for the greater number of them were members of some sick benefit club, but Owen's ill-health rendered him ineligible for membership of such societies. (RTP 226)*

His friend Edward Cruttenden provided evidence that Robert still had the manuscript in April 1910. Cruttenden was also a friend of George Meek, the Eastbourne socialist who embarked on a walking tour of Sussex and Kent SDF branches to spread the word. At Sandgate in 1906 or 1907 he called on the eminent H.G. Wells who suggested that he wrote a book about his experiences. That book, *George Meek, Bath Chairman*, was published by Constable in April 1910. Cruttenden gave Robert a copy and Robert's verdict was "too Meek and mild."

Fred Ball, after interviewing an elderly Cruttenden in the early 1950s, mistakenly added to the myth that Meek's book inspired him to do better and the result was RTP. But by then Robert had virtually completed his, but had yet to send it to a publisher. Ball put the record straight: "It couldn't have been Meek's *book* which fired Robert because his own book was by all accounts then completed, but he would have known about Meek's book in the making; Meek was well acquainted with Robert's friend Cruttenden and I'm sure that when Cruttenden told me that Meek's *book* fired Robert he meant that when he heard that a man he knew and a man in extremely humble circumstance, a bath chairman, was actually writing a book and was talking of getting a man as famous as Wells to write a preface he *was* fired – by this knowledge. And *that* even if he had already begun on his own." (4)

Incidentally, Ball disagreed with Robert's verdict that Meek's book was too mild: "...it is a much better book than I expected to read, it contains a damning indictment of social conditions and much social history of his life period, much of it very sad, and it is completely honest, if a little self-centred. It was one of the first genuine accounts of working class life written by a genuine worker, one of the lowest in the social scale at that. In this Meek is more 'genuine' than Robert himself who had the advantage of some education and of not coming quite from off the floor." (5)

Shortly after April 1910 Cruttenden recalled Robert completing the final manuscript: "I could always find him on Sunday morning seated at a desk busy with his classic. He never told me the title but he assured me it was to be something better than George Meek's, which I had lent him."

In the writing, Robert had already dubbed the working class as society's real philanthropists who worked a lifetime to benefit others. J.H. Poynton wrote: "I think the reason he gave the book such an unusual title was that the local press at the time was boosting up a gentleman who had given large sums to the hospital. Bob used to say that the workers were the real Philanthropists but didn't know it." (6) Robert had also read Wordsworth who in his youth had planned to produce a Republican Journal to be called *The Philanthropist*.

Robert first considered calling it *The Ragged-Arsed Philanthropists*, but changed it to *Trousered*. Robert and his workmates would never have themselves used such a prissy phrase, but he either realised himself, or was persuaded by another, that such crudity would not be accepted by respectable potential publishers.

Robert, in completing his book, was also well aware that it was, in legal terms, libellous to Hastings bigwigs, employers and public figures, critical of friends and acquaintances, and revealed many public and private scandals. He had to live and work in the town and could not do that if he was blacklisted or prosecuted or both. His answer was to slightly change the geographical location and disguise the main characters with Dickensian names such as Slyme, Sweater, Grinder and Crass.

Another safeguard was to adopt a pseudonym. At first he considered calling himself Robert Croker but was afraid that people would say "Croker by name and Croaker by nature." The inspiration was all around him in the trestle tables which are used by by house-painters and sign-writers. He signed himself 'Robert Tressell' (although that was later misspelt as 'Tressall).') It is measure of Robert's confidence that his book would be published and sell well that he went to such lengths.

The final draft was around 250,000 words in 1,674 pages plus a title page, a five-page list of chapter headings, a five-page preface and a five-page unfinished chapter entitled "Mugsborough, Sweater, Rushton, Didlum and Grinder." (7) There were also several drawings and Kathleen suggested that he intended to create more illustrations. The draft was written with different inks and pens, and several half-page passages were deleted. There were minor alterations: most children's names were changed; the Great Money Trick was originally performed by Barrington; and the term' government' was replaced with 'State.' Abbreviations for 'bloody' were sometimes restored, sometimes changed to 'damn'. There were few spelling mistakes, and those there were carefully corrected.

Kathleen said: "Then he had someone make a tin box with a handle in which to keep the manuscript for sending to publishers. So far as I know it was just packed consecutively. I don't know whether it was in chapters or not – my memory is just of a box of loose paper."

After interviewing Kathleen at length, Ball wrote: "Into this manuscript he had put all the honesty and fervour he had. He had written a unique book, the only one of its kind. Perhaps it would make history. Perhaps he could now emancipate himself from drudgery, poverty and perhaps even from ill-health and give Kathleen a new life." (8)

Robert and his daughter discussed what they would do with the money they earned from it. They agreed that first they would travel around the world together, not on a luxury liner, but as the only passengers on a little tramp steamer which would stop at all the out-of-the-way ports, and "after wards they would see."

Kathleen went on: "Once when we were talking about investments and interest, I said to him. 'Supposing something happened to you and I got the money for the book, aren't I entitled to have that?', and he said. 'Yes, you are, but if you wanted to invest it, before you could touch the interest you'd have to make sure that the workers who were providing that interest were being properly paid.'" (9)

It was a fantasy, of course, if an understandable one. Robert and his daughter were emboldened by the joy of completing a five-year literary project and encouraged by the success that year of Robert Blatchford's *Merrie England* which celebrated the growing working class movement.

Robert sent off his massive, beautifully hand-written document of nearly 1,700 quarto sheets in the tin box to the first publisher they could think of. Soon after it was returned unread with a note saying that it was too long and that the company insisted on typescript.

Robert may have sent it to Blatchford – although Ball could find no reference to it in the Manchester central library's archive of Blatchford papers – and to Henry M. Hyndman. He certainly sent it to Constable's but it was again rejected as 'unwieldy'. His unfinished preface may have been an attempt to explain it to potential publishers and to vouch for its authenticity, but the fact that it is unfinished is evidence that he quickly lost heart. Kathleen said: "When the book had been returned from some three publishers with the same comments, Robert did not even try and read it again, overcome by its faults and lack of typescript. It would probably have had the same fate as the model of the airship if I hadn't rescued it." (10) She told her father: "You can't destroy that – I want it."

To add to disappointment and despair, Robert's health was deteriorating fast. Gower said that he was coughing up blood before he finished the manuscript, and a passage in RTP describes the feelings of Owen suffering a similar condition and worrying about the impact on his family:

Owen went out into the scullery to wash his hands before going to bed: and whilst he was drying them on the towel, the strange sensation he had been conscious of all the evening became more intense, and a few seconds afterwards he was terrified to find his mouth suddenly filled with blood. For what seemed an eternity he fought for breath against the suffocating torrent, and when at length it stopped, he sank trembling into a chair by the side of the table, holding the towel to his mouth and scarcely daring to breathe, whilst a cold streamed from every pore and gathered in large drops upon his forehead.

Through the deathlike silence of the night there came from time to time the chimes of the clock of a distant church, but he continued to sit there motionless, taking no heed of the passing hours, and possessed with an awful terror.

So this was the beginning of the end! And afterwards the other two would be left by themselves at the mercy of the world. In a few years' time the boy would be like Bert White, in the clutches of some psalm-singing devil like Hunter or Rushton, who would use him as if he were a beast of burden. He imagined he could see him now as he would be then: worked, driven, and bullied, carrying loads, dragging carts, and running here and there, trying his best to satisfy the brutal tyrants, whose only thought would be to get profit out of him for themselves. If he lived, it would be to grow up with his body deformed and dwarfed by unnatural labour and with his mind stultified, degraded and brutalized by ignorance and poverty. As this vision of the child's future rose before him, Owen resolved that it should never be! He would not leave them alone and defenceless in the midst of the 'Christian' wolves who were waiting to rend them as soon as he was gone. If he could not give them happiness, he could at least put them out of the reach of further suffering. If he could not stay with them, they would have to come with him. It would be kinder and more merciful. (RTP 333-334)

Clearly, Robert never contemplated child-murder, but his own personal desperation is clear. Kathleen denied that her father ever suffered haemorrhages in Hastings, but Gower wrote: "the chapter in which Owen is stricken with haemorrhage is literally true; he told me of the occurrence and of his fears for the future." (11)

Robert's sick leaves grew longer and longer. Noakes would deliver the pauper coffin plates to his home when he left Adam's and Jarrett's at 5.30 and he described how Robert would sometimes be in bed. Noakes would wait while Robert wrote out the inscriptions propped up with pillows.

Robert would take extra care out of respect and fellow-feeling for the paupers.

He told Noakes that he had previously "thought what a wonderful place England was and that is why he came." But he had suffered a decade of disillusionment and he feared he would die a broken man. Even in work, he said, he only had the status of a "beast of burden" compelled to toil to keep alive until it was time to die. He said that he had written his book to reject that path, but the book had in turn been rejected. But he wouldn't give up all hope while he still breathed.

Robert had made the extraordinary decision to emigrate again. (12)

LEAVING

"vanished into the surrounding darkness"

As always with Robert's life story, there are conflicting reasons given for his decision. All of them, to differing degrees, may be right.

Raymond Postgate concluded: "Ill health, tyranny, poverty and disgust at the work he, an admirer of William Morris was forced to do, made him decide to try and work his way to America." Canada then became his intended destination, Postgate concurred, because "his asthma was getting worse" and he was advised medically that the Canadian climate would suit him best.

Kathleen gave three different, but not necessarily conflicting, reasons for the momentous decision. She had taken Oxford local examinations before leaving St Helens teaching school and won honours in English, French, history, geography and maths. She and her father made enquiries and Whitelands College agreed to accept her, but there was no money to finance such an education. "I think this is what started the Canada project," she told Ball.

But she also said: "Since the book was no good, and we couldn't get around the world, we'd go to Canada and make a fresh start, this time forgetting his ragged-trousered philanthropists who would not listen to sense and for whom he had written the book. He would make some money to leave me in more comfortable circumstances. He was sure he would be able to get his own kind of decorative work with good wages and a good home for both of us."

And again: "I think he was sometimes tempted to give up his crusade and set out in business on his own as he finally decided when he made up his mind to go to Canada." (1)

Disillusionment, if not with the Cause then with those it was intended to liberate, must have been a factor. Robert, in the book's penultimate chapter, expressed his disappointment from the viewpoint of Barrington: *The revulsion of feeling that Barrington experienced during the progress of* the election was intensified by the final result. The blind, stupid, enthusiastic admiration displayed by the philanthropists for those who exploited and robbed them; their extraordinary apathy with regard to their own interests; the patient, broken-spirited way in which they endured their sufferings, tamely submitting to live in poverty in the midst of the wealth they had helped to create; their callous indifference to the fate of their children, and the savage hatred they exhibited towards anyone who dared to suggest the possibility of better things, forced upon him the thought that the hopes he cherished were impossible of realization.

`You can be a Jesus Christ if you like, but for my part I'm finished. For the future I intend to look after myself. As for these people, they vote for what they want, they get what they vote for, and, by God! they deserve nothing better! They are being beaten with whips of their own choosing, and if I had my way they should be chastised with scorpions. For them, the present system means joyless drudgery, semi-starvation, rags and premature death; and they vote for it and uphold it. Let them have what they vote for! Let them drudge and let them starve!' (RTP 573)

It is hard to believe, given his nature, that Robert believed that, but the fact that he put those words on paper is a pointer to his own bitter angst. Robert could also be haunted by a sense of guilt, as he showed when describing Barrington's exit from Hastings: *Barrington was specially interested in the groups of shabbily dressed men and women and children who gathered in the roadway in front of the poulterers' and butchers' shops, gazing at the meat and the serried rows of turkeys and geese decorated with coloured ribbons and rosettes. He knew that to come here and look at these things was the only share many of these poor people would have of them, and he marvelled greatly at their wonderful patience and abject resignation.*

But what struck him most of all was the appearance of many of the women, evidently working men's wives. Their faded, ill-fitting garments and the tired, sad expressions on their pale and careworn faces. Some of them were alone; others were accompanied by little children who trotted along trustfully clinging to their mothers' hands. The sight of these poor little ones, their utter helplessness and dependence, their patched unsightly clothing and broken boots, and the wistful looks on their pitiful faces as they gazed into the windows of the toy-shops, sent a pang of actual physical pain to his heart and filled his eyes with tears. He knew that these children - naked of joy and all that makes life dear - were being tortured by the sight of the things that were placed so cruelly before their eyes, but which they were not permitted to touch or to share; and, like Joseph of old, his heart yearned over to his younger brethren. He felt like a criminal because he was warmly clad and well fed in the midst of all this want and unhappiness, and he flushed with shame because he had momentarily faltered in his devotion to the noblest cause that any man could be privileged to fight for - the uplifting of the disconsolate and the oppressed. (RTP 573-574)

Ball's verdict was: "In Canada he would have needed his health above all to stand any chance of settling. Perhaps he thought there would be better opportunities for Kathleen there, though I am more inclined to believe that he could no longer stomach the suffocating class structure and snobbery of England and longed to get to somewhere where a man was a man, in the greater freedom of the dominion."

It is also easy to forget that during those hard times, Robert's decision was hardly uncommon. His friend Alf Cobb had seriously considering emigrating five years before. During Robert's decade in Hastings there was a serious exodus from Hastings by those fleeing hunger and destitution. As early as spring 1902 the council housing chairman said that the sooner a working man could leave, the sooner he could find employment for his children. No other south coast town of comparable size saw such a high proportion of its citizens moving to Canada and Australia. The Sussex Colonising Association reported in 1911 that "considerably more people have left the town recently than ever before." (2) The highest numbers left from the poorer districts of Ore and Hollington.

Having made up his mind, Robert acted swiftly. He arranged to go to Liverpool where he aimed to get work to pay for his passage. He persuaded his sister, Mary Jane, who had little love for him, to take in Kathleen. Mary Jane with her six children ran a special school for blind and mentally-handicapped children in Kenilworth Road. He told her it was a temporary arrangement. "I only expected to be at my aunt's for a few weeks," Kathleen said. Later Kathleen admitted: "What puzzles me is , with their attitude towards my father, why should he leave me with them except that they were the most well off of the family and perhaps for shame's sake she would treat me well and I would be fed and clothed and perhaps after a while she might have paid me a salary." (3) Robert told none of his workmates about his planned emigration.

Ball raised pertinent questions about his state of mind: "Could he really have believed he would ever get to Canada? Why leave Kathleen when he knew his health was so precarious? Had he given up all hope for his book?

Why the secrecy of his departure? Did he fear he was going to die, and feel that he couldn't die slowly in his lodgings? Kathleen couldn't be kept at home indefinitely to nurse him, and he and his sisters were not on such terms that he would care to be upon their hands. And perhaps he shrank from the idea of being forced to seek relief or of creeping to the workhouse under the eyes of those to whom he had so savagely denounced those institutions." (4)

Kathleen, however, said: "I do not think he had any dread of ending up in the workhouse. He would often say, 'well. This won't buy the baby a new coat,' or he would probably say, 'If I don't get something soon we'll end up in the workhouse.'" It was nothing more than a saying, Kathleen implied. And his niece Alice insisted that he was not a broken man: "We knew he would suffer anything to be independent of others and follow his inclinations."

Ball concluded: "He had no stable place in the world, he possessed nothing, the world was again gone from under his feet and perhaps he really believed that he could make another start."

Writing more than a century later, my belief is that love and concern for Kathleen outweighed his disillusionment with his fellow workers, and that his natural verve and optimism outweighed his poor health.

In the penultimate page of RTP Owen, facing death from tuberculosis, and his child watch George Barrington depart for a new life:

In a very few minutes they heard the whistle of the locomotive as it drew out of the station, then, an instant before the engine itself came into sight round the bend, the brightly polished rails were illuminated, shining like burnished gold in the glare of its headlight; a few seconds afterwards the train emerged into view, gathering speed as it came along the short stretch of straight way, and a moment later it thundered across the bridge. It was too far away to recognize his face, but they saw someone looking out of a carriage window waving a handkerchief, and they knew it was Barrington as they waved theirs in return. Soon there remained nothing visible of the train except the lights at the rear of the guard's van, and presently even those vanished into the surrounding darkness. (RTP 586)

That is certainly wistful, but Barrington had left them a note, enclosing £10, to show that he is not alone. And the book concludes on an optimistic note despite all that has preceded it. The final page illustrates both despair and hope for the future and can be seen as a fair indication of Robert's own emotional and mental state:

As they remained at the window looking out over this scene for a few minutes after the train had passed out of sight, it seemed to Owen that the gathering darkness was as a curtain that concealed from view the Infamy existing beyond. In every country, myriads of armed men waiting for their masters to give them the signal to fall upon and rend each other like wild beasts. All around was a state of dreadful anarchy; abundant riches, luxury, vice, hypocrisy, poverty, starvation, and crime. Men literally fighting with each other for the privilege of working for their bread, and little children crying with hunger and cold and slowly perishing of want.

The gloomy shadows enshrouding the streets, concealing for the time their grey and mournful air of poverty and hidden suffering, and the black masses of cloud gathering so menacingly in the tempestuous sky, seemed typical of the Nemesis which was overtaking the Capitalist System. That atrocious system which, having attained to the fullest measure of detestable injustice and cruelty, was now fast crumbling into ruin, inevitably doomed to be overwhelmed because it was all so wicked and abominable, inevitably doomed to sink under the blight and curse of senseless and unprofitable selfishness out of existence for ever, its memory universally execrated and abhorred.

But from these ruins was surely growing the glorious fabric of the Co-operative Commonwealth. Mankind, awaking from the long night of bondage and mourning and arising from the dust wherein they had lain prone so long, were at last looking upward to the light that was riving asunder and dissolving the dark clouds which had so long concealed from them the face of heaven. The light that will shine upon the world wide Fatherland and illumine the gilded domes and glittering pinnacles of the beautiful cities of the future, where men shall dwell together in true brotherhood and goodwill and joy. The Golden Light that will be diffused throughout all the happy world from the rays of the risen sun of Socialism. (RTP 586-589)

Kathleen was certainly not worried about his state of mind or health. She was used to his illnesses: "He was always up and down and was seemingly well at this time and full of hope that it would not be long before we were on the high seas to Canada."

She remembered packing up their possessions in their London Road lodgings: "Our books, pictures and other properties were packed in packing-cases and I don't think Robert sold anything when he left except perhaps some of his books. More probably he gave things away. The manuscript was left with me. There was too much looking forward to the plans he would make for us to go to Canada to think about the manuscript." Robert never gave her any advice or instructions about what to do with it, contrary to some later reports that he "told her he had no money to give her but perhaps his writing would be worth something one day." (5)

Kathleen was 18 and painfully shy outside her home, school and close circle of friends, as befitted a young Edwardian lady.

She recalled: "Dad sending me down to the station to get his ticket and me coming back without it because it was a man at the ticket office. That will show you what I was like. My life must have been too sheltered and home-bound. I don't remember him scolding me for it." He got the ticket himself

Robert left Hastings in August 1910, although the exact date is not known. Kathleen said: "He took with him a lot of art things and drawings, originals by William Morris, his pounces and designs to use in any work he might get to earn the money for our sea fare, and his clothes."

Not even Gower and Cruttenden, his closest friends, knew he was going, the latter saying: "He just slipped away, unbeknown to anyone." Another friend, John Whitlock, said: "He just faded out overnight."

Only Kathleen saw him off from Warrior Square station, St Leonards. She said: "We were quiet and sad at parting but looking forward to soon meeting again for our journey."

Ball wrote: "So, as in his boyhood, he was to set off again into the unknown. In periods of feeling better his spirits must have risen and he must have felt capable of undertaking the journey." (6)

That confidence was tragically misplaced.

A LIVERPOOL TRAGEDY

"filled with a burning zeal"

Even Robert's journey to Liverpool is the subject of conflicting accounts.

Jack Mitchell wrote in 1969 that a friend of Robert's, Frank Jackson, told him that Noonan stopped in London and was present at a send-off in a pub in the capital where money was collected to send him on his way (1). This seems unlikely, given that Robert had not told even his closest workmates in Hastings that he was leaving. On the other hand, Robert may have broken his journey for a drink with London friends.

Ball was told by a correspondent, C. Jones, that Robert stopped at Wrexham and told him he was on his way to Canada.

Whatever route he took, Robert was certainly in Liverpool during August, the month he left Hastings. Kathleen initially assumed he was staying with his sister Ellie, but instead he took lodgings with James and Mary Anne Johnson at 35 Erskine Street, and got some sort of short-term work nearby. Relations with Ellie had been strained for some time, and there is no evidence that he even called on her, much less stay with her. James Johnson was a labourer and although the house at No 35 was modest, he needed a sub-tenant to help pay the rent.

John Nettleton wrote: "The area was well known as a dwelling place for building workers, in those days, when the so-called 'tramping system' – whereby workers would be assisted by the union to travel the country in search of work – was still in force in the building industry. And it seems fair to assume that the local branch of the Painters' Society recommended that address to Bob Noonan as a place where good and economical lodging could be found, though whether he would have received financial assistance from the Society remains uncertain." Nettleton conceded that Robert's few months in the city are "a mixture of mystery, rumour, legend and a few established facts. (2)

Liverpool in 1910 was outwardly a rich city but suffering from a depression which would within a year see numerous large-scale strikes. Once again,

Robert would have found it difficult finding work. According to one story, Robert found work for the builders' firm Joseph Barracloughs, in Juvenal Street close to his lodgings. As the work entailed one of Robert's specialities – engraving coffin copperplates – that has the ring of truth but is impossible to prove as the firm disposed of its records from that time. Another story has him repainting the emblems of the Liverpool Tram Company which was in the process of being taken over by the Corporation. Given Robert's artistry, that is also plausible but no employment records have been kept.

Robert wrote to Kathleen and Gower during his first three months in the city, but the letters were lost and remembered details were sketchy at best. Robert Quigley, later the Irish Nationalist leader Michael Collins' personal envoy, is said to have heard Robert speak publicly at Liverpool pier head and another person claimed that Robert was pointed out to him by the syndicalist S.H. Musten, but neither reports have been corroborated. (3)

Given what we know of Robert, it is impossible to imagine him not getting involved in political activism. The Clarion Fellowship ran a café in Lord Street in the city centre and it is easy to imagine him conversing with local socialists. It appears certain that Robert attended the regular meetings at the Edge Hill Lamp, a short distance from Erskine Street, a favourite spot for socialist orators. The contemporary socialist writer-critic insisted that at one such meeting he was approached after making a speech by a "short, dapper man in a grey suit" who congratulated him and said, referring to the audience, "They'll come around to our way of thinking eventually." (4)

It is also highly likely that Robert would have been a regular visitor to Islington Square, later known as Red Square, to listen to orators as he ate his supper in a small café. The trade unionist Billy Kelly's uncle was a pavement artist and told him that in the square he had "met a man who talked to him about his paintings. Years later, on seeing a picture of Robert Tressell, he came to believe, and remained fixed in his belief throughout his life, that his conversation partner was Robert Tressell." (5)

Nettleton admitted in 1981: "Some of the stories that have been told of Tressell today in Liverpool cannot be verified. All that can be guaranteed is that they tend to be told whenever Tressell's name comes up in socialist discussion, as it so often does on Merseyside. And in one sense it doesn't matter if they are true or not, because legends are really stories which people tell themselves because they may be more true than truth itself. It may be that these stories are an attempt to flesh out the bare bones of the Tressell-Liverpool connection, and to make him seem more of a citizen of Liverpool, the recognition of the great role he and his book have had in developing and shaping the political consciousness of the Liverpool labour movement." (6)

What can never be disputed, however, is that Robert's health deteriorated fast in Liverpool.

On November 26 1910 he was admitted to the Royal Liverpool Infirmary, part of the city workhouse, and registered in the general ward of its hospital. His condition was almost certainly tuberculosis. Hospital authorities told Ball: "It was quite common to nurse tubercular patients in a side ward off the general ward. This would be counted as an admission to a general as opposed to a private ward where the patient would pay for the treatment." (7) Despite his assurances to Kathleen, he was effectively dying in a workhouse.

On the day of his admission, Robert would have been heartened by news of a meeting in Manchester of 200 delegates representing 70 groups, 16 trades councils and 60,000 workers to form the Syndicalist Education League.

By 1910 conditions in workhouses had massively improved but could still be grim. In the 1860s a genuine philanthropist, William Rathbone had provided in Liverpool at his own expense a superintendent nursing assistants and 12 trained nurses, but no doctor. Fifty-four paupers who acted as ancillary nurses during an epidemic were sent back to the wards as confirmed drunkards. In 1909 a Commission found that up to 3,000 paupers continued to act as nurses in such institutions across the country. Robert had no complaints about the treatment he received and wrote to Gower saying that the nurses had been very kind to him.

But as weeks turned into months Robert was overcome by loneliness. Nobody visited him. Kathleen explained: "When he became ill and was taken to hospital I was not unduly worried. When a person is ill on and off for years, one does not expect them to become suddenly worse and not recover. I had no money of my own, I was working in the school teaching handwork and helping with the care of the children, dressing and washing them, but I got no salary. I just lived in my own dream-world thinking of what we would do when we got to Canada. I'd get a job as a teacher and

Dad would paint and write. He wrote cheerfully from hospital about decorating the ward for Christmas and being friendly with the other patients." (8)

To Gower, however, he wrote that "his health had gone all to pieces and that he wouldn't mind much when the end came."

Robert certainly hid the seriousness of his condition from Kathleen and it may be that his sister Mary Jane colluded with the loving conspiracy. Kathleen said: "Robert never gave me any idea about the finality of his illness – had he done so I'm sure my aunt would have helped me to go to him. One of the symptoms of TB is optimism and after all his other illnesses he probably expected to recover..."

But a letter to Kathleen written before his hospital admission speaks volumes in retrospect:

"I feel so unhappy at being away from you and miss you more than I can say. It makes me very miserable to think of all you used to do for me and of how unkind and irritable I often was in return and although I know that you always made allowances for the worry that caused me to be like that, I cannot forgive myself and try in vain to comfort myself with the thought that you know I never meant to be unkind and that you know I love you more than anything else in the world.

"I have thought of nothing but you since I lost sight of you on the platform and the world seems a dreary place to me because you are not here. I cannot write down here all that I feel and want to say to you but if it were true that circumstances compelled us to live apart from each other permanently – then I would much prefer not to continue to live at all... Je vous aime toujours. Dad" (9) Only a scrap of the document remained because it fell to pieces as Kathleen constantly "treasured" it and read and re-read it during her lifetime. It is the only known surviving piece of personal correspondence from him, and retains the power to move both spiritually and emotionally.

On February 4 1911 Kathleen received a telegram: "Your father died at 10.15 last night." The cause was "bronchial pneumonia," she was told by a nurse who wrote her "a very nice letter" telling her how much Robert was liked in the hospital." In fact, Robert's death certificate gave cause of death as "phthisis pulmonalis", a wasting of the lungs caused by tuberculosis.

Kathleen later believed that the nurse's misinformation was "probably dad's instructions ...preventing them from telling me how terminal his illness was in order to delay my heartache. No mention was made of TB."

Whatever the cause of death she believed, Kathleen was devastated. She said: "The bottom fell out of my world and I do not remember much of the days immediately following. I was absolutely shocked and stunned. It *really* took my breath away. All I remember was just sitting on my bed for about three days, no getting undressed or doing my hair or anything. I suppose they must have brought me food but I do not remember any trays.

"The hospital wrote and asked what arrangements should be made and my aunt told them to make the 'usual arrangements.' They must have wondered what kind of creature I was. I don't remember writing the reply. I was completely dependent on my aunt."

Aunt Mary Jane appears to have washed her hands of her brother. There is no record of the Liverpool hospital informing Kathleen, his nearest relative, of the seriousness of his condition; equally there is no record of any responsible adult asking Liverpool how he was. Mary Jane appears to have been a remarkably callous woman. Ball was more generous in his opinion, suggesting that Robert may have asked all his aunts to keep his daughter in the dark.

None of the rest of Robert's family, his brothers and sisters, including Adelaide, got in touch. The family was clearly divided. But Kathleen said: "I think Mary Jane was the only one who was hostile, probably because she didn't want to be linked to a working man, especially in her own town. She resented his choice of life and also possibly there was a guilt complex as she may have had most of the family fortune though most of it was tied up in Chancery (10).

Robert was uninsured and was so buried on February 10 in an unmarked pauper's grave along with 12 others a few yards from the walls of Walton Gaol. Such graves were for those interred wholly at public charge and some whose relatives could afford a coffin and funeral service, but not a burial plot. They were up to 25 feet deep and could take several weeks to fill. (11) Kathleen was not told its location. She had no tombstone to visit, no place in Liverpool to mourn, even if she had had the wherewithal to visit. None of his property was returned to her. His letters from Kathleen, Gower and others, his tools, his William Morris originals and his design patterns were lost forever, possibly taken by his last landlady in lieu of outstanding rent.

Robert had always had a horror of the workhouse and a pauper's grave. In RTP old Jack Linden suffered both, as shown when the workmates had buried Philpot: *On their way they saw another funeral procession coming towards them. It was a very plain-looking closed hearse with only one horse. There was no undertaker in front and no bearers walked by the sides. It was a pauper's funeral.*

Three men, evidently dressed in their Sunday clothes, followed behind the hearse. As they reached the church door, four old men who were dressed in ordinary everyday clothes, came forward and opening the hearse took out the coffin and carried it into the church, followed by the other three, who were evidently relatives of the deceased. The four old men were paupers - inmates of the workhouse, who were paid sixpence each for acting as bearers. They were just taking out the coffin from the hearse as Hunter's party was passing, and most of the latter paused for a moment and watched them carry it into the church. The roughly made coffin was of white deal, not painted or covered in any way, and devoid of any fittings or ornament with the exception of a square piece of zinc on the lid. None of Rushton's party was near enough to recognize any of the mourners or to read what was written on the zinc, but if they had been they would have seen, roughly painted in black letters

J.L.
Aged   67
and some of them would have recognized the three mourners who were Jack Linden's sons. (RTP 525-526)

There were no death notices in the Hastings newspapers. But he lived on in the memories of those who knew him. Fred Ball, interviewing them up to 50 years after his death, was struck that they all referred to him as "dear old Bob" or "dear little Bob."

Len Green remembered until he died in the 1970s seeing three redoubtable little men, all about the same height and all wearing dark trilby hats, walking along Robertson Street in deep conversation. They were dockers' leader Ben Tillett, Alf Cobb and Bob Noonan.

Even his niece Alice, who never liked Kathleen and whose mother Mary Jane coloured her judgement, saw something of his worth, albeit from a rather snobbish viewpoint: "I have told you quite truthfully that Robert was not born into the working class. He would have had a much happier life, no doubt, had he been.

"He felt that the working class had been grievously wronged beyond all measure and he also believed that before he formed any judgement or expressed opinions he would find out the smallest details and the innermost secrets from his own practical experience and life, and therefore he took upon himself and became the class he so earnestly desired to help." *(12)*

But perhaps Robert's best epitaph was spoken by his daughter Kathleen to Ball more than half a century after his death:

"I wouldn't have had him any different except that I wish he had not had so much physical suffering – filled with a burning zeal for justice and the betterment of mankind no matter what the personal cost. He was an agnostic but surely lived the most Christian life I have ever come into contact with, who hated sham and hypocrisy and who loved children and all weak and helpless creatures and who suffered agonies when he contemplated their probable futures and his inability to alter them." *(Ibid)*

KATHLEEN ALONE

"politeness and curiosity"

Kathleen was left alone in a household that was unconventional while adhering to strict Edwardian mores. She was a teenage orphan take in on sufferance by a family which had never liked her father.

Her aunt, Mary Jane, was married to John Bean Meiklejon, a draper who later became a house furnisher's salesman. They had three daughters – Alice, whom Ball interviewed, Olive and Ruby – and three sons – Paul, Percy and a third who remains nameless. Mary Jane ran her special school in 48 Kenilworth Road, and 37 Carisbrooke Road, St Leonards, properties which were linked by back-to-back gardens. But father John lived in London, visiting St Leonards only for occasional weekends.

Kathleen and her cousins were given board and lodgings and some pocket money, but no pay, for as long as they stayed at home. That arrangement, with the youngsters doing the work of teachers and servants, caused frictions, but Mary Jane was unbending. The family was constantly fracturing. Olive was forbidden to train as a nurse because her mother considered it a lowly profession, and the young woman eventually went to America to fulfil her ambition. Older sister Ruby and brother Percy had travelled to Canada for new horizons. Percy upset his mother when he married a girl in the laundry business. Kathleen said: "I can't understand why my aunt, who was the wife of a linen-draper, should have been so upset. She said to me she wouldn't have cared how poor the girl was if only she had been a lady." (1)

Paul, a "delicate" young man whose leg had been amputated below the knee after a childhood fracture had been badly reset, lived with his father in London but visited his mother and siblings more frequently. Kathleen said: "His second name was Alexander and his mother used to say: 'Paul was born to command.' He was waited on by mother and servants." Only Alice appears to have put down permanent roots in Hastings.

Such a household must have been stifling for both Kathleen and her cousins. Kathleen recalled: "I was with my aunt for over two years until my cousins convinced me that if I had to work for a living it was better to work for strangers and be properly paid than to remain at home for practically nothing. Olive and Ruby had left home for the same reason, although Ruby had returned to England after years in Canada."

"Ruby and Olive had left home possibly because, being family, they were expected to work without salary, and after Robert died my aunt treated me in the same way and perhaps instead of being a niece she regarded me as a daughter…" (2)

Her female cousins put out recommendations in London and Kathleen secured a job in the capital as nurse-governess to one child. When she told her aunt, Mary Jane was furious, claiming that Kathleen was ungrateful for all she had done. Kathleen left and Paul and Ruby paid her train fare to London.

Kathleen could never remember the name of the family she worked for perhaps a couple of months except they were "very nice people." There was some minor row over her precise duties and she stormed out. "It was my first experience of being on my own and perhaps I was a bit touchy," she recalled. (3). For Kathleen, the 19-year-old's move was critical on two fronts.

Firstly, her switch in employment, or her predicament, saw her reunited with her crippled cousin Paul Meiklejon. The young man, limping on a peg leg after the girl he had been courting died, came to visit. "It was a case of misery loves company," Kathleen said. The two fell in love and reached an understanding that they would marry and emigrate to Canada whenever that could be possible. Mary Jane, as mother of one and aunt to another, was kept in the dark about the arrangement. She found out, however, and she encouraged Paul to go to Canada "to remove temptation," little realising that that was the couple's intention anyway. Much later Kathleen said: "If my aunt had had any sense (it's easy to be wise after the event) she would have arranged for me to meet some other young men for I suppose I was at the ripe time to fall in love with any nice young man. As it was I was grieving for Dad, and Paul was grieving over the loss of his girl-friend." (4)

Secondly, Kathleen's second job was with Mr and Mrs Mackinlay, tasked with looking after their five children. Mrs Mackinlay, said Kathleen, "was very nice and so was her mother who lived in another suburb and I used to cycle over there…" Kathleen was taken on family holidays to North Devon. The Mackinlays knew it was a short-term arrangement because Paul had headed off to Canada and Kathleen would join him when they could. Paul would write every week.

However, Mrs Mackinlay noticed that Kathleen had a small tin trunk under her bed and asked what "treasures" in contained. Kathleen told her that it was her father's manuscript. The family's next-door neighbour was Miss Jesse Pope, a writer of children's books and a professional lady journalist who regularly contributed to *Punch* and who knew the London literary Establishment. Miss Pope came for tea and the mistress of the house told her about the manuscript. Kathleen recalled: "I took the two young boys into them and was introduced. Mrs Mackinlay had evidently told Miss Pope about the manuscript and she asked to see it and she took it away with her." (5)

Miss Pope later wrote: "A few months ago a friend asked me to look at the manuscript of a novel, 'The Ragged Trousered Philanthropists,' a work of a socialistic house painter, who wrote his book and died. I consented without enthusiasm, expecting to be neither interested nor amused – and found I had chanced upon a remarkable human document." (6)

Miss Pope sent it first to Constable's publishing house, who that year had published George Meek's book. They rejected it for being too "unwieldy." But Miss Pope mentioned it to Pauline Hemmerde, the sister of the Recorder of Liverpool and secretary to another publisher, Grant Richards. "Why not let Mr Richards see it?" Miss Hemmerde said. "It can't do any harm." Grant Richards was a well-established entrepreneur with a reputation for taking risks with new or risqué authors and a track record of occasionally dodgy dealings and see-sawing fortunes – often he forgot to pay his own adoring secretary. Miss Pope took her advice.

Richards wrote: "It was from a friend that I first heard of that mountainous manuscript… My secretary Miss Hemmerde had a cousin, Miss Jessie Pope. One day I heard that Miss Pope had heard from a neighbour that her children's nurse had confessed that her own father had written a book – well not exactly a book because it wasn't in print, but a story in the sensed that it was a novel, the novel of his own life that wanted to get itself into print and to be a book. Politeness and curiosity made Miss Pope promise to read the book and it was brought to her." (7)

Kathleen Noonan

Miss Pope sought a meeting with Richards and admitted that it was "ever and ever so much too long," full of repetition and needed to be cut down severely. Eventually she took it to show Richards who agreed to publish it if she agreed to reduce it from an estimated 250,000 to around 100,000 words (In fact she cut it by about 40 per cent to around 150,000 words).

"She discussed the matter with the owner," Richards said. "She told her what she and I must have sincerely believed, that its chances of success were very slight. But the opportunity of publication appealed to Miss Tressall (sic)… The book was damnably subversive, but it was extraordinarily real, and rather than let it go I was willing to drop a few score pounds on it." (8)

Kathleen said that the meeting "resulted in an interview with Mr Richards, when he told me that he had sat up all night reading it, that he had never been more impressed by a book, and was willing to publish it, but that it would have to be cut down because there was a lot of repetition in it. I explained the reason for the repetition – that my father felt that he had to hammer home his message to get the workers to see it – but that made no difference…

"He also wanted to change the title but I held out for that and would not consent. He explained that publication was a gamble – it might be successful or a complete flop, He would pay me £25 for all rights, including dramatic rights and if it was a success would pay me more but would not bind the firm to that. I was getting £12 a year at Mrs Mackinlay's and £25 outright seemed a fortune. It was explained to me that it would be costly cutting it down to make it possible to publish. Miss Pope probably got more for her work than I did for the manuscript." (9)

Kathleen's interview with Richards was on August 22 1913 and the same day he wrote to her confirming his offer, promising publication no later than June the following year. He wrote to her: "I will tell you now …that I do not remember reading any manuscript which affected me more deeply than this work of your father's. I should like to have known him."

Miss Pope strongly advised Kathleen to accept the offer and on August 28 wrote to Richards that she had told her "I consider it a very generous one, and she certainly feels she is being very well treated. Personally I don't think anybody could read that MS and treat the daughter of the man who wrote it, badly." In the same letter Miss Pope also confirmed her role as editor, on the basis of 100 hours-worth of cutting and shaping over six weeks. Her fee was certainly close to Kathleen's £25. Many have queried Miss Pope's tactics in ensuring her own profitable role. But Ball was generous, and right, when he wrote: "We must pay tribute to Miss Pope who had sent the book to a number of publishers and acted as an unpaid agent all through for Kathleen." (10)

More problematic, with the benefit of hindsight, is the question of whether Richard's. a known chancer in the piratical world of publishing, exploited Kathleen. She said: "Apart from my ignorance, I was only 20 and a very young 20 at that, my upbringing was far too sheltered."

But for the times the payment, whether or not it was intended to be a one-off, was more than many copyright deals secured by established authors. Ball wrote that "even an author destined to become a best-seller might have been pleased to begin so well." He added: "And of course, while publishers will often gamble on a young writer hoping for reward in the success of his later work, few will invest in one who being dead can produce no more. Even then a publisher could lose as many as two or three hundred pounds on a book and half a dozen failures for an under-capitalized but adventurous publisher like Richards might have been very serious." (11)

Jessie Pope set about editing and cutting. In her preface she wrote: "In reducing a large mass of manuscript to the limitations of book form it has been my task to cut away superfluous matter and repetition only. The rest practically remains as it came from the pen of Robert Tressall, house-painter and sign-writer." Later generations queried that claim, as Pope slashed and burnt, removing completely sub-plots which showed the depth of Robert's humanity.

In a letter to Richards she said: "In going through the m.s. again I find the last few chapters are in my opinion the weakest part of the book and with your permission I should like to cut out all the matter about Ruth's intrigue with Slyme. It is not that I think the public will be offended at the sordidness of the story – I suppose they have put up with many worse ones – but the long-drawn-out description of Ruth's misfortunes, the birth of the baby, the description of Easton's and Owen's attitude regarding the affair, in fact the whole of that particular part of the narrative is written in a melancholy maudlin manner far below the standard of other parts of the book.

"I think the book would gain if it could all be cut out... Perhaps you will let me hear from you as soon as possible on the matter, as I am approaching that part of the story with scissors and paste-pot." (12)

Richards agreed. Her scissors also completely removed cut out the pivotal figure of Barrington, the educated, middle class worker who gave Owen moral support and who was part of Robert's own composite character. And, inexcusably, she reshaped and changed the story's ending. She moved to the climax Owen's wild speculation, following a lung haemorrhage, of committing suicide and taking his family with him so that they would not leave them in poverty. That section was originally in the middle of the book, and Robert ended his own manuscript on a note of hope.

Fred Ball found that unforgiveable, saying that it "changes Owen's humanity and moral stature, bringing him finally to personal despair and moral cowardice (he wasn't shown by Tressell as either unbalanced or capable of murder). But he also said that Pope's actions may have been unintentional rather than malicious because "she simply didn't understand." (13)

Another casualty was Robert's hand-drawn title page. The new version would misspell his pseudonym as "Tressall", a mistake which stayed with the book for decades.

The book was published, price six shillings for 400 pages, on April 23 1914, and six copies were given to Kathleen. Shortly afterwards, newly enriched in comparative terms, she sailed to Canada to join Paul. They married and both reportedly worked on the stage. They had one daughter. A relative told Ball that every Christmas they hung presents on a tree for the children of a local institution or orphanage which their toddler daughter would hand over.

Family connections with Hastings swiftly faded. It was reported in Hastings that Paul joined a flying service and was killed. Just as Robert had feared, Kathleen and her baby were left alone.

Then, just after the Great War ended, in 1918 or 1919, Kathleen and daughter were reported dead in a motor accident.

Robert's worse fears appeared to have been justified in a way he never would have imagined.

HOME FROM THE WARS

"Men still fight like wolves..."

In May 1918 Grant Richards published an even more truncated version of RTP selling at just a shilling a copy. He was by now aware of the book's popularity amongst working men and had an eye on soldiers returning from the front.

Robert's Hastings workmate, Len Green, returned from the Great War via Portsmouth hospital. An orderly mentioned RTP which "didn't mean a thing to me," Green recalled. "But he started to tell me about different parts of the book, and then when he said something about an Absconding Secretary of the Light Refreshment Fund ...that jogged my memory."

On his return he bought a copy from W.H. Smith's on Hastings Station. "The wife read it out to me, and we stopped up nearly all of Christmas Eve, listening, and I knew all the characters that he meant them to be," Green said. "He didn't mean that they should have all their real names there to embarrass their families." (1) The character on which Old Philpot was based borrowed the copy, as did others of Robert's old workmates, until it became ragged. None had known that Robert had written a book, but all recognised either themselves or others in it.

An apprentice called Crudduck remembered the book being passed around at Adam's and Jarrett's: "I heard the men talking about Tressell's book and tittering amongst themselves. Bob Noonan was supposed to have written it but he had never talked about it." (2)

The working-class dramatist Tom Thomas wrote: "Seeking the real cause of that ghastly blood bath (the Great War), I heard of meetings at Finsbury Park on Sunday mornings. At these, which were organized by the Herald League, I listened to anti-war speakers who sometimes received quite a rough handling from some of the crowd... It was here that I bought my first copy of *The Ragged Trousered Philanthropists* which was to me as to many others both a revelation and an inspiration." (3)

Jack Jones, later to become general secretary of the Transport and General Workers Union, said that the first book to open his eyes to the wrongs of society, aged 12, was called 'Our Old Nobility' and was lent to him by a ship-repair worker. "To suddenly realise that the 'noble lords' were descendants of cattle robbers, land thieves and court prostitutes was a devastating revelation," he wrote. "A few years afterwards a good old socialist and trade union fighter in Garston and the south-end, Bill Bewley, lent me *The Ragged Trousered Philanthropists*. I couldn't lift my eyes from its pages. It was so real in its exposure of much of the life around me and which I was beginning to experience in my first job after leaving school. But the great significance of the book for me was the simple, clear explanation of socialism."

Throughout the turbulent 1920s and 1930s RTP was read widely. It began to be known amongst British and Irish building workers as The Painter's Bible. Brendan Behan wrote some years later that it was his "family's book." He added: "On every job in Dublin you'd hear painters using the names out of it for nick-names, calling their own apprentice The Walking Colour Shop." Every foreman was called Nimrod "even by painters who had never read the book, nor any other book either."

But it went beyond the building trade. The steward of a Methodist mission bought 10 copies for friends and associates. A Quaker couple in Birmingham gave a young woman a copy. Intellectuals both embraced and dismissed it. But for many struggling through the Depression it, according to numerous testimonies, turned them into socialists.

An apprentice coach-builder, given RTP by his father, and recognised much in it: "Jokes were made of the Joiners Coat of Arms consisted of toasting a bloater over the fire and the poor painter holding a slice of bread underneath the fish to catch the fat whilst being cooked. They would also joke about the painters 'skeleton kits' of tools they had brought on the job, which made me pity them more than ever. I can see now the small lad pushing the truck with the step ladders up the hill. The sacking of men at an hour's notice, or less." (4)

That young man became a committed socialist, Labour councillor and, above all, a trade unionist. And for generations RTP became a trade union bible and, as Harker pointed out, an "activist's tool kit."

In December 1922 the house-painter's union executive member for Liverpool, J. Walsh, recommended RTP for all his members, urging them to "risk half a crown" on a book which "once read cannot be forgotten." Walsh was convinced that such chapters as The Long Hill had "done more to compel both operatives and employers to recognise their duty to the lads than all the speech-making on the same subject." Walsh rejected any empty gesture of appreciation for the book's author, saying that "to keep his memory green, and the most practical way of appreciating the service that he has rendered, in exposing the seamy side of our trade in particular, is to devote our energies towards abolishing root and branch, the wretched conditions which he depicts." (5)

During that period it was also clear that little had changed in terms of working conditions. In 1924 a house-painter who had been apprenticed in Hastings in 1908 and who had known Robert said: "Men still fight like wolves to get a job that gives them a bare existence ...no security, no peace of mind, no certainty for the future."(6) Trade unionism may have grown stronger and education improved, but only a tiny minority had the energy after work to fight against the system. Without RTP that minority would have been tinier.

By 1932 George Hicks, the newly-elected Labour MP for West Woolwich, warned that the Depression was having "disastrous effects" on the building industry. He went on: "The curse of unemployment is with us to an alarming and terrible extent. The continuous introduction of new machines and methods is, in addition, making employment for the 'Ragged Trousered Philanthropists' more precarious. Perhaps the future is not so dark and hopeless as it was in the bad old times, but it is gloomy enough in all conscience." (7)

RTP in its cheap abridged form became an essential part of a young socialist's small library, from the son of a Mersey tug boat engineer to a young council worker in Glamorgan. London Communist Jack Dash read RTP the weekend before he started work on a Stepney building site. He was "all stirred up and ready to have a go" and by the end of the week the site was unionised. (8) A refugee German doctor's daughter read the "haunting account of the exploitation of the poor" after she joined the anti-Fascist movement.

Many years later John Nettleton spoke of the book's particular affinity with Liverpool: "The secret of RTP is its pure simplicity. Karl Marx wrote *Das Kapital*. I've been a shop steward for 20 years. If I were to go on the shop floor and read *Das Kapital*, I wouldn't be a shop steward for long – I'd be out in five minutes. But the chapter on the Great Money Trick is *Das Kapital*, simplified into the working men's understanding. I first heard it on a ship. These few pages are still done at branch meetings and they are still done in what they call the 'hut' at building sites whenever they're rained off, because it is as relevant today as the day that he wrote it. I know lads that have got that off by heart. And every new apprentice whoever comes on the building site at Liverpool Cathedral, that's his first lesson. And he learns that before he learns about the trade..." (9)

In 1990 Ron Todd, general secretary of the giant Transport and General union, said that the book inspired succeeding generations of union leaders. "I cannot remember any general secretaries who have not, as part of their learning, read *The Ragged Trousered Philanthropists*," he told Steve Peak. "It's been a stock book in every trade unionist's home that I can remember. When I first read the book it was when I was a Ford shop steward, and quite frankly it had a great impression on me." (10)

RTP also inspired working class theatre. The first of many versions was staged by Tom Thomas of the Workers' Theatre Movement in Hackney in 1927 or 1931. The group, made up mainly of building trades workers, put it on after a dramatized version was turned down in the West End. The show ran for 40 performances and was instrumental in the creation of the Unity Theatre. It then went on tour (11) Mark Cheney, who took part, recalled: "I shall never forget the show that we did in Braintree – we rolled up to the town hall in a coach provided by the Labour town council, who gave us a right royal welcome and incidentally a high tea, and then we all paraded the town with bell, book and candle, with leaflets and posters, and the audience literally crammed the hall....

"Although this play was direct and open propaganda, we managed to penetrate the Labour clubs and institutes around London and when one considers the significant fact that that we had to compete with the usual club turns and the beer-swillers, who sometimes left hurriedly before ten to get their drinks, it is surprising the success we managed to maintain with these honest-to-God working class audiences.

"It is due, no doubt, to the fact that the humour was typically working class, the homeliness of the dialogue with the fifteen 'bloodys' allowed us by the censor (which we expended in the first two scenes and sprinkled a few more for good measure) won their attention and support.

"We also did many shows for strikers who were particularly impressed by the 'Join the Union' appeal at the end; at one historic show at the Hackney Manor Hall for the first Hunger Marchers, who marched into the hall to the stirring music of a drum and fife band during the first scene of the play, we cheered with the rest of the audience and started the show over again for their benefit."

In 1937 the Reading Labour Dramatic society staged a version as its contribution to their local trade union recruitment week. By then RTP was regarded as a milestone for the stage as well as the printed word.

RTP grew by reputation during raucous and turbulent times. Fred Ball wrote: "Like another book of dissent before it, The Pilgrim's Progress, saved and kept alive by the movement of religious dissent against the Establishment, so RTP was saved and kept alive by a movement of social and political dissent, the Labour Movement; and particularly the socialists and more particularly the various unofficial anti-war, industrial shop-floor and rank and file movements."

The book in 1939 struck a chord with the teenaged Hertfordshire carpenter Eric Heffer – a friend of mine later in life when he was a Labour firebrand in the Commons. "Everything in the book I recognised around me," he said. "We had a Misery for a foreman. We could be sacked on the spot. The bosses wanted us to be bodgers because the quicker the job, the higher the profits. Any sense of pride in the job was knocked out of us. The book made me understand the true nature of capitalism." (12)

Heffer probably bought the October 1938 abridged edition published by Martin Secker who had bought the Richards Press. In April 1939 when its 25-year unrestricted copyright ran out, Penguin negotiated to publish it in paperback. It was this edition that arguably had the greatest impact. Another war widened its audience.

Penguin's sixpenny paperback was published in April 1940 and, despite wartime paper restrictions, around 50,000 were printed. By then the Nazis had overrun Holland and Belgium, but the print run was sold within a month. It was reprinted in May in a slightly smaller format, and again sold astonishingly well. Various reasons have been put forward. There were favourable reviews in *The Times* and *The Daily Telegraph*. The book came out at a time when other books, including Michael Foot's Guilty Men, were attacking the pre-war national government. And there was a mood that if Britain was again at war, the mistakes of the previous one should not be repeated, including the treatment of workers on the home front. Penguin reported that the most persistent and effective factor in sales of RTP was word of mouth.

But the biggest factor must have been conscription. Men from all backgrounds – industrial, crafts and clerical – were called up. They left behind them varying degrees of squalor and comfort. And RTP fit neatly into knapsacks.

In January 1941 Penguin again reprinted. That summer saw a surge in demand for all books as bombing raids had destroyed an estimated 20 million of them, and service personnel bored stiff in barracks contributed to the demand.

Penguin and Pelican Books supplied paperbacks for Red Cross parcels and also reached a distribution deal with the Forces Book Club. The Penguin edition carried the words: "For The Forces. Leave this book at any Post Office when you have read it, so that men and women in the services may enjoy it too." (13) Demand for RTP both at home and on active service abroad outstripped supply. A former Bradford labourer ran a rudimentary lending library in the Egyptian desert and his solitary copy of RTP was very much in demand. An Irish RAF man borrowed it and "by the time I got to it it was very limp, dog-eared and decrepit." (14)

The book was passed from hand to hand in the Parachute Regiments in "semi-secrecy" because officers did not approve. A Grenadier Guardsman took a copy into educational classes where a comrade claimed he had been ordered to shun such "subversive literature." A young Liverpudlian serving in the jungles of Burma, however, reported that his officer lent it to so many of those serving under him that it fell apart. And a "politically unaware" RAF officer who had been unaware of the extremes of poverty it depicted, read it and was "convinced of the rights of the common man." RAF fitter John Sommerfield was posted to a forward airfield in Burma where "there wasn't much to read ...but I had a sort of little library that travelled with us, disguised as a box of 20-millimetre cannon shells." It included the RTP Penguin which "unfortunately, didn't last long, being handed around and read and re-read until it literally fell to pieces." (15)

RTP was read in all branches of the armed forces, and Socialist and Communist groups within them also played their part in the book's circulation. On the home front also there was a voracious appetite for books as the war dragged on. Working class people were increasingly literate and, in the pre-TV era, read up to five hours a week.

Richards Press issued hardback reprints in August 1943 and again in April, July and December 1944. The dust jacket plugged it as a "faithful picture of working men, driven by misery and want, ignorance and fear, into an anti-social attitude of helplessness and despair. Their lives, their thoughts, their work and leisure, their politics, their reaction to the message of a workmate who tries to help them understand the causes and cure of their poverty and squalor, are depicted with the stark realism possible only to one who has taken part in their struggle and has known at first hand their puny hopes and their ever present fears."

Penguin also reprinted on thinner paper in 1944 and copies were sold across the Dominions, including Australia.

Why did it become a forces' favourite? Shortage of other material may have been an issue in some circumstances. But overall it caught the mood of desperate times. Service personnel from all backgrounds were thrown together in an atmosphere of "ever present fear." They were determined that they, unlike their fathers after the trenches of the Western Front, would return to a better land. They were exposed to new ideas, and new pressures of both conscience and expectation. The political message hit home.

But a major factor is that it chimed with the experiences of squaddie life. Nostalgia for their homes – they knew the characters portrayed -, bolshieness in all its senses, and a constant guerrilla war to get the better of their ruling class, that is, the officers. And perhaps above all, the irreverent humour of the ordinary squaddie or naval rating. In RTP tragedy and squalor sits alongside biting, sarcastic, and sometimes vicious, humour. In that context it is a very funny book and it is easy to imagine some bumptious officers or NCOs garnering surreptitious nick-names from RTP.

The impact of the book on servicemen in particular continued to be freshly felt to the end of the war and beyond.

In October 1944, following the D-Day invasion, the Labour party announced that once hostilities ceased it would leave the cross-party wartime coalition and stand in the subsequent general election as an independent party.

That election duly took place in July 1945, although it was some time before the votes of personnel still serving overseas were counted and the results declared. Winston Churchill and the Conservatives thought they had it in the bag, and so did most commentators. The Communist Party saw an opportunity to make gains, but their hopes were also shattered by a surge to Labour, especially amongst the forces. Clement Attlee's party won almost 12 million votes and 400 Parliamentary seats in the "khaki election." Churchill, the war leader, was deeply shocked by the "ingratitude" of the nation, although he had contributed towards his own defeat when he, during the election campaign, had compared Labour politicians, who had shared the dangers and deprivation of the war as well as helping to win it, as akin to the Gestapo.

Communist Mervyn Jones, himself disappointed by his party's lack of progress, reported that "what people mostly said in explaining why they had voted Labour was that they were guarding against a return to the unemployment and poverty of the 1930s."

And RTP, although an Edwardian book, plugged into such fears. In 1947 Alan Sillitoe was conscripted and posted to Malaya as an RAF wireless operator to fight insurgents. A signals corporal from Glasgow handed him a copy, saying: "You ought to read this. Among other things it is the book which won the '45 election for Labour."

That claim is impossible to wholly sustain. British voters admired Churchill's wartime record but did not trust the Conservatives. Labour figures such as Attlee, Herbert Morrison and Ernest Bevin had, during the war, proved their competence. They seemed better able to rebuild the country after six years of total war.

But *The Ragged Trousered Philanthropists* did its bit.

FRED BALL AND THE MANUSCRIPT

"like small boys detected at scrumping apples."

One Sunday morning three men met in a small café at the Elephant and Castle Tube station. Sixty guineas were handed over in return for two parcels. It seemed a cloak and dagger affair, the men talking in hushed whispers. Inside the parcels were sheaves of papers. Not, however, secret documents, but the complete, hand-written original transcript of *The Ragged Trousered Philanthropists.*

The purchaser was Fred Ball, a Hastings man who would become Robert Tressell's first biographer. Born in the Old Town in 1905, Fred came from a line of wheelwrights, ironsmiths and building workers. His mother was a dressmaker and seamstress at Plummer Roddis, the town's biggest drapers, and his father was a gardener at Telham Hill House. Fred left school aged 14, and although he wanted to be a gardener himself, he was apprenticed to a plumber. That did not bring in enough earnings for his family so in 1920, aged 15, he was became a counterhand in a London branch of Sainsbury's. He returned to Hastings in 1928 and set up a small grocer's shop. It swiftly went bankrupt. He attended Workers' Education Association classes in music and literary appreciation, wrote poetry and grew increasingly political. In 1936 he became secretary of the Hastings Left Book Club's poetry group. The outbreak of the Spanish Civil War and a local vicar telling him he was "too prejudiced in favour of the working class" were the catalysts for his joining the Communist Party.

A local house-painter told him that RTP was "one of the books that was most lent... a book you ought to read." (1) Ball did so and it was an eye-opener. Ball said that it was the first English novel he had read "in which men at work was the basic setting, and the working class the basic characters, and treated as real people, the kind of people I'd been brought up among, and not as 'comic relief.'"

Ball was introduced to two of Robert's old workmates and on May 1 1937 went to London with his brothers carrying Robert's hand-painted SDP banner. Ball was amazed that while in some Hastings circles 'Robert

Tressell' was well known, in others he was invisible. He could find no copy of RTP in Hastings Library. It had never been mentioned in Ball's own family when he was growing up. The idea of a biography began to form.

Ball wrote: "The central characters were building workers and I had several relations in the building trades and had myself worked for a local builder when I was a lad of fourteen and, exactly like Bert, the apprentice in the book, had often worked in the paintshop cleaning out paintpots and had pushed a heavy hand-truck about the town and this only nine years after Robert Tressell was himself working in the trade here.

"Then the book was actually written by a working house-painter and not by a professional writer looking in from the outside. And I was a worker trying to be a writer. And finally this book, I was told, was written and set in Hastings and I was a native of Hastings. Yet, despite all these local associations, I had never heard of it." (2) Ball began digging deeper and, crucially, began interviewing Robert's contemporaries.

During the war, in 1942, it occurred to Ball to get in touch with Grant Richards. In tentative correspondence, he asked Richards about Tressell's original manuscript and whether it could be bought for a modest sum.

"I had no idea what happened to it after publication," Ball wrote. "Perhaps it had been left in Canada... Grant Richards settled the question. First he wrote to me asking what I meant by a 'modest sum.' Having no idea what he thought it might be, or what such a manuscript would fetch, I knew what I meant and suggested, with little hope, the sum of £50. He soon wrote back saying he didn't have the manuscript but thought it might be acquired for something like that. He would make enquiries." (3)

Later it emerged that Richards, in financial difficulties and approaching retirement, had been concerned he could make no provision for his long-time secretary, Pauline Hemmerde. He gave her the Tressell manuscript, which she accepted gratefully and later sold it to an anonymous stranger for £10. (4)

Richards' alleged enquiries dragged on until the war had ended, which was something of a relief for Ball, who didn't have £50 and didn't know where to get it. Eventually, in November 1945, Ball received a letter from a Robert Partridge, presumably the anonymous purchaser who was stationed at RAF

Harwell, offering the manuscript for 300 guineas. Partridge, a collector of some sort, reckoned he could get more than that in the US market.

Such a sum was way beyond Ball's reach – his employment was erratic and he was married to Jacqueline with four daughters - and he did not reply. But nine months later, at the end of August 1946, Partridge wrote again saying that Richards had "pleaded so ably" on his behalf that Ball could have it for 50 guineas.

This was still beyond Ball's reach but earlier, as friends returned from active service with back pay, he had half-formed a syndicate of like-minded people who might buy shares to save the manuscript for working class Britain. The other members were Peter Blackman, George Jackson, Ernie Bevis, Gregory Gildersleeve and Mr and Mrs Andrew Kelt. They were still willing and Ball suddenly had 50 guineas. Partridge then wrote raising the price to £60 and then, at the last moment, 60 guineas. Ball scraped together the difference and, with one of the shareholders, travelled to London on September 29 1946 to make the purchase from Partridge.

"After a nerve-racking wait he arrived and the two parties satisfactorily identified each other," Ball wrote. "To save carrying out this momentous transaction in the street Mr Partridge suggested that we do it in a nearby tea shop, a far from pretentious one at that, and there upon the little tea shop table we opened the parcels and set eyes upon the actual hand-written manuscript of *The Ragged Trousered Philanthropists*. And it was a large MS – about nine inches high...

"We had no doubts about its genuineness – only a prodigiously patient and industrious forger would dream of copying such a work... after the three of us had stayed about an hour on two cups of tea each and talking at sixteen to the dozen we began to draw the attention of the proprietor and his staff. So we hurriedly packed up the manuscript and got outside feeling like small boys detected at scrumping apples." (5)

Ball later recalled: "The manuscript was in two parcels, one just a little larger than the other and we wondered why... at home I discovered why it was in two parcels. The smaller one, about two-fifths of the whole, I found combed out and not included by Grant Richards and it contained characters and episodes which were vital to the author's own." (6)

At the time Ball and his partners had no idea what they were going to do with it. They thought of a trade union museum or research facility. But in the short term Ball would retain it as he wrote his biography of Tressell.

Ball, by-lined F.C. Ball, wrote *Tressell of Mugsborough* during a period of unemployment and, eventually, in his spare time while reading meters for the Gas Board. It was published by Lawrence and Wishart in October 1951 to favourable reviews.

By then Ball and his friends had investigated whether Tressell's entire book could be published. One problem was copyright, the other the huge amount of work needed to piece together Tressell's work from the loose piles of folios, some ditched by Jessie Pope, others cut and pasted, others switched from the original running order.

Ball and his friends certainly saw publication in full as a holy grail. He wrote: "I thought, and the shareholders agreed with me, that it was outrageous that the public should only have Grant Richards' version of the book and not the author's own. I urged that somehow we must get this original published. But how? The copyright, even for the unpublished parts, belonged to Richards Press and we were bound by that. The Richards version was still being printed and they weren't likely to start all over again with a much longer book. And even if we managed to find a willing publisher, how would he get round the law of copyright? The reality of that law I discovered when I finally published *Tressell of Mugsborough*, and had to pay Richards Press for passages quoted from the unpublished parts of the manuscript of which I possessed the only copy!" (7)

But the publication of Ball's own biography, imperfect and full of unanswered questions, he readily admitted, sparked wider interest, particularly his references to the full manuscript. There was long, and ultimately abortive, correspondence with the trade union movement, particularly the National Federation of Building Trades Operatives. Ball was invited to speak to a Federation rally in Hastings and drafted a motion for the National Society of Painters' annual conference in June 1952 pledging "all support in its power to ensure the success of a full edition." It came to nothing. Ball wrote after reading the minutes of the 1952 conference: "It is clear that the many confusions among platform and delegates arose not from lack of interest in Tressell, but from lack of familiarity with the ways of the publishing world, and a suspicion that I have never been able completely to dispel, that I must have had some personal advantage to gain through publication." (8)

Ball's own publishers, Lawrence and Wishart, also expressed interest and the commercial world delivered where the trade union movement had not. The full version was published by them on October 6 1955, nine years after the manuscript had been bought. Because the original copyright did not expire until 1964 they paid Richards Press suitable compensation.

However, the above paragraph does not do justice to the Herculean efforts of Ball, his wife Jackie, their daughters, friends and family, in piecing together the fragmented, bowdlerised piles of paper, with pages and additions stuck together, into Robert's initial work.

Ball told me: "For a year it was spread across our kitchen table. The kettle was constantly on the boil to steam apart pages glued together 40 years previously. There was a constant stream of visitors – writers, students, teachers, trade unionists, Scottish pitmen on one occasion – who called in to see it. Progress was slow, but it was a real labour of love. There were long discussions with Maurice Cornforth, of Lawrence and Wishart, over the running order of chapters. Eventually we had two typescripts which conformed, as closely as we could ever tell, with Tressell's concept and vision." (9)

Ball also wrote of the difficulties making sense of the order of chapters, as the Grant Richards edition was parcelled separately from the rest and the whole was in a damaged condition. As previously stated, Jessie Pope had excised whole chapters. Ball, his wife and helpers inserted the missing chapters having first decided where they should go. Having got the shape of the whole book, they then had to restore the original text to what it was before altered by Pope. "Some pages were cut through with scissors, a few were missing altogether ..." Ball wrote. "In some places where she (Pope) had pasted stiff card over the original we steamed Tressell's pages off the card... In other cases, where we found this was damaging the original, we left the card on and read his text from the back with the aid of a hand-mirror and copied it out. In restoring the cut pages, many parts of which were taken out and stuck in other ;parts of the manuscript, we had to search many times to find exactly where the pieces had come from, and sometimes this was only possible by matching the two edges left by her scissors." (10)

The first print run was of 5,000 copies – 1500 in a hard-cover 'library' edition costing 30 shillings, and 3,500 in a soft-cover 'trade union' edition priced at 10 shillings and sixpence. Both sold out within three months. Over the next decade or so Lawrence and Wishart reprinted six times, all in hardback. In 1965 Panther Books published it its Classics series with an introduction by Alan Sillitoe, one of Britain's most popular novelists since the filming of his working-class masterpiece, *The Loneliness of the Long Distance Runner.* That version was constantly reprinted, and the full version has never been out of print since. In 1967 a special edition was published to link with a BBC production of RTP, using a colour still from the production on the front cover. It has been recognised as one of the "steadiest sellers" in the book trade, both in the UK and abroad. Full editions appeared in America, Canada, Australia and South Africa, and it has been translated into Russian, German, Czech, Bulgarian, Japanese and Swahili.

It was, and remains, a publishing phenomenon.

A MASTERPIECE?

"a working class Vanity Fair"

The publication of the full version of RTP rekindled the old debate of whether it was the work of a journeyman or a genius. The mangled version had already proved its worth in terms of inspiration and longevity. But now Tressell's full work was on display the question of whether or not it is literature in the fullest sense came to the fore again. The argument still rages.

Ironically, given the books nature and purpose, it was Establishment publications which first awarded it qualified literature status, and the Left, forever riven by obscure ideological differences and plain jealousy, which was the most critical.

The *Times Literary Supplement* had said of the abridged version: "It is not a work of genius but it has talent." (1) When the full version came out that opinion changed: "Tressell was a literary artist and knew precisely what he was doing. The long half-baked speeches on politics, anti-capitalism and the hope of the workers are all moving and tell the reader more about the rise of the British Labour Party, its instincts, traditions and future, than all the fireworks of Bernard Shaw or the blueprints of the Webbs. But it is as a story and a work of art that *The Ragged Trousered Philanthropists* has lasted so far - and will continue to last. The characters are too alive to be swamped by anything. It is true that it is because what Noonan recorded was sober fact that we are still bedevilled by labour relations. Robert Noonan's book is the voice of the poor themselves." (2)

Tressell's book had, especially in its abridged form, always divided the Radical Left , particularly Soviet-era British Communists. Sometimes those divisions were reflected in the same review. In September 1927 the printer Tommy Jackson wrote in the *Daily Worker* that RTP's popularity was in literary terms inexplicable: "In form a novel, the book is in fact a series of sketches of proletarian existence strung together by the merest thread of a plot. It has no exciting episodes, and its one and only sex episode is quite momentary and leads nowhere. It does not end, but breaks off hinting at horror. Its character-drawing is unaffectedly crude, and its hero is not beyond suspicion of sentimental priggishness. Quite half of its bulk is occupied with frank propaganda speeches presented as such – altogether a book which breaks every rule and ensures its damnation from the first." But Jackson continued: "Yet it has gone through nine large editions, and will probably go on selling indefinitely until the Revolution. The reason for this is plain – the book is true. The propaganda may be old-fashioned, but it is sound and the general background and atmosphere are such as every Worker can recognise and sympathise with at sight." (3)

When the full version came out many on the Left believed that the alleged flaws outlined above had only been magnified. Mervyn Jones, writing in *Tribune*, even claimed there was no artistry in RTP: "Now if you stand in Oxford Street for four hours with a camera, you do not succeed in making a film of the life of London. A film, a novel, a play is a work of selection, emphasis and contrast, brought out by ruthless cutting and editing." (4)

Almost 50 years later, Ray Farrar, an overall fan, wrote: "The "Philanthropists" lack feelings of class solidarity and the novel is hazy about how they may attain class consciousness to forward the struggle for socialism. Occasionally the idea of the impoverished masses driven by their wretched conditions to overthrow the capitalists in a bloody uprising is proffered, at others an appeal to "reason", to vote for Revolutionary Socialists. Owen's 'lectures' of course mirror the socialism of his day, a convincing analysis of capitalism coupled to the drawing of a wonderful vision of a socialist future, but somewhat vague as regards the transition between." (5)

Peter Miles found that RTP "has no place in the received academic literary canon... Tressell has proved a prickly candidate for admittance to the pantheon of English Literature." (6) He regarded RTP as a "self-contained kit for the dissemination of ideas." (7) And he concluded: "Pessimism about the dependence of working-class culture forces Tressell towards direct political education rather than struggle through cultural forms – where the battle is already lost." (8)

Miles also pinpointed RTP's position outside mainstream literature which relies on academia and bookshops: "Marked by familiarity, affection and enthusiasm, this history comprises recorded anecdote and the still living, although socially delimited cultured consciousness fostering such anecdotes. From this communal perception it is evident that continued reading of Tressell owes much to a popular tradition of interpersonal recommendation and dissemination, largely at the grass roots of the British labour movement. Unlike normative transactions over the bookseller's counter, this tradition of transmission possesses, or has been endowed with, qualities of intimacy and engagement. These reinforce the character of the tradition as the expression of an active desire that others should share the experience of the book..." (9)

Raymond Williams focused on the RTP as part of a previously-scarce tradition of work as the basis of literature, a tradition notable for honourable attempts rather, until Tressell, with complete success. George Eliot had tried it in *Adam Bede* and *Felix Holt*, while Thomas Hardy had achieved it in *The Woodlanders, Tess of the D'Urbervilles* and *Jude the Obscure*... and later it was the "decisive matrix" of much of D.H. Lawrence's work. Tressell's book was crucial, Williams wrote, "for it is not only to his literary ancestors – and especially to dickens – that we must go to appreciate him, but also to that largely unrecorded, anonymous culture of the ordinary people, in characteristic jokes, idioms, gestures, mockeries, entertainments, styles of speech: that largely sardonic, sometimes sentimental world in which over the years and the generations, thousands of ordinary people have defined their experience and their responses to it: that social creation which is as general and powerful as a language itself, and from which Tressell draws so much of his strength. Writers of his kind, and on his subject, are sustained by this culture at the same time as they organise and articulate it in individual works. It is in his access, unrivalled in his period, to just that popular culture, that Tressell finds ways of creating his unique and memorable world, in a mode which then has this inbuilt power to get through to many thousands of ordinary readers, who have kept and are keeping his novel alive." (10)

Williams was writing the forward to Jack Mitchell's book, the first full-scale critical appraisal of RTP. Mitchell knocked flat the critiques of literary snobs on both the Left and Right. He wrote that Tressell had avoided the traditional plot line and instead opted for a "wheel-like" arrangement which builds up rising suspense. The lack of "love interest" also made it unique, as there is no other important novel in the last 200 years where the author has dared to leave this out."

Mitchell went on: "There is a striking 'otherness' about the book's subject matter and construction. Add to this Tressell's avoidance of all the accepted tricks of the professional writer for titillating the reader's interest, an occasional surface amateurism about the writing, plus a tendency at times to long-windedness and repetition in the polemical passages, and you have that 'sound barrier' through which so many well-meaning scholars have failed to pass to a full recognition of Tressell as an artist. But there has been no problem on this score with the workers." (11)

Mitchell saw a clear connection from Thomas Carlyle to John Ruskin to William Morris to Tressell. Carlyle (1795-1881) was a bourgeois prophet of doom who despised industrial modernity and harked back to the Middle Ages. Unlike Robert he had no understanding of class struggle but believed in the dignity of work and believed that idleness, whether enforced by unemployment or the outcome of privilege, was a sin. Ruskin (1819-1900) was a middle class reformer who, below the surface, believed in the traditional strata of society. But like Robert he believed that work should be used to create beauty rather than the pursuit of profit, luxury or war. Morris (1834-1896) put together elements of the other two, but championed sincerely the working classes and democratic ideals. Morris, as we have seen, had a profound effect on Robert's physical and working art, but was a greater influence on his mastery of the written word. Morris believed, as Robert clearly did, that the mundane details of a working life were themselves instruments for social change and literary endeavour.

Mitchell wrote: "Thus the fact that our first real proletarian novelist was a skilled craftsman in the house-decorating trade, that he put the problem of man and labour ...in the centre of his picture, while owing something to Ruskin, bears the unmistakeable imprint of Morris." (12)

The Socialist Alliance activist and writer Dave Harker was critical of many aspects of RTP but was sure of its benevolent impact:. The RTP, he wrote, "is clear, straightforward and eminently readable, but in many ways it is a very odd book. After all, novels do not usually explain key points of Marxist theory. True, it has humour, parody, pathos, irony, rage, little victories, defeats, arguments and ideas. And it is brimful of hatred and contempt for the capitalist 'System', the ruling classes and their hangers-on. But surely capitalism is irreversibly triumphant in the 21st century? And anyway, the book is very hard on workers... Are all its readers sentimental masochists?"

Harker pointed out that some jaded readers see in RTP support for the idea that the working class is "too selfish, short-sighted and downright stupid to act in its own interests." But he concluded that RTP "is about hope. It is about socialist values and their continued relevance when we are being told that capitalism is here forever... The RTP was produced, reprinted, distributed and put to work throughout the labour movement and after a century is still used as a weapon in the struggle." (13)

As the years drifted towards the close of the century and into a new one, the re-assessment of Robert's work, both literary and political, was unabated.

Alan Sillitoe, writing in 1965: "I read an abridged edition of *The Ragged Trousered Philanthropists* when I was nineteen and with the Air Force in Malaya. It was given to me by a wireless operator from Glasgow, who said: "You ought to read this. Among other things it is the book that won the 1945 election for Labour." It had been cut to half the length of the present full version, made to end on a note of despair suggesting that cranks who believed in Socialism could do nothing better than think of suicide. The present edition ends the way the author intended.

"It isn't easy to say precisely the effect this book had on me when I first read it. It certainly had a great one, because it has haunted me ever since. Those whose life has touched the misery recounted by Robert Tressell can get out of it many things: a bolstering of class feeling; pure rage; reinforcement for their own self-pity; a call to action; maybe a good and beneficial dose of all these things.

"The soul of Robert Tressell, in its complete rejection of middle-class values, seems forged in the formative years of the English working-class, during the Industrial Revolution of 1790-1832. Tressell no doubt inherited this feeling from his early days as a more independent workman in South Africa. The working people in his time did not have the same clarity, violent outlook, nor intellectual guidance of those earlier men of the Industrial Revolution. Never before or since were they so spiritless or depressed.

"England was stagnating, eddying in a cultural and material backwater of self-satisfaction and callous indifference, in which those who had hoped it would go on forever, and those who had not were beginning to curse the day they were born. But by the time the first great English novel about the class war was published, the power of those who might act was being cut down on the Western Front. The Great War drained off the surplus blood of unemployment, and definite unrest. It proved once more the maxim that war is the father of a certain kind of progress - in certain societies. I imagine also that Robert Tressell's destitute workers welcomed it, for a while."

The year before, reviewer Oliver Edwards wrote that RTP has "no neatly worked out plot. It reaches no climax and comes to no conclusion. When Noonan is writing about the classes he did not know from the inside – it is there that his scoundrels are to be found – he can only caricature. Barrington, the wealthy man's son turned socialist, is a shadowy figure. There are a few pages here and there where the socialism becomes tedious. But all the rest more than compensates. It is salutary to be reminded that in our own lifetime men have been paid under £1 a week, that dismissal could be instant, and that the alternative to a job was starvation. *The Ragged Trousered Philanthropists* rings far more true than many of the better known 'condition of the people' novels of its day. That is why it has lasted." (14)

Novelist Margaret Drabble, writing in 1987: "The action takes place during one year in the lives of a group of working men in the town of Mugsborough, and the novel is a bitter but spirited attack on the greed, dishonesty, and gullibility of employers and workers alike, and on the social conditions that gave rise to these vices. Debates on socialism, competition, employment, and capitalism are skilfully interwoven with a realistic and knowledgeable portrayal of skilled and unskilled labour in the decorating and undertaking business, and with the human stories of the families of the workers. Noonan's coining of names for local worthies - Sweater, Didlum, Grinder, Botchit, etc. - indicates his attitude towards the widespread corruption and hypocrisy that he exposes, and the book has become a classic text of the Labour movement. The ironically named 'philanthropists' of the title are the workers who toiled for pitiful wages while making no effort to understand or better their lot." (15)

Andy McSmith, writing in *The Independent* in 2010, said: "George Orwell called it a "wonderful book." When I worked in a radical book shop in Newcastle upon Tyne, years ago, it was our best-selling title. Yet it is difficult to imagine that anyone has ever settled down to read the unabridged version of *The Ragged Trousered Philanthropists* from cover to cover for sheer pleasure. It is long, it is by an author about whom so little is known that he bordering on the anonymous. It is a story of a bunch of people doing a job they do not enjoy much, painting and decorating.

"But it is an astonishing creation for all that. Before it was published, just a few working-class characters had turned up in English literature, such as *Jude the Obscure*, in Thomas Hardy's novel of that name, or some of Charles Dickens's creations, but they were being observed from the outside by writers who had never had to do manual labour. It is also extraordinary how little work intrudes upon pre-20th century literature. You could spend a lifetime studying great novels in which no one is depicted doing any paid work at all. In English literature, there seemed to be an unspoken convention that work – particularly menial, monotonous work – made people less interesting.

"Some of the author's comments on his characters are notoriously scathing, but that is because he is berating them for undervaluing themselves. He calls them "philanthropists" because they allow themselves to be exploited. He wishes that they would stand up for themselves. It is a novel that celebrated the dawn of working-class consciousness."

D.J. James, reviewing Harker's 2003 book, wrote: "As literature, Tressell's work falls neatly into George Orwell's famous category of 'good bad books': novels that are full of faults – in this case repetition and tedious explication – but whose human qualities allow them to survive long after more exalted productions have gone to the remainder bin. Personally, I would cheerfully back *The Ragged Trousered Philanthropists* to outlast the complete collected works of Virginia Woolf and Iris Murdoch. Tresssell is a pattern demonstration of one of the great axioms of modern politics – that some of the worse advertisement for socialism are socialists." (16)

On the centenary of Robert's death the playwright Howard Brenton, whose adaption of RTP had just been staged at the Liverpool Everyman, described the book as "a working class *Vanity Fair*." He went on to address both literary merit and the novel's political relevance:

"The novel's 750 pages teem with comic and tragic incidents. Tressell uses wildly varying styles. He describes life on the edge of the abyss of destitution, a place he knew all too well, with a tender naturalism. But he is never sentimental. Ruth Easton's husband Will sinks into alcoholism, they rent out a room to the religious Slyme, who seduces her. Finding herself pregnant she goes to drown herself in the canal. But Tressell knows chance and death go hand in hand. Ruth finds that where there was a gate to the canal towpath there is now an iron railing. Almost farcically, she can't find a way through. She gives up and goes to Nora Owen, Frank's wife, for help and survives.

"Tressell relished writing set pieces sometimes of farce, sometimes of great eloquence. Vivid scenes among the bosses on the town council read like a berserk Dickens. In contrast there is "The Great Oration", a mighty 30-page speech given by the renegade son of a rich Manchester manufacturer (shades of Engels). In crystal-clear prose, it covers the history of capitalism from the middle ages to the end of the 19th century, then sweeps on to describe how a just socialist society could be achieved. There is a children's birthday party at which Bert White entertains children and parents with "the grand pandorama", a toy theatre he has made using newspaper and magazine cuttings that mix patriotic scenes of empire and royalty with pictures of appalling factory conditions and riots.

"The workers are "philanthropists" because they give the value of their work away to their employers. Tressell sees them as stunted, their potential blocked, ignorant of their predicament. They are forever having to hurry and botch jobs to keep costs down, suppressing their natural creativity. From the firm's owner Rushton to his manager Hunter, the foreman Bob Crass, to the workers, the system brutalises and squeezes the humanity out of everyone. *The Ragged Trousered Philanthropists* is the working-class *Vanity Fair*.

"In the 1900s the two paths socialism could take were already mapped: revolutionary and parliamentary. The party Tressell joined, the SDF, was revolutionary. We know that path led to the disaster of the Soviet Union. But the reformist path taken in Britain has led, after the successes of the 1945 Labour government, to the watering down and sluicing away of all socialist aspirations by New Labour. Does Tressell say anything to us? Can we compare our world to the Hastings of 1905?

"In "The Great Oration", Tressell describes the creation of a new kind of state: the co-operative commonwealth. It is a communist vision, utopian, even quaint, but deeply moving. Writing a stage adaptation made me think, paradoxically, that everything is different but nothing has changed. We too are enmeshed in a feckless and dangerous capitalist system. Tressell's wonderful book convinced me that it's time to begin the struggle for the co-operative commonwealth all over again." (17)

Fred Ball, who had so painstakingly put back together the original manuscript, said simply: "I have never changed my opinion that Tressell is a true original in our literature, whose personal story could not be allowed to die…" (18)

My own view is that it is a masterpiece of its time with continuing relevance today. It is a vivid depiction of a bygone age, and no-one should pretend that the horrors it contains in terms of the day-to-day poverty is wholly true today. I'm sure Robert would not approve of the "feckless" underclass who are more concerned with flat-screen TVs, computer games and Ipods than meaningful employment.

One of the strongest elements in the book showed the love of a single father for his child. His fiction imitated the real-life bond with his daughter which shines through century-old memories of those who are themselves now dead. Robert certainly fostered the joys of childhood learning, as Kathleen attested to in what she regarded as a blissful, if poor, childhood without a mother, and that comes through loud and beautifully clear in RTP. Robert also saw educations, from basic numeracy and writing to balloon-making and the identification of flora and fauna on country rambles, as a way out of poverty and exploitation.

Robert also had astonishing ear for the spoken word. A few lines, whether said in an office, on a site or in a pub, pins down instantly character and background. The punctuation may now seem archaic, but Robert was a master at capturing speech patterns. His obvious delight in recording the authentic voices of working men is never patronising, except when applied to bosses' narks, crawlers and those with pretensions to emulate their "betters."

The times may have changed, but Robert's Edwardian analysis of that exploitation and the market force cruelties of capitalism. He would not have been surprised at the credit crunch, sub-prime mortgages, the bonuses enjoyed by greedy bankers as the prize for failure, the state bail-outs, the collapse of economies, the global recession and the emergence of new competitors with their own selfish agendas. And reading his account of a general election and a by-election, he certainly would not have been surprised by a Tory-Lib coalition government which increased penalties on the poor while rewarding the rich.

I also believe that RTP merits its category as literature. Its vivid use of language means that we can hear all the characters as they work, rest and play. Robert also had astonishing ear for the spoken word. A few lines, whether said in an office, on a site or in a pub, pins down instantly character and background, the punctuation may now seem archaic, but Robert was a master at capturing speech patterns. His obvious delight in recording the authentic voices of working men is never patronising, except when applied to bosses' narks, crawlers and those with pretensions to emulate their "betters."

Its characters are positively Dickensian, but all believable, and with only the merest hint of exaggeration for effect. Its episodic structure also reflects both Dickens's serial style and the best of today's TV serialisation. More *The Wire* than *Eastenders. Cathy Come Home* rather than *Big Brother*. And its mix of humour and tragedy, and its willingness to find humour and spirit in tragedy, puts it with the best of all genres.

The full version may not be "the best book ever" but for inspiration it is among the best. It is, as Amazon tags it, "the first great English novel about the class war." Which, by my definition, makes it a genuine piece of literature with claims to masterpiece status. That may not be an unqualified answer to this chapter's title, but it is close enough.

BACK FROM THE DEAD

"The Girl Mystic"

Fred Ball concentrated on finding a permanent home for the manuscript. In the late 1940s he had had discussions with the associated Society of Woodworkers, Wortley Hall Memorial College and the National Council of Labour Colleges, but they all drew a blank. A deal was virtually done in 1954 with the Electrical Trade Union, but just before it was clinched the union's general secretary, Walter Stevens, was killed in a motor accident and his successor did not follow it up.

Late in 1957, however, Peter Blackman, one of the shareholders and secretary of the Sussex Federation of Trades Councils, made a scatter-gun pitch at several other unions. The first to bite, having previously turned Ball down, was the Nation al Federation of Building Trades Operatives. The union's executive agreed a price in May 1958: the original 70 guineas cost to the shareholders, plus 20 guineas to compensate them for expenses over the years, plus 2.5 per cent compound interest. That came to £129 10s and 10-and-a-half d, which was rounded up to £130. Ball wrote a history of the manuscript and in August he and his wife took it and the manuscript, packed in a cardboard box marked "processed peas", to the Clapham HQ of the Federation. They handed it to H. Heumann, editor of the Federation Journal. Ball wrote: "There was no ceremony, just a simple in and out with a couple of minutes' chat during which Mr Heumann expressed his preference for the Richards version of the book." (1)

The Federation donated it to the TUC where it was displayed in Congress House as part of the heritage of the whole trade union movement. It was handed over, in a simple ceremony to which Ball was not invited, to TUC general secretary Sir Vincent Tewson. Ball confessed he was "selfishly sorry to lose sight of these historic hand-written pages of our house-painter." But it had finally reached "an honoured resting place."

Over roughly the same period Ball tried to locate the banner which Robert had painted for the SDF depicting the serpent of capitalism being strangled by a worker. It had first been used at a Hastings beach meeting in 1910 addressed by Tom Kennedy. Robert's friend and fellow-activist possessed it for years and in 1929 it was handed over to the new Hastings branch of the Independent Labour Party, with SDF changed to ILP. In 1937 it was carried from Blackfriars to Hyde Park in a May Day procession. When war came, it disappeared. Ball was told that it was sent to Birmingham in 1940, as Hastings was then in the front line during the Nazi invasion scare. After the war officials were unable to find it. "It may well be stored in someone's attic," Ball said. (2)

Meanwhile the reprints of RTP finally saw some recognition in Mugsborough, albeit on a small scale. In 1962 the local trades council donated a seat made by Corporation carpenters which was placed in Carlisle Parade. The trades council also won permission to install a marble tablet on the wall of Robert's old residence at 115 Milward Road. Ball, supplied with more information about the family background and identity, started writing an updated biography of Tressell.

At the end of May 1967 he received astonishing news which delayed publication of his follow-up for several years.

Late in May 1967 the *Radio Times* gave details of an upcoming BBC TV production of RTP, dramatized by Stuart Douglas and produced by Michael Bakewell. The following Monday he received a telephone call from his brother telling him that *The Times* had carried an interview with ...Kathleen Noonan. He couldn't believe it until he saw the newspaper's photograph and it was undoubtedly recognisable as an elderly version of the portraits he knew so well. Kathleen was living in Gloucestershire, and had done so for many years. Furthermore so was her daughter Joan, also reported killed in a Canadian road crash. Robert sent Kathleen a copy of his book, *Tressell of Mugsborough*, and with his wife took a train to meet her.

In Gloucestershire they cordially were met by Kathleen, her daughter and her son-in-law Reg Johnson, who had seen the *Radio Times* preview and written to *The Times* to tell them that Tressell's daughter was alive.

Kathleen, a sprightly, laughing-eyed septugenarian told the Balls, in the first of many interviews, her extraordinary story.

She had used the £25 from the sale of the book to buy her passage to Canada and three trunks of clothing, one of them full of stockings, ready for a colder climate. Her aunt still disapproved of her impending marriage to her son Paul, but offered her best wishes nevertheless. She later sent a Queen Anne silver tea service as a wedding present. Kathleen was waved off from London by Mrs Mackinlay and her two daughters, and she set sail in June 1914 from Bristol on the Royal George. The ship docked first at Quebec and then at Montreal from which Kathleen took a train to Regina, Saskatchewan. She met Paul on July 1 1914 and they were married by special licence four days later at St Peter's Church. Kathleen gave her parents' names as Robert and Madeline Noonan. Paul was described on the certificate as a gasoline engineer.

Within a month war was declared and Paul was laid off by his firm Massey Harris of Regina where he had been servicing farm equipment. The young couple saw an advertisement for a theatrical company which was recruiting a cast for a transcontinental tour. The company wanted a "heavy" to play serious parts and an "ingénue" to play innocent girls. The couple were hired after reading for the director. Paul adopted the stage name Edward Lynne and Kathleen became Mrs Lynne in the company and Gabrielle Devereaux on the stage. Kathleen recalled: "We studied and rehearsed in a small Ontario town. We couldn't have been out of work for long, as it was while we were studying one day in the cemetery I lost my wedding ring and we had only been married for three months when that happened." (3)

The company performed one-night stands through Saskatchewan and Alberta, and three weeks of repertory at Brandon, Manitoba, including two performances on Christmas Day 1914. "Part of our proceeds were supposed to go to the Red Cross," Kathleen said. "At some towns we did very well and stayed longer and at others the halls were half-empty. It was a very interesting life for me – seeing Canada on the way, dashing from one station to another to make connections; having to put up scenery when we arrived, for we carried, and had to use, our own in most places, as it was only an occasional town that had a real theatre." (4) They stayed in hotels and boarding houses, buying food from farms and village shops.

The travelling life stopped when Kathleen became pregnant and her condition became evident on stage. Joan was born on November 7 1915 in Winnipeg. At the railway station the couple could not afford to redeem a trunk they had left to go on tour. Lost with it were family papers, manuscripts, letters, family photographs and copies of the *Evening Ananias*, the 'newspaper' her father had produced when returning by ship from South Africa. The couple lived in a succession of furnished rooms and.

Despite their baby, the marriage soured. Kathleen jumped at the offer of a free railway ticket to Toronto with Joan, where they joined the husband-and-wife managers of the touring show. Paul sold their few possessions and eventually joined them and obtained an office job, which he clearly hated. "Whether it was confinement to routine or whether his liver was affected then I didn't know but I used to dread his return at night as I never knew what mood he would be in," Kathleen said. "It was just that we were mentally incompatible, he had been spoiled and I suppose I had been too."

Paul was offered a place in a vaudeville show and there was a position for Kathleen, but she would have had to wear tights on stage. She refused, to Paul's chagrin. "Imagine Katie, who wouldn't shake a duster out of the window without first pulling down her sleeve, in tights with a frill round the middle," Kathleen said. "The pay was very good and Paul was furious because I wouldn't do it." The vaudeville entrepreneur, however, taught the couple mind-reading tricks which was to have been part of the show. The couple, for reasons which Kathleen could not remember, nevertheless took the act on the road themselves, mainly giving performances at the new picture houses between one and two-reel films. Kathleen, in flyers circulated by Paul in advance, became 'Gabrielle Devereaux, the Girl Mystic.'

Their show eventually folded and they found themselves in a small town with virtually no money left. Paul could not get a job and Kathleen worked in a hotel kitchen in return for bed and board. The marriage was by then virtually over but Kathleen felt she could not leave him while he was in dire straits. Eventually Paul was taken on by a small show company and Kathleen, with 16 dollars for a train fare, told him she and Joan were leaving. He refused to believe the split was permanent and saw them off at the railway station, saying that if any relatives asked after him she should tell them he was dead. Kathleen arrived at Toronto and stayed with friends until she found work. She vividly remembered Armistice Day 1918 in Toronto: "Excitement was wild, everyone waving flags, banging pots and shaking talcum powder over passers-by. I got Joan a small flag and she waved it as I pushed her in her go-cart. Saying "Peace, Peace." (5)

Paul visited their flat in Toronto and tried to persuade her to get back together again. When that failed he threatened to take Joan away from her. Such threats came to nothing, and the truth finally dawned on him. He advertised for a girl to join him in a mind-reading act, specifying that she had to have "long fair hair and be really pretty." Kathleen said: "My friends teased me about that. But he never bothered me again and I suppose that was when he invented the motor accident. It was unheard of to think that I should leave him. He might have said we'd died from the influenza epidemic which was raging just then, but that would not have been so dramatic." (6)

Kathleen stayed in Toronto for several years and continued to call herself Mrs Lynne, partly because her married name, 'Meiklejon,' was unusual and would have made it easier for Paul to trace her if he returned from his theatrical travels. She did not claim a penny in maintenance from her husband, believing strongly that she had no right to it because she had left him. For a while she cared for an invalid, and then found a job at St John's Hospital run by Anglican nuns. She stayed there for seven years. She and Joan never starved but had to watch the pennies. Paul had reported back to Britain that they had been killed, so contact with her remaining family was non-existent. But Grant Richards had not heard the bogus reports and sent Kathleen another £25 for her father's book during the early post-Great War years when it was clear that he had a best-seller. "It is still selling well," he told her in a letter.

In 1923 Joan became seriously ill with rheumatic fever and was in bed for a year. That made her work at the hospital increasingly difficult and she enrolled with the public health division of the Victorian Order of Nurses which allowed her greater flexibility over her working hours. She remained with that organisation for 15 years. During that time she became, like her father, an ardent social reformer.

Kathleen, and later her daughter, joined St John's social service study group, attached to the Diocesan Synod of Montreal, and the Anglican Fellowship for Social Action. Helped by a like-minded reporter on the Montreal Daily Star, she produced a pamphlet exposing the city's slums and the conditions of the poor. Her original title, *Dirty Old Montreal*, was changed to *Hovels for God's Children* on the grounds that the original version might have been libellous. The tract exhorted church-goers to see for themselves their brothers and sisters "rotting in infested hovels fit for but rats and lice" and find out who owns and operates the properties, who exploits the poor. It also urged congregations to find out if they or their diocese derived any income from the slums, adding: "The time has come that judgement must begin in the House of God."

Joan's health deteriorated and in 1945 mother and daughter set off for warmer climes, travelling to Tampa, Florida before boarding a ship to Kingston, Jamaica. When Kathleen applied for a passport she put her name as Mrs Meiklejon-Lynne, but was told that another application had been received for a Mrs Lynne-Meiklejon for a journey to England. She discovered that Paul had married in 1922, apparently bigamously, and had died of a liver complaint in 1942. Kathleen told the passport office nothing and the similarity of names was put down to coincidence.

In Jamaica Kathleen quickly found work in the Nuttall Hospital, while Joan worked in hotel offices. But both developed painful throats which they blamed on dust and in 1947 they returned to Canada. Kathleen was hired as assistant matron at Trinity College, Toronto, where she stayed for seven years. Joan, who had always wanted to be a missionary and was offered training in England in 1956. Joan tracked down her surviving relative, Robert's niece Alice, and from her learnt that she and her mother had been reported dead almost 40 years earlier. In 1958 Kathleen joined Joan for a holiday, the first time she had been in England since 1914. By then she was working at the women's College Hospital, Toronto. She and Joan returned to Canada. In 1962 Alice died and Joan received the balance of her father's share of the family estate. She and Kathleen decided to return permanently to England.

None of Robert's circle of friends ever knew of Kathleen's return from the dead. The only family member who knew, cousin Alice, who had kept the secret for decades for reasons she never shared, was herself dead for real. Gradually Kathleen pieced together the fate of others she had known as a child. She had not seen Arthur, the little cousin she had shared homes with, for several years before she first set sail for Canada, and was nine or 10 the last time she remembered seeing him in St Leonards. She discovered that Arthur had signed up during the First World War as an 18-year-old aircraftman in the Royal Flying Corps. He was killed and the name First Air Mechanic G.A. Rolleston is carved on the war memorial in Alexandria Park. Hastings. His is one of 1,250 names of men from Hastings and St Leonards – 707 of whom died in 1914-198 - etched into the Portland stone, topped by a bronze by Margaret Winser, a pupil of Rodin. The £2,000 memorial was due to be unveiled in Autumn 1921 but that was delayed until March 1922 due to difficulties with the bronze casting and "industrial action."

In England Kathleen realised for the first time the extent of her father's fame and the sales of his book in numerous forms. Lawrence and Wishart sent her a copy of the full version and it was only after reading that she realised how badly the 1914 editor had "mutilated" her father's work. The publisher and the BBC sent her cheques, even though the RTP copyright had expired. She certainly held no grudge against Grant Richards, telling a reporter: "It was a lot of money to me and the publishers were taking a chance. Nobody knew whether it would be a success so I suppose it was a very fair price/ I keep kicking myself for my own stupidity, but I don't think that there is anything I can do about the book now." (7) She then dropped her own little bombshell, saying that she could not afford a TV and had therefore missed the screening of the BBC version. It was that, it emerged, that had led her son-in-law, Joan's husband Reg Johnson, to write to the media and reveal that Tressell's daughter was alive and well and living in Gloucestershire. Kathleen told Ball: "If I had had a TV set I would probably still be 'dead' and we would never have met."

In August 1968 Kathleen, with Joan, returned to Hastings for the first time in 54 years. She was filmed revisiting her old homes and other places associated with her father. A few months later she was presented with a TV set, following a fund-raising effort by Hastings trades council, at the railway staff association club in St Leonards, along with a cheque. The following June she was able to watch the BBC version of her father's book when it was reshown. In the meantime she was reunited with her old childhood friend Rose Cruttenden.

Fred Ball, in a number of long interviews, grilled her on her father and her childhood and everything since, for his updated Tressell biography. The pair hit it off from the start, and Ball reciprocated by filling her in on the missing parts of her own family history, not least her mother's real name.

Kathleen died in Bristol on March 12 1988, aged 95. Ball wrote her obituary, starting: "Kathleen Noonan, the only child of 'Robert Tressell' who wrote *The Ragged Trousered Philanthropists*, herself earned a permanent niche in the literature of socialism. Robert Noonan's novel (1914) would never have seen the light of day but for his daughter's devotion after the Irish house-painter and sign-writer's death in 1911." (8)

Kathleen, during a colourful, improbable life on three continents, found peace through her religion and zeal for social reform. Robert would have understood the former, and warmly approved of the latter.

THE MURAL

"falling slates and rubble"

My own walk-on part in this story came late in 1970 when I was a 17-year-old trainee reporter on the *Hastings and St Leonards Observer*, described in RTP as *The Obscurer*. I knew nothing of that epithet at the time.

 My parents had settled in Hastings when my father Jimmy, a professional footballer since his mid-teens, having played for such teams as Leicester City, Bolton Wanderers, Grimsby Town and Watford, was signed up for the Southern League after age and professional fouls had knocked him out of the top ranks. Although he was the son of a Lanarkshire miner and of good socialist stock, he rarely talked about anything other than football, bless him. I had joined the local paper in 1969, a few months into my A-Levels, after walking out of Hastings Grammar when I was told that my eyesight was not good enough to be an RAF fighter-pilot. I was taken on by a great, old-school editor, J.V. Cornelius, who believed that his reporters, male and female, should witness everything – from flower shows to infanticide inquests, from bring-and-buy sales to murder investigations. I was the youngest on the staff which meant that when I was in the office in Cambridge Road, I was expected to pick up any ringing telephones.

Such a call came, in August or September 1970, from Fred Ball. Did I know that Robert Tressell's only surviving pictorial masterpiece was about to be demolished? he asked. Robert who? I almost asked, but didn't. I was swiftly enthused by Fred's own enthusiasm.

It emerged that David Haines, a local writer, had noticed a gang of demolition men starting to dismantle St Andrew's Church, where in 1905 Robert had worked so long and so hard on decorating the chancel. Robert's artwork had long been covered in whitewash and plaster, but Haines scratched at a surface and uncovered gold-leaf and colour. He called the curator of Hastings Museum, Mainwaring Baines, and Fred who then called the *Observer*. Luckily I was the lad who picked up the phone.

It was clear that Robert's original artwork was about to be smashed to smithereens. But did anyone care? A rescue campaign was started. To help, and to encourage interest in the campaign, I interviewed the local vicar, the Reverend T.H. Walters, to discover why Tressell's work had been covered over in 1966. He told me that French vandals had daubed it "in bright orange paint with French slogans and obscenities."

He went on: "I came in early on Sunday morning and could hardly hold the service with this filth in the background… Some parishioners hastily set about scrubbing the walls and as they did this, inevitably a great deal of damage was done to the painting… It had been a drab dark area, the prevailing colour being a gloomy green. The church council decided that it should be repainted in mid-white emulsion. This transformed it into an attractive, light and airy sanctuary." The vicar also told me that he had little knowledge of Tressell and no idea of the mural's significance. (1)

Ball, his 10-year-old daughter and the Haines family scraped at the lower portions of the chancel and, instead of a gloomy green, they found bright, vivid colour. Ball wrote: "We had to make a quick decision. The demolition men were about to pull the roof down and were already removing slates and, with the huge beams and stonework, the church floor would soon be several feet deep… We were told, quite rightly, that demolition could not be held back for us, delay was a costly business, but the workmen told us we had about two days before the roof came in. We rapidly began cleaning off to try to find a definite part of the design and came up with an outline of one of the 14 panels which formed the lower half of the mural Working over the week-end with such doubtful aids as paint removers and detergents we uncovered part of the panel… after the week-end we could only get to work when the demolishers weren't actually taking the roof off and even then we managed sometimes to be tucked away in the chancel while parts of the main roof were coming down and the whole place was filled with clouds of dust and falling slates and rubble." (2)

I remember it well. I was there with a photographer, having persuaded the editor that it was a story worth covering, and we were on site when masonry tumbled – health and safety rules were pretty lax then. I did not join in physically – I only had one suit and that was for work, not demolition rescue – but I like to think my contribution was to generate publicity. My coverage sparked interest with the *Guardian,* who sent its

star foreign correspondent, Martin Woolacott. I picked up him from the railway station and took him to the demolition site. I then remember leaving him for an hour in a greasy-spoon café where he scribbled out a page lead for the following day's edition. It was headline "Hastings still fails Robert Tressell" and read in part: "A massive fresco by Robert Tressell, sign painter and decorator extraordinary, and author of the Socialist classic, *The Ragged Trousered Philanthropists*," is about to be destroyed.

"The fresco is the only surviving example of Tressell's work as a decorator. It was covered over a few years ago but is still intact beneath a coat of distemper. Demolition contractors began to knock down the church last week and are due to start on the chancel within a couple of days. Barring a miraculous intervention, all that is likely to be saved of the fresco are a few fragments that two local writers hope to remove before the chancel is knocked down.

"Hastings, whose citizens were outraged some 50 years ago to discover that the Mugsborough of Tressell's book was their own town, has received the news with total indifference. The "Hastings Observer," which figures in Tressell's book as the "Obscurer," gave the story six inches on an inside page. The council – which Tressell called the "Forty Thieves" or "The Brigands" – has evinced no interest in the affair. Everybody on the church side connected with the demolition of St Andrew's seems either to be on holiday or unaware of what is happening.

"No claims are made that Tressell, who worked in Hastings between 1901 and 1910, was a great painter. But he had talent in that direction, a talent which saved him from losing his job on more than one occasion. And the fresco clearly also has a historical and sentimental interest.

"Readers of "Philanthropists" will remember that Owen, the character closest to Tressell himself, avidly seizes the occasional opportunities to do artistic decorating work, as when he agrees to decorate the drawing room of "The Cave" in Moorish style. Tressell did many such jobs for the four or five Hastings building firms he worked for in his 10 years in the town. At one time, there were 30 or 40 "Tressells" in the town – murals and frescoes in restaurants, public-houses, churches, and private homes.

"Hastings has never been proud of Tressell. Nothing is made of him in the schools, and the education committee even turned down a recent offer by a London school to put on a dramatised version of "Philanthropists" for Hastings children. Tressell's centenary year – he was born in 1870 – has been marked in Hastings by a minuscule display in the central library. The director of the town's museum has, however, offered a few pounds towards the cost of the do-it-yourself rescue operation." (3)

Woolacott was a bit harsh on the *Observer/Obscurer*, but created a fuss which resulted in a modestly happy outcome. The council took an interest, particularly after my editor wrote in a leader column: "The goings on in St Andrew's and in particular certain Press reports have aroused a great deal of controversy both locally and nationally. Local residents seem bent on proving that Hastings is interested in Tressell. Both Mr Ball and the Observer have received countless phone calls offering assistance. The report angered officials in the Church Commission, who claimed that all this had been going on behind their backs." (4)

Over the next week offers of help and money came from the trades council, unions, local people and the BBC, while the Public Works Department of the council loaned equipment. Ball and Haines insured themselves – that

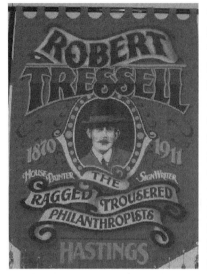

was compulsory – and cut the panel, along with plaster and brickwork, from the now roofless church. Workmen shared £40 to give them time to do so, something which would have tickled Robert. The pieces of the panel were carried away in cardboard boxes and stored in the museum until they were reconstructed over a period of several years when money was available. The panel is on display still as the last known physical reminder of Tressell's work. Ball said: "For this reason above all, and irrespective of any intrinsic merit the murals may have possessed, was the salvage operation undertaken."

Later it transpired that the original templates for the St Andrew's mural had been found in company stores and unwittingly destroyed because no-one recognised their value.

Also towards the end of 1970, and prompted by the BBC documentary which followed Kathleen on a tour of Hastings, Robert Noonan's last resting place was finally found.

Ball had long before obtained a copy of his death certificate which showed that he had been buried with others in a pauper's grave near the walls of Walton Gaol, Liverpool. The cemetery superintendent, William Marsden, tracked it to plot T.11. The camera crew were shown to a grassy, overgrown patch. There was nothing to mark the spot, but after measuring 11 paces to the right spot the cameraman placed an empty jam pot to focus on.

A few yards away was a grave containing the bones of a family called Owen.

***

That was not the end of the story of Robert's grave.

When Fred Ball's book was published in 1972 it sparked much interest amongst Liverpool trade unionists and activists, including seaman John Nettleton, local hero Billy Kelly and Labour councillors. They agreed that a headstone must mark Robert's last resting place. It was not easy.

First the local vicar at St Nicholas's, which included the cemetery, referred their bid to the Church of England's upper echelon, who refused unless permission was given by all the remaining relatives of those buried with Robert, an impossible task. After six months, the church authorities accepted permissions from Irish relatives who may or may not have been related to the dead paupers. Nettleton and his allies paid the Church £36 for bureaucracy. Their next task was to raise the money for a headstone. They formed a committee which included such luminaries as Jack Jones and Eric Heffer. The stone cost over £1,000, paid for by unions, pensioners and people from as far away as Australia. The collection included Japanese yen and Yugoslav dollars.

The stone was quarried in Sweden and brought to Hull by members of the National Union of Seamen. From Hull it was taken by union drivers to be polished by union members in Aberdeen. From Aberdeen it was ferried by trade unionist drivers to Liverpool. "We wasn't having no scab working on that stone," said Nettleton.

But there remained a problem, despite the certainty of the TV camera several years earlier, of where exactly to put it. Nettleton recalled: "We found from an old grave-digger that the way they marked the pauper's section was that they had an architect's mark and they run out a plumbline and he also told us that paupers were buried differently from anyone else. Where an ordinary grave had four foot between a pauper's grave was six foot by four foot and only two foot between. And you know what they done? They used to bury them in the opposite direction. They worked them to death, and then they used them as a drainage system after they died." (5)

Liverpool trade unionist poet Tony Bradburn visited the approximate site and wrote:

Wintry roots comfort the workhouse waste
Forgotten men and women bone to bone
Briars, weeds, bare shooting canes and dank earth
Entomb the source of Noonan's self-erected stone.

A desolate church, a man-made shell, turns
Aside from the prison towers.
And each in turn think they've claimed his soul
That escaped in the darkest hours.

The site was indeed overgrown, with grass three feet high, and it took Nettleton and Kelly weeks to find a small sandstone marker with the correct burial number on it. The grave had been pinpointed and the headstone was finally placed over the grave in 1977. On it, at Fred Ball's suggestion, were carved not just Robert's name but also those of the others who shared the pauper's grave:

Elizabeth Mary Davies. Anna Brown. Margaret Bethell. James Cribb. William Ash. May James. Ann Ashton. William Ducksberry. William Barnes. Mary Davidson. Lily Harrison. Richard Donald.

POSTSCRIPT AND CONCLUSION

"on a par with the Tolpuddle Martyrs"

In Hastings a culture grew around Robert Tressell. Talks were given, memorials erected, research undertaken and societies formed, most notably the Robert Tressell Workshop.

The fragments of Tressell's mural lay in cardboard boxes as the local museum could not afford the £1,500 needed to restore it. An appeal was launched by Mrs Irene Wright, a former Lewisham gardener who had read RTP when she discovered she lived opposite one of Robert's lodgings. Unions donated between £50 and £100, and the rest of the money came from small amounts, mostly under £5, from members of the public. By 1982 the appeal had raised £2,500 and the restoration was completed that Easter. It shows the bible resting on Tudor roses open at Psalm 119 with, illuminated in gold leaf, the words: "Thy word is a lamp unto my feet and a light unto my path." It was unveiled in Hastings Museum by Eric Heffer who described Robert as "the greatest Socialist writer that Britain ever produced ...he should be honoured every year on a par with the Tolpuddle Martyrs."

Fred Ball, whose second biography, *One of the Damned*, was published in 1973, was involved in much Tressell-related activities. His dream of being a writer himself had been realised – apart from the two Tressell books he had also published his childhood memoirs, *A Breath of Fresh Air* and the fictionalised *A Grotto for Miss Maynier*. The latter had been inspired by his gardening work as a teenager. Fred, who always wanted to be a "pastoral poet" and had some poetry published, admitted to me that he was "painfully slow" writing prose. He wrote out his copy in longhand and it was typed up by his wife Jackie. In 1977 BBC Radio 3 broadcast his dramatized documentary *A Search for Robert Tressell*.

But as he got into his 70s the work and the tasks he set himself wore him down. He lived in a modest house in Fearon Road, Hastings, the same road as my parents, but complained of "blood pressure brought on over the years by tension, anxiety and such." (1) He felt that all his work on Tressell, including his books, had not done much for himself and his family.

He died on April 14 1988, a month after writing Kathleen Noonan Lynne's obituary. Fred more than anyone ensured that Bob Noonan's real story would be told. I am certain they would have liked each other a lot.

Joan Johnson, Robert's granddaughter, was taken seriously ill in 2000 and died on October 8. There was talk of making a feature film of RTP but, as always, money and copyright proved problems. Her husband, Reg Johnson, collected a substantial Tressell archive at their East Grinstead home, set up the Robert Tressell Foundation, and campaigned vigorously that at least some of the royalties due from a book which has gone into 111 editions and which still sells globally. At the 2005 Hay book festival he spoke of his chagrin that a granddaughter of the late publisher Martin Secker was receiving RTP royalties from the HarperCollins estate. He pointed to RTP in which capitalism always seems to defraud the workers, in this case through the generations. "The family, like the characters in the novel, has paid the price," he said. (2)

I left the *Observer* in April 1972 to run the Rye office of the *Sussex Express*. In between gymkhanas and tracking down a runaway Hong Kong police chief I covered bread-and-butter issues, some of which would have slotted easily into RTP. Rye Tory MP Bryant Godman Irvine, for example, told his local Conservative Association that he was pressing in Parliament to cut benefits for all strikers by £4 a week. He told me that it didn't matter whether a striker's union was paying strike pay or not. And he slammed the gas men over their current industrial action, one of many during Ted Heath's premiership. "The gas industry has been paying a wage about £2 above the average wage of this country, which is not low," he said. "If it were not for these industrial troubles we should have greater hopes of reaching our national objectives. (3)

After a year on the *Express*, I left Hastings to get on in newspapers. After covering murders, terrorist trials and the Middle East, and after six months on a union picket line, I reached the House of Commons as a Lobby correspondent in 1978 and got stuck.

I lost touch with Fred Ball and others then alive who played parts in the Tressell story, but I never lost interest in the subject. Several readings of RTP and Fred's books stayed in my mind. During the 18 years that Margaret Thatcher and John Major reversed many of the advances which working class people had made since Robert's day, I talked with those on both the Left and the Right of the Labour party about RTP's influence.

In Annie's Bar I had many conversations with MPs influenced by RTP, including Eric Heffer. And Ron "Red Ron" Brown, MP for Leith from 1979 to 1992. Ron was suspended from the house on several occasions, including once for hurling the Mace to the floor during a 1986 debate on the poll tax, for which he was also presented with a £1,500 repair bill. I'm sure that Robert would have approved of such behaviour. Not so much, perhaps, of the consequences of a conversation I had with Ron in 1991 about RTP. I gave him the names and addresses of pubs which Robert was known to have frequented, including the Cricketers and the Cambridge. Ron embarked on an away day pub crawl which led to a prosecution and £1,000 fine for smashing the furniture in the Hastings flat of ex-lover Noona Longden. He was expelled from the Labour Party and lost his seat in the following year's elections.

In 1985 the Robert Tressell Museum of Local history was opened in Walton Park Cemetery, Liverpool in a red sandstone building erected in 1852 close to Walton Gaol. Writer Tony Birtill reminded readers that Brendan Behan, a remand prisoner at the Gaol after being arrested in 1939 for IRA activities, regarded RTP as his favourite book. "Little did he know that his favourite author was buried but a stone's throw away," Birtill wrote. Irish nurses in the hospital and workhouse sent their children to the nearby Blessed Sacrament Junior School. Birtill was one of them, writing: "We often used to play in the pauper's cemetery. Strange to think, we were running all over Robert Noonan's last resting place.

"The cemetery is now the base of the Rice Lane city farm and so is as popular as ever with local kids who believe that he was a Robin Hood figure who was hanged in Walton Prison. His memorial is regarded with awe. One local kid was heard describing Noonan to a friend in a sweetshop: 'I'm not sure what his real name was but they called him the Ragged Arsed Rascal.' Noonan would have liked that." (4)

***

The Union Castle liner *SS Galacian* on which Robert, Kathleen and the rest of his little family has sailed from South Africa to England was renamed Glenart Castle in September 1914 and saw service as a hospital ship during the Great War. She was torpedoes by a U-boat on February 26 1918 and 162 people on board died. She remains on the sea floor 10 miles west of Lundy Island. (5)

***

Hastings' history since Robert left has been eventful.

The period after the Great War was dismal as returning servicemen were promised jobs which didn't exist and a reconstruction that never happened. In Hastings the only growth industry was that of street-hawkers. After the death of Alf Cobb, socialism in Hastings continued to battle against the tide. Frank Willard, in response to a Conservative cleric, wrote: "The Socialist is not at all a nice man. He bawls unpleasant truths from the housetops; he forces upon the public mind the ghastly inequalities of our social system. The Socialist agitator of today merely does what an unlettered carpenter did more than nineteen centuries ago, and like Him he is faced with the hatred and enmity of the professors and preachers of his time...." (6)

The 1930s saw another rejuvenation when the council finally realised they had to up their game to b ring in the tourists. Seaside resorts were looking tired and shabby, few more than Hastings, but the borough embarked on an ambition development programme along the sea shore. Most of the promenade was rebuilt, including a two-tier section near the pier. At the far St Leonards end an Olympic-sized swimming pool was built and the open-air complex was reckoned to be one of the best in Europe for swimming and diving. Marine Court, an Art Deco block of flats resembling the superstructure of an ocean-going liner, was also erected.

The Second World War put Hastings on the front line. The harbour arm and the pier had sections blown up to prevent them being used by Nazi invaders, the beach was fortified and placed out of bounds, and as air raids intensified many children were sent away.

In the post-war years the borough's fortunes see-sawed, and the cycle of relative prosperity followed by decline continues today. New developments, increasingly out of town, exist alongside boarded-up shop fronts, closed pubs and areas of semi-dereliction. Most local firms employ fewer than 10 people, and unemployment is almost double the East Sussex average. The population is ageing and major infrastructure projects remain elusive. The pier is a wreck, victim to both offshore speculators and arsonists. But the Old Town, once regarded as the pits, is a tourist magnet again.

Politically, the town swings back and forth in a way which Robert would have recognised. During the early 1970s the council had no overall control; in 1976 the Conservatives took power until 1980 when it reverted to a hung authority; it was taken by the Liberal Democrats in 1996 who lost it two years later following Labour's landslide 1997 general election victory; two years later Labour lost overall control; the Conservatives briefly took over for a year; between 2007-10 there was no overall control. Labour won it back in 2010.

In the 2012 council election Labour listed as its achievements: reducing street drinking, protecting allotments from developers, compulsory purchase of derelict homes, a crackdown on bad landlords, and the publication of the salaries and perks of all councillors. Robert would have approved, but he would also have hoped for something more. That election manifesto promised more decent homes and licencing of landlords, which would have ticked Robert's boxes. But he might have been puzzled by the prioritising of CCTV and war of dogs fouling the footpaths. However, he would have understood the council's frustrations at a 50 per cent cut in central government funding, the highest in the South East. (7)

In 1970 I covered the election of Hastings Conservative MP Ken Warren before I was old enough to vote myself. The flamboyant Warren had a personalised number-plate - MP 1066, what else?- and held it until he retired and it was handed on a plate to newcomer Jacqui Lait who promptly upset the fishing community by agreeing with EU quotas. She lost it to Labourite Michael Foster in 1997, the Conservative's second least likeliest loss in that election. Foster was an equality minister in the run-up to the 2010 election when Amber Rudd regained the seat for the Conservatives.

***

The Robert Tressell Workshop posed the obvious question: "What would Robert Tressell think if he were to come back from the grave and visit Hastings today? Once again he would find capitalism undergoing a crisis. Unfortunately, he would also find the Labour Party in crisis as well. I think he would be depressed to find that... although materially better off, we, the working people of Hastings, are still philanthropic. Indeed, we appear to be giving back what gains we have made over the years." (8) That question was posed in 1982.

Tony Benn, at a memorial lecture in Hastings in 1986, said: "Tressell's contribution to the reawakening of hope is that he gave us a torch to pass on from generation to generation. He gave us a lamp to light the way. He showed us that there is a light at the end of the tunnel. Robert Tressell is a teacher for our time who speaks from the past to give us hope for the future." Benn, regarded as a grand old man of British politics before his death, did more than most to keep Labour out of power during the Thatcherite era and papered over his time in a Labour Cabinet which rubber-stamped Trident. But was he right in this case?

Steve Peak wrote in 2011: "A beauty – and weakness – of *The Ragged Trousered Philanthropists* is the way Tressell describes the problem of capitalism in a graphic, powerful and simple manner. As he intended, the problem could then be understood and related to by the least literate of working people. But largely missing from his description are the complexities of racism, imperialism, environmental awareness, feminism and the power of the freemasons. Readers did not have to come to terms with any feelings they might have at not relating to black or Irish people, of a lack of interest in the environment or of difficulties there might be in male/female relationships… The absence of these complex issues from the drama of the book made it easier to read and understand, but may ultimately have played a role in making the powerful novel unsuccessful in its basic aim of overthrowing the intricate and self-perpetuating capitalism." (9)

Peak may have overstated his case by referring to the absence of "green" issues and racism – they were simply not a matter of concern in regional English communities of the time. But he has a point with Ireland and feminism. There are only a few glancing references to Ireland in the book and none at all to suffragettes – two of the dominant issues in the decade within which he was writing. There is no direct attack on the monarchy, although that is implicit in his denunciation of inherited wealth and landed aristocracy. And there are few references to foreign affairs and no sense of the slide towards global war, apart from a reference to German military police charging unemployed workmen. (RTP 302)

Peak raised questions about whether RTP, by avoiding uncomfortable issue, somehow contributed to the circumstances in which generations of activists went into "the dead end of the 1997 Labour government." That appears a ludicrous charge.

But Peak was closer to the truth when he wrote: "Many New Labourites after 1997 found the book uncomfortable: its sentiments were too blunt, its story-line unsophisticated, the emotions too crude and the whole thing apparently out-of-date. But the Labour government's failure to fulfil the hopes of the working class brought a renewed interest in the novel..." (10)

The book's contribution to Britain in the 20th century has already been discussed, but should never be under-estimated. The key was its influence on Labour's 1945 election triumph, of which the creation of the NHS is its most enduring, though now threatened, legacy. Robert wrote of workmen collecting their wages: *On the ledge of the little window through which their money was passed there was always a Hospital collection-box. Every man put either a penny or twopence into this box. Of course, it was not compulsory to do so, but they all did, because they felt that any man who omitted to contribute might be 'marked'. They did not all agree with contributing to the Hospital, for several reasons. They knew that the doctors at the Hospital made a practice of using the free patients to make experiments upon, and they also knew that the so-called 'free' patients who contribute so very largely directly to the maintenance of such institutions, get scant consideration when they apply for the 'free' treatment, and are plainly given to understand that they are receiving 'charity'. Some of the men thought that, considering the extent to which they contributed, they should be entitled to attention as a right. (RTP 221)*

But Robert would have had trouble with much of what has happened since. At the unveiling of her grandfather's mural, Joan Johnson said: "I often think that it is a good thing granddad died when he did. He would have had a fit at Stalinism and tower blocks. One of his great messages was that people should always do a good job, as his mural shows."

Robert would have had even less truck with those parents, certainly not all poor, who send their children to school unable to converse, sit still or go to the toilet on their own, never mind the first idea of the alphabet, colours and numbers. He would be truly shocked by the account of a south east teacher who wrote of her five-year-old pupil: "They wear nappies, drink cola from baby bottles, and don't know how to open a book... I put it down to parents dumping their children in front of the TV rather than interacting with them. These parents seem to believe that giving their children fundamental life skills isn't their responsibility... surely the joy of childhood is about the incredible journeys of discovery that children make. Surely the wonder of being a child lies in the abundance of learning – from the colours of the rainbow to how to eat like a grown-up. Tragically, many of the youngsters in my classroom are experiencing a horribly stunted childhood. They are painfully aware of adult concepts like binge drinking, yet can't recite a single nursery rhyme." (11)

However, many have pointed out that the political climate and attitudes of the ruling classes depicted in RTP have a particularly strong resonance today. One correspondent, Denis Keogh of Glasgow, wrote: "Cameron, Osborne and the sycophantic Clegg remind me of the story of the Pied Piper. The people of the South East followed the Tory tune and the rest of us fell in the same pit. Robert Tressell's book depicted the very same demise of the downtrodden, and that was 100 years ago." (12)

Robert would also have felt vindicated today in his view that the Tories and the Liberals were indistinguishable, merely cronies feathering their own bed. That view is held widely to apply to the recent Conservative-Liberal Democrat coalition, and not just by the Left.

At the time of writing the first draft of this book, 2012, newspapers and other media were reporting premier David Cameron trying to limit the damage caused his government by 'lobbygate' in which meals with him were sold to fat-cat donors and commercial special interests. There was more flak about the impact of the previous month's Budget, including a "granny tax" which will hit the part-time earnings of pensioners to pay for a 5p cut in income tax for the super-rich. Recession-hit families were also reckoned to be £511-a-year worse off because of child benefits curbs, Utility company bosses pocketed £millions in bonuses which cutting jobs and services. Bankers continued to be rewarded for failure. And it was revealed Tory London Mayor Boris Johnson raked in £900,000 from second jobs. All of the above echoed scandals in RTP, and each would have slotted in easily with Robert's vision.

I am writing this, the final draft, after the unexpected Tory win on May 7 2015 after five years of a coalition which undermined the National Health Service, used "austerity" cuts on public services and the poor to pay for more tax breaks for the rich, and introduced such abominations as the bedroom tax which impacts most heavily on the disabled and their carers. Yet millions of working class voters backed the Tories, or the UK Independence Party, or various complexions of nationalism, rather than Labour. The great-grandchildren of Robert's "Philanthropists" kept the Tories in power, and he would have found that truly shocking. Along with the fact that up to five million potential voters are unregistered, presumably because they either can't be bothered or see politics as an irrelevance to their daily lives. Yet all is not lost.

During my time reporting Parliament, new generations of politicians have rediscovered RTP because, while much of its polemic appears outdated, it speaks directly to ordinary, hard-working men and women struggling to make ends meet. There is nothing patronising about it, which is why it has lasted so long, and hopefully an upcoming generation will go back to it.

It is worth reminding ourselves again of Robert's final paragraphs, in which darkest night is replaced with some sunshine:

"But from these ruins was surely growing the glorious fabric of the Co-operative Commonwealth. Mankind, awaking from the long night of bondage and mourning and arising from the dust wherein they had lain prone so long, were at last looking upward to the light that was riving asunder and dissolving the dark clouds which had so long concealed from them the face of heaven. The light that will shine upon the world wide Fatherland and illumine the gilded domes and glittering pinnacles of the beautiful cities of the future, where men shall dwell together in true brotherhood and goodwill and joy. The Golden Light that will be diffused throughout all the happy world from the rays of the risen sun of Socialism."

It's a long time coming.

NOTES

All page number references to RTP in the text are from the Flamingo Modern Classic 1992 edition.

All page references to Fred Ball are, unless otherwise stated, from the 1979 Lawrence and Wishart edition of *One of the Damned*.

INTRODUCTION

1 Conversation with author, 1982
2 Introduction to Flamingo editor of RTP, 1983
3 Harker 227
4 Tribune, Oct 21 1955
5 Mitchell 1

CHAPTER 1 CHILDHOOD

1 Harker, 1
2 Ibid, 1-2
3, Ball 5
4 Harker,2
5 Ball, 5
6 Ibid, 6
7 Ibid 5-6
8 Ibid, 6

CHAPTER 2 SOUTH AFRICA

1 Ball, 9
2, Hopper, 10
3 Ibid, 10
4 Hyslop, 71
5 Ibid, 81
6 Ball 15-16
7 Harker, 6
8 Ball 18-19
9 Harker, 6

10 Hopper, 12
11 Ball, 22
12 Hopper, 13
13 Hopper, 8
14 Ball, 17
15 Harker, 9
16 Ball, 27
17 Ibid, 27
18 Ibidl, 28
19 Ibid, 26

CHAPTER 3 HASTINGS

1 Walsh, 9
2 Thornton, 16
3 Ibid, 18
4 Ibid 21-24
5 Hastings Mail and Times, July 7 1906
6 Ball, 9
7 Matthews 9
8 Ibid, 16
9 Hastings Mail and Times, Nov 23 1907
10 Hopper, 49
11 Matthews, 17
12 Peak, 8
13 Robert Tressell Workshop, 55
14 Hastings Mail, Nov 21 1903
15 Justice, Feb 8 1908
16 Matthews, 22

CHAPTER 4 MISERY

1 Ball, 33
2 Ball, 34
3 Ball, 43

CHAPTER 5 FAMILY LIFE

1 *Hopper, 39*
2 *Ball, 43*
3 *Ibid, 45*
4 *Ibid, 46*
5 *Harker, 12*
6 *Ball, 155*
7 *Ibid, 49*
8 *Ibid, 47*
9 *Ibid, 131*
10 *Ibid, 49*
11 *Ibid, 61*

CHAPTER 6 PAINTING AND BURYING

1 *Ball, 54-57*
2 *Peak, 7*
3 *Ibid , 17-18)*
4 *Ball, 54*
5 *J. Walsh, Painter's Journal 1922*
6 *Harker, 12*
7 *Ball, 59-60*
8 *Hastings and St Leonards Observer, Nov 6 1905*
9 *Harker, 13*

CHAPTER 7 ART AND OTHER TALENTS

1 *Ball, 63*
2 *Ibid, 62*
3 *Interview with author, Nov 1970*
4 *Robert Tressell Family Papers, The Evolution of the Airship article online*
5 *Ball, 69-70*
6 *Ibid. 67*

CHAPTER 8 RELIGION

1 *Ball, 68*
2 *Mitchell, 131*

3 Ball 94-95
4 Mitchell, 101
5 Ball, 93

CHAPTER 9 DRINK

1 Charles Booth, Life and Labour of the People of London, 305
2 Hopper, 35

3 Peak, 51
4 Hastings Observer, Feb 27 1909

CHAPTER 10 ELECTION

1 Ball, 81
2 Maclean, 88
3 William Morris. Manifesto of the Socialist League 1885
4 Ball, 82-85
5 Robert Tressell Workshop,, 39
6 Hasting Mail, Nov 5 1904
7 Ball, 80
8 Ibid, 72
9 Hopper, 20

CHAPTER 11 BIRTH OF A BOOK

 1 Ball 88
2 Raymond Postgate, The Builder's History
3 Hopper, 32-33
4 Hastings Observer Jan 15 1907
5 Hastings Mail, Feb 2 1907
6 Matthews,23-24
7 Justice, Feb 2 1907
8 Matthews, 35
9 Hopper, 22
10 Matthews, 24
11 Hastings Observer, Sept 1906 10
12 Peak, 20

13 Ball, 82-83
14 Matthews, 8
15 Hastings Observer, April 1 1905
16 Peak, 22
17 Richards press release 1914
18 Ball, 142

CHAPTER 12 THE PROFESSOR

1 Ball, 118
2 William Morris, How I Became A Socialist, article 1894
3 Ball, 137

CHAPTER 13 PLAY AND POLITICS

1 Ball, 136
2 Ibid, 127
3 Ibid, 127-129
4 Robert Tressell Workshop, 73
5 Ball, 133
6 Ibid 133

CHAPTER 14 SWEATER AND OTHER BOSSES

1 Postgate, 369
2 Ball, 115
3 Ibid, 116-118
4 Matthews, 10
5 Ibid
6 Ball, 116
7 7 Peak, 24
8 Ball, 116
9 Ibid 105

CHAPTER 15 FATHER AND DAUGHTER ALONE

1 Ball, 102
2 Ibid, 104
3 Hopper, 7
4 Ball, 104

5 Ibid, 132
6 Hastings Mail, Oct 5 1907
7 Labour Leader, Aug 13 1909

8 Justice, Aug 28 1909
9 Thornton, 21
10 Justice, Oct 10 1910

CHAPTER 16 THE BY-ELECTION

1 Oxford Dictionary of National Biography. Online edition
2 Robert Tressell Workshop, 42
3 Hastings Observer, Feb 29 1908
4 Journal of Liberal History, summer 2008
5 The Sun, Feb 18 1905
6 Hastings Observer, Feb 29 1908
7 Hastings and St Leonards Weekly Mail, March 3 1908
8 Ball, 125
9 Justice, March 14 1908
10 Hastings Observer, March 4 1908

11 Oxford Dictionary of National Biography, online edition

CHAPTER 17 CROOKS, THIEVES AND COUNCILLORS

1 Matthews, 1
2 Ibid, 3
3 Ibid, 8
4 Ibid, 10
5 Ibid, 12
6 Ibid, 110
7 Justice, March 1909
8 Ibid
9 Ibid

CHAPTER 18 COMPLETION AND DECLINE

1 Ball, 150
2 Ibid, 151-152
3 Ibid, 145

4 Ibid, 143
5 Ibid, 144
6 Daily Worker, May 10 1936
7 Harker, 42
8 Ball, 147
9 Ibid, 147
10 Ibid, 149
11 Gower letter to the Daily Herald, 1927, exact date unclear
12 Ball, 151

CHAPTER 19 LEAVING

1 Ball, 153
2 Matthews, 20
3 Ball, 163
4 Ibid, 154
5 Poynton, undated article
6 Ball, 154

CHAPTER 20 A LIVERPOOL TRAGEDY

1 Mitchell, 13
2 Nettleton, RT memorial lecture, Hastings 1981
3 Harker, 45
4 Nettleton
5 Ibid
6 Ibid
7 Ball, 157
8 Ibid, 159
9 Ibid, 162
10 Ibid, 160
11 Harker, 47
12 Ball, 161

CHAPTER 21 KATHLEEN ALONE

1 Ball, 164
2 Ibid
3 Ibid, 165
4 Ibid, 237
5 Ibid, 166

6 Jessie Pope, Preface to RTP 1914 edition
7 Grant Richards, Author Hunting, 280-281
8 Ibid
9 Ball, 167
10 Ibid, 169
11 Ibid, 171
12Jessie Pope correspondence, Oct 29 1913
13 Ball, 212

CHAPTER 22 HOME FROM THE WARS

1 Harker, 89
2 Ball, 187
3 Tom Thomas, 114
4 Harker, 102
5 Ibid
6 Ibid, 103
7 Ibid, 124
8 Ibid, 136
9 John Nettleton, Robert Tressell memorial lecture, Hastings, March 1985
10 Peak, 8
11 Ball, 214
12 Eric Heffer, conversations with author, 1985
13 Ball, 186
14 Harker, 139
15 Ibid, 140

CHAPTER 23 FRED BALL AND THE MANUSCRIPT

1 Harker, 132
2 Robert Tressell Workshop, 11
3 Ibid
4 Frank Swinnerton, Adventures of a Manuscript, article, Dec 1956
5 Ball, 192
6 Robert Tressel Workshop, 19
7 Ibid, 19-20
8 Ball, 200-201
9 Interview with author, 1971
10 Ball, 207-209

CHAPTER 24 A MASTERPIECE?

1 *The Times Literary Ssupplement, Feb 22 1952*
2 *Ibid, March 1 1957*
3 *Daily Worker, Sept 1927*
4 *Tribune, Oct 21 1955*
5 *Ray Farrar, socialistworld.net*
6 *Miles, 1*
7, *Ibid, 10*
8 *Ibid, 17*
9 *Ibid, 2*
10 *Mitchell xiii-xiv*
11 *Ibid, 22-23*
12 *Ibid, 158*
13 *Harker, xvii-xviii*

CHAPTER 25 BACK FROM THE DEAD

1 *Ball, 226*
2 *Ibid, 227*
3 *Ibid, 233*
4 *Ibid, 234*
5 *Ibid, 233-235*
6 *Ibid, 236*
7 *The Times, May 1967*
8 *The Guardian, March 17 1988*

CHAPTER 26 THE MURAL

1 *Interview with author, Sept 1970*
2 *Ball, 246*
3 *The Guardian, Aug 20 1970*
4 *Hastings Observer, Aug 29 1970*
5 *Nettleton, Robert Tressell Memorial Lecture, Hastings 1988*

POSTSCRIPT

1 *Harker, 218*
2 *Guardian, June 4 2005*
3 *Irish Times, Nov 10 1984*
4 *Peak, 12*

5 *Hastings Observer,* July 30 1921
6 *Hastings and Rye Constituency Labour Party, 2012 local government election manifesto*

7 *Robert Tressell Workshop,* 83-84
8 Peak, *8*
9 Ibid, *5*
10 *Daily Mail,* Feb 15 2012
11 *Daily Mirror,* April 4 2012

BIBLIOGRAPHY AND OTHER SOURCES

BALL, F.C, *Tressell of Mugsborough* (Lawrence & Wishart, London 1951); *One of the Damned* (Weidenfeld and Nicholson, London 1973), *Introduction to Robert Tressell Workshop* publication of The Robert Tressell Papers (WEA, 1982)
COLE, G.D.H., and POSTGATE, RAYMOND, *The Common People 1746-1946* (Methuen, London),
HARKER, DAVE, *Tressell - The Real Story of The Ragged Trousered Philanthropists* (Zed Books, London and New York 2003)
HICKS, GEORGE, *Preface* to 1927 edition of *The Ragged Trousered Philanthropists*
HOPPER, TREVOR, *Robert Tressell's Hastings – the Background to The Ragged Trousered Philanthropists* (Fanter Books, Lewes 2005)
HYSLOP, JONATHAN, *A Ragged Trousered Philanthropist and the Empire: Robert Tressell in South Africa,* History Workshop Issue 51 (Spring 2001) pp
JOHNSON, REG and HARKER, DAVE, *Working Bibliography* (2006, www.unionhistory.info)
LAYBOURN, KEITH, *The Rise of Socialism in Britain* (Sutton Publishing, Stroud 1997)
MATTHEWS, MIKE, *Alf Cobb: Mugsborough Rebel – The struggle for justice in Edwardian Hastings* (Christie Books, Hastings 2011)
MCLEAN, IAN, *Keir Hardie* (Allen Lane, London 1975)
MEEK, GEORGE, George Meek, Bath Chairman (Constable, London 1910)
MILES, PETER, *The British Working-Class Novel in the 20th Century,* (Edited

by Jeremy Hawthorn (Edward Arnold, London 1984), Chapter One, The Painter's Bible and the British workman: Robert Tressell's Literary Activism

MITCHELL, JACK, *Robert Tressell and The Ragged Trousered Philanthropists* (Lawrence & Wishart, Surrey 1969)

MORRIS, WILLIAM, *William Morris by himself – Designs and Writings*, edited by Gillian Naylor (Guild Publishing. London, New York, Sydney and Toronto 1988); articles: *Why I Became A Socialist* (1893); lectures: *The Lesser Arts* (1877), *The Art of the People* (1879), *Art and the Beauty of the Earth* (1881)

NETTLETON, JOHN, *Robert Tressell and the Liverpool Connection* (Memorial lecture, Mastings, March 1981)

PEAK, STEVE, *Mugsborough Revisited – author Robert Tressell and the setting of his famous book, The Ragged Trousered Philanthropists* (Speaksbooks, Hastings 2011)

PELLING, HENRY, *A History of British Trade Unionism* (Penguin History, London 1992)

POSTGATE, R.W., *The Builders' History* (National Federation of Building Trades Operatives. London 1923)

RICHARDS, GRANT, *Author Hunting by An Old Literary Sports Man* (Hamish Hamilton and Coward-McCann, London and New York 1934)

ROBERT TRESSELL WORKSHOP, *The Robert Tressell Papers - Exploring 'The Ragged Trousered Philanthropists'* (Workers Educational Association, Kent 1982)

SILLITOE, ALAN, *Introduction* to 1965 edition of RTP

SWINNERTON, FRANK, *The Adventures of a Manuscript* (The Richards Press, London 1956)

THOMAS, TOM, *A Propertyless Theatre for the Propertyless Class* (History workshop Journal 4, 1977)

THORNTON, DAVID, *Hastings: A Living History* (The Hastings Publishing Company, 1987)

TRESSELL, ROBERT, *The Ragged Trousered Philanthropists* (Grant Richards 1914,Lawrence & Wishart, London 1955; Panther Paperbacks 1965, HarperCollins 1993)

WALSH, J, *Editorial Remarks*, NSP Monthly Journal (1922)

The Clarion
Daily Telegraph
The Guardian

Hastings News
Hastings and St Leonards Observer
Hastings and St Leonards Weekly Mail and Times
Justice
Liverpool Echo
Painter's Journal
Primitive Methodist Magazine
The Sun
Sunday Telegraph
Sunday Times
Sussex Express
The Times
Times Literary Supplement
Tribune

INDEX

Adam's and Jarrett's, builders, Hastings, 123, 127, 147, 163, 164, 169, 171, 187, 190, 204, 213, 237
Arnold, Edward, writer, 68

Bailey, the Rev. John, Liberal supporter, 121
Balfour, A.J., Liberal prime minister, 121
Ball, Fred, author and Tressell biographer, 5, 14, 15, 30, 58, 68, 70, 84, 123, 155, 209, 226, 234, 240, 244, 258, 260, 266, 268, 272, 274, 275, 277, 287   Jacqueline Ball, wife of Fred, 247, 249
Barracloughs, Joseph, builders, Liverpool, 222
Bassett, Polly, florist and firebrand, 190
Beehive team rooms, Hastings, 111, 124
Beney, Charles Alfred, cycle shop owner, 150, 174
Birtill, writer, 278, 279
Blackman, Peter, secretary of the Sussex Federation of Trades Councils, 261   Blatchford, publishers, 211
Boer War, 25-31
Booth, Charles, social reformer, 104
Braamfontein disaster, 19
Brenton, Howard, playwright, 257-259
Brown MP, Ron, 278
Bruce and Company, sanitary engineers and builders, Hastings, 47, 49, 50, 58
Burke, Thomas Henry, Irish permanent under-secretary, assassinated, 15
Burrows, Herbert, socialist and teetotaller, 110
Burton and Company, builders, decorators and funeral directors, Hastings, 70-73, 77, 78, 80, 83, 123

Edwards, Oliver, reviewer, 256
electricity and gas companies scandal, Hastings, 198-200

Fabians, 112
Farrar, Ray, critic, 252
Fenians, 11, 15
Foster, Michael, Labour MP for Hastigs and Rye, 287
Freeman-Thomas, Freeman, Liberal MP for Hastings, 114, 118, 119, 121
free school meals, 102, 103
free trade, 117
funeral business, 78, 79

Galacian, S.S., passenger ship, 30-31, 279
Gillingham, Sol, baker and Republican, 26
Gladstone, William, prime minister, 17
Godma Irvine, Bryant, Conservative MP for Rye, 277
Gower, Bill, apprentice, 48-50, 55, 61, 62, 65, 66, 68, 69, 84, 89-91, 111, 131, 136, 138, 150-152, 181, 182, 204, 212, 219, 222-224, 226, 293
Great Famine, 15
Green, Len, painter and decorator, 69, 72, 174, 227, 236, 237
Griffiths, Arthur, later President of Sinn Fein, 26

Haggard, the Misses, possibly daughters of the writer Sir H. Rider Haggard, 68

Haines, David, writer, 269
Hardie, Keir, 112
Harker, Dave, Socialist Alliance activist and writer, 254, 255
Hartel, Elizabeth, Tressell's wife, 18-20
Hastings and St Leonards Observer, 5, 35, 82, 124, 126, 179, 182, 268, 289, 297

Hastings, battle of, 33
Hastings fishing fleet, 33, 37
Hastings News, 34
Hastings pubs frequented by Tressell, 106, 278

suicides, 44, 78

Swift, Dean, writer, 68

Syndicalist Education League, 223

Temperance halls, 106

Tewson, Sir Vincent, TUC general secretary, 261

theatre and TV productions of RTP, 241, 250, 262

Thomas, Tom, dramatist, 237, 240

Thompson, James, organiser of unemployment marches, 128, 129

Times, The, 262

Todd, Ron, general secretary of the Transport and General union, 240

Tomlinson, Ricky, actor and activist, 10

Tone, Theobald Wolfe, Irish nationalist, 15

trades council, Hastings, 108, 113, 117, 124, 128, 223, 260, 261, 266, 272, 262   Transvaal, 17

Transvaal Federated Building Trades Council, 24

Tressell, Robert, *see Noonan, Robert*

Tribune, 252

Trinity College, Dublin, 14

TUC, 261

Uitlanders, 17, 25

unemployment marches, 126, 127

United Irishmen, 25

Val Mascal, mansion, Hollington Park, 72

Verrier, Marie le, miniaturist painter, 68

wages (in 1906), 116

Walsh, J.,Liverpool house-painters' union activist, 80, 239

Walters, The Reverend T.H., vicar of St Andrews, 270

Warren, Ken, Conservative MP for Hastigs, 287

Webb, Beatrice and Sidney, socialists, 112

Weston, Stanley, Hastings mayor and greengrocer, 190

Willard, Frank, ILP activist and shopkeeper, 111, 124, 126-128, 278

Williams, Raymond, writer, 253

Rebel Road is a section of the Unite education website that celebrates trade union and labour movement heroes that have been publicly recognised by a statue, plaque or building named after them. You'll also find pubs with historical connections and a list of museums and exhibitions that anyone wanting to know more about labour history should consider visiting. Help needed - please make contact with details of anything we might have missed so that we can regularly update the site. We intend using the information to develop campaigns to increase the public recognition of trade union and labour movement heroes. http://www.unitetheunion.org/growing-our-union/education/rebelroad/ !

Book of the month. Tutors on Unite education courses often get asked what books they would recommend reading. We have thus launched a book of the month service for Unite members. The subjects chosen are very varied and include politics, sport, social and labour history and economics. There is review of each book and details of how readers can obtain copies.

http://www.unitetheunion.org/growing-our-union/education/bookofthemonth/ !

Trade union heroes books: Unite education has started publishing an extensive series of short books on trade union heroes from Unite's past and present. Tom Jones - a fighter for freedom and working people: Spanish Civil War Volunteer and Welsh TGWU general secretary and Julia Varley - trade union organiser and fighter for women's rights are already out as of March 2015. These books are free to download online and in print format.

For more information on all these projects contact Mark Metcalf on 07952 801783 or email **markcmetcalf@btinternet.com**

Jim Mowatt - Unite Director of Education

UNITE Education has published a number of booklets written by Mark Metcalf that are free to download.

1) THE GREAT DOCK STRIKE OF 1889
http://www.unitetheunion.org/uploaded/documents/The%20Gr
eat%20Dock%20Strike%20of%201889%20%20web%20booklet11-
23272.pdf

2) TOM JONES - A fighter for freedom and working people:
Spanish Civil War volunteer and Welsh TGWU general secretary
http://tinyurl.com/k9q8e3m

3) JULIA VARLEY - Trade Union organiser and fighter for
women's rights
http://www.unitetheunion.org/uploaded/documents/Julia%20V
arley11-22098.pdf

Printed in Great Britain
by Amazon